THE GREAT CHALLENGE

THE GREAT CHALLENGE

The Myth of Laissez-Faire
in the Early Republic

FRANK BOURGIN

Foreword by Arthur Schlesinger, Jr.

GEORGE BRAZILLER • NEW YORK

Published in the United States in 1989
by George Braziller, Inc.

For information address the publisher:

George Braziller, Inc.
60 Madison Avenue
New York, NY 10010

Library of Congress Cataloging-in-Publication Data

Bourgin, Frank, 1911-
   The great challenge : the myth of laisse- faire in
the early republic / by Frank Bourgin.
     p. cm.
   Includes index.
   ISBN 0-8076-1217-0
   1. United States—Economic policy—To 1933. 2. United States—Economic
conditions—To 1865. 3. Laissez-faire. I. Title.
HC105.B77 1989
330.15'3—dc19   88-31184
                                           CIP

Produced in the United States
by Ray Freiman & Company
Stamford, Connecticut

First Printing, February 1989

To My Mentors

Since this study is finally seeing the light of day, I wish to dedicate it to those who most left their imprint on my thinking.

To my parents, Marel and Morris Bourgin, long since departed, who as recent immigrants knew nothing about Jefferson, but who brought up their three sons to trust and revere his values.

To my wife Dorothy, who suffered with me through my defeat and frustration of a half-century ago, who shares with me the joy and satisfaction of seeing this work finally accepted.

To Professor Allan F. Saunders, my first teacher of political science in 1928, and my very dear friend who at age ninety from his retirement in Honolulu encouraged me not to give up, and suggested that I read Arthur Schlesinger's *The Cycles of American History*.

To the memory of Professor Paul H. Douglas, my first teacher of economics, and my good friend in his last years, for the inspiration of knowing him—a great mind and a great heart, who helped set my course.

To the memory of Professor Charles E. Merriam, whose idea it was to write this study, who at a very early stage encouraged me to pursue my research on laissez-faire, and who challenged his students to reach out for new ideas.

To Professor Arthur Schlesinger, Jr., whose *Cycles of American History* provided the first confirmation and substantiation of my ideas in almost fifty years, and who in acknowledging me as a "pioneer" in restructuring our early American economy, with his encouragement and support, has brought this work out of the shadows.

Acknowledgments

Trying to recall who assisted me in preparing the writing of this dissertation almost a half-century after the fact is neither productive nor satisfying. I have searched my memory endlessly and without much effect. If others than Professor Merriam were involved, they have unfortunately slipped my memory. As I recall, it was a lone job, and others in the Political Science Department staff who knew about my project probably doubted that it was on sound historical ground. I must confess that when it was not accepted, I too felt some qualms of self-doubt—not about my factual basis, but whether I had gone too far in my conclusions.

I owe thanks to a number of people who helped bring the dissertation out of the darkness where it slumbered. To Mrs. Meryl Thulean of the American University Institute of Learning and Retirement, who typed the long summary that I used in teaching a course on the subject in the spring of 1986. To Joe James, who typed the manuscript, for his care and helpfulness in relieving me of some of the chores. To Barbara E. Stinchcomb and Dr. Geoffrey C. M. Plampin of the University's Office of Dissertation Secretary, for their punctilious editing of the manuscript. To Shirley Kessel, for her help in preparing the index. To my brother Simon, who read the manuscript in the unrevised version, for his helpful comments and his encouragement that I persevere. To Marilyn and Roger Israel and Claudia Sandonato, who offered their father constant moral support. My thanks, too, to C. Herman Pritchett, professor emeritus of political science at the University of California at Santa Barbara, for his generous appraisal and for his honesty in recalling events of a half-century ago; to Professors Gary Orfield and Joseph Cropsey of the Political Science Department for reading and evaluating the manuscript; and to Professor Cropsey for overseeing details of other requirements for graduation. Above all, my thanks to the University of Chicago and its Political Science Department for their integrity and honesty in admitting a mistake and taking steps to rectify it.

Contents

FOREWORD by Arthur Schlesinger, Jr   xi

PART I
THE CONSTITUTION MAKERS:
THE FEDERAL CONVENTION AND THE CONSTITUTION

CHAPTER I   Introduction: Clearing the Mind of Cobwebs   19

CHAPTER II   The Federal Convention Assembles   27

CHAPTER III   Mercantilist Influences in Designing
Our Constitution   37

CHAPTER IV   The Convention Designs a Strong
Executive Office   49

PART II
THE NATIONAL PLANNERS

CHAPTER V   Alexander Hamilton: Credit and Finance   67

CHAPTER VI   Alexander Hamilton: Industrial Development   86

CHAPTER VII   Thomas Jefferson: Public Land Policies   107

CHAPTER VIII   Thomas Jefferson: Internal Improvements   127

CHAPTER IX   Albert Gallatin and John Quincy Adams:
Internal Improvements   148

NOTES   177

SELECTED BIBLIOGRAPHY   205

INDEX   217

Foreword

The strange adventures of this book illustrate both the risks of scholarship and the convoluted ways of the academy. Behind the book lies a touching drama of dashed hope, derailed careeer, and belated vindication in the life of an individual scholar.

Frank Bourgin was born in Ely on the Iron Range of Minnesota in 1910. He intended to become a lawyer, but fascination with political science soon diverted him to an academic career. He graduated *magna cum laude* from the University of Minnesota in 1930 and took an M.A. at the Claremont Colleges in 1932. The next autumn he entered the Ph.D. program at the University of Chicago. After teaching for three years each at the Ely Junior College and at the Duluth State Teachers College in Minnesota, he resumed his studies in Chicago in 1939 under a research fellowship. He now became a student of Charles E. Merriam, perhaps the leading American political scientist of the day, a prolific writer, a famed teacher, and a genial but busy man who shuttled back and forth between classes in Chicago and conferences with President Roosevelt and New Deal officals in Washington.

Merriam's concern in Washington was with what the 1930s called national planning. National planning for Merriam and his associates in the National Resources Planning Board did not mean a regimented society governed by edict and decree. It meant advisory planning, the systematic application of research and intelligence to social problems, a procedure decentralized in approach, flexible in operation: coordination, not command.

But the very mention of national planning excited passionate opposition. "Plan" was a fighting word, filled, in conservative minds, with subversive connotation. Critics assailed the New Deal as an un-American departure from the ancient traditions of the republic. The men who founded the nation, the critics claimed, thought that government best which governed least and would be appalled by the idea of government seeking affirmatively to shape the nation's future.

Merriam, who knew history as well as political science, believed that the planning idea had ample precedent in the American experience. Frank Bourgin was now looking for a subject for his Ph.D. dissertation. Merriam suggested that he immerse himself in the writings of Alexander Hamilton, Thomas Jefferson, and James Madison and analyze their thoughts on national economic policy.

As Bourgin dug into the sources, he discerned patterns of public intervention

in the economy sharply contradicting the received idea that the American republic was conceived, born, and reared under the star of laissez-faire. Scholars were
willing to concede that Hamilton was in some ways a planner; but Jefferson had
seemed safely in the camp of laissez-faire and states' rights. Bourgin's research
now showed that Jefferson's land policies and internal-improvements proposals
envisaged a purposeful planning role for the national government.

In anticipation of Jefferson's bicentennial on April 13, 1943, Merriam arranged for the publication by the National Resources Planning Board of Bourgin's
heretical views on Jefferson. Then the project was abruptly canceled for fear of
political reprisals from so-called Jeffersonian Democrats representing the conservative wing of the Democratic Party. Merriam subsequently published a con-
densed version of a Merriam-Bourgin collaboration in *Ethics* in July 1943 under
the title "Jefferson as a Planner of Natural Resources."

Hamilton and Jefferson, Bourgin demonstrated, were not alone. Other
statesmen of the early republic—he laid particular emphasis on Albert Gallatin
and John Quincy Adams—proposed a leading role for government in promoting
economic development, in building a transportation network, and in supporting
education and science. Bourgin's research uncovered and documented a positive
governmental policy in the first forty years of the republic using national power
and resources for national purposes with long-term goals—in short, national
planning.

These conclusions were not so altogether heterodox as Bourgin rather
fearfully supposed. Forty years earlier the economic historian Guy Stevens
Callender had brilliantly delineated the role of governments, both state and
national, in guiding American economic development. But Callender's work was
not known at all to political scientists and had even been forgotten by historians.
So far as he knew, Bourgin was breaking new ground, and he was unquestionably
challenging entrenched orthodoxies and established wisdom.

Bourgin's original intention had been to write a chronological account of the
historical antecedents of national planning. Now finding himself committed to a
critique of a cherished national myth, he decided that further research would be
necessary for Part III of the book. This delayed completion of the dissertation for
another year. Married and running out of money, he had already withdrawn from
graduate school in the war years to take a job as historian in the Chicago office of
the quartermaster general. He plugged away at his dissertation during evenings
and weekends, however, and in the winter of 1944–45, by which time he was
employed as a purchasing agent in a war production plant, he submitted a massive
manuscript of 617 typewritten pages to the Chicago department of political
science.

In March 1945 he received a disturbing letter from Leonard D. White, the
chairman of the department and a political scientist almost as distinguished as
Charles Merriam. "Three members of your thesis committee, Messrs Merriam,
Pritchett, and White," it read, "have just finished reading the new draft of your

study. We had a long conference yesterday afternoon with respect to it, and I am sorry to report that it does not yet seem to be in satisfactory shape." It was their "unanimous opinion," White added, "that the best way to push it forward is to take time off from your business affairs . . . return to the University, and give all of your energy and thought to the thesis."

It is impossible to unravel after forty years what in fact happened to the Bourgin dissertation. Merriam had retired from active teaching, though he occasionally performed departmental chores. It seems improbable that he would have disapproved a dissertation by a student whose topic he had initially proposed and with whom he had published the *Ethics* article two years before.

The third member of the committee was C. Herman Pritchett, then a junior assistant professor, later to become chairman of the department and a distinguished authority on American judicial practice and procedure. In 1988 Professor Pritchett expressed some doubt that Merriam, well into academic retirement, would even have read so long a thesis. As for Pritchett himself, he had no recollection of having read the Bourgin thesis nor could he recall the "long conference" mentioned by White. No comments by either Merriam or Pritchett appeared on the manuscript when it was returned to Bourgin, and marginal notes by White occur on only one chapter.

Professor Pritchett's "reluctant conclusion" is that Leonard White made a unilateral decision and that Pritchett himself, as a very junior political scientist, simply deferred to one of the eminences in his field. White, all agree, was in Pritchett's words "a man of the most scrupulous rectitude." His concern, Pritchett surmises, was that absence from the university, if further prolonged, might disqualify Bourgin from an academic career. But Bourgin, now father of a one-year-old child, had a family to support. Becoming a full-time student again was out of the question.

Could White, a Republican, have been shocked by Bourgin's exposure of the myth of laissez-faire and his contention that national planning was an old American habit? Perhaps; yet in his magistral three-volume administrative history of the United States in the nineteenth century White himself soon made clear the surprisingly large role the national government played in economic life. One can only conclude that in the confusions of March 1945, under pressure of war work in Washington, White plunged ahead, thinking by harsh reprimand to reclaim Bourgin for academic life, unaware that in Bourgin's case returning to graduate school was an economic impossibility.

Bourgin was devastated. His dream of an academic career was shattered. With his dissertation disapproved, he even began to doubt his own research. Did the evidence really sustain his conclusions? Who was he, a young and unknown student, to challenge the leaders of his profession? He saw himself as a failure in scholarship, put his dissertation away into a black steel file box, and entered the men's clothing business in a small Minnesota town.

Over the next thirty years he held a variety of jobs, first in business, then in government, raised a family, and lived a proud and relatively successful life—always haunted, one must suppose, by intermittent visions of what might have been, yet never embittered by an embittering experience. As the family moved from place to place—seven times in forty years—the black steel box moved with them, a grim reminder of failure, placed in the basement in each new residence, never opened.

Retired in the 1980s and living in Washington, Bourgin taught occasionally at the American University Institute for Learning and Retirement. As the bicentennial of the Constitution approached, his curiosity revived about what he had written about the Constitutional Convention so many years before. At last he opened the steel box and took a fresh look at the yellowing manuscript in faded type. It seemed to him a solid piece of work. Nor was his argument any longer so heretical within the historical profession.

After the Second World War, the rising interest in problems of economic development in the Third World had prompted scholars to try to figure out why economic growth had taken place so rapidly in the United States. This led to a rediscovery of the role of the public sector. Carter Goodrich, a Columbia economist, and the Committee on Research in Economic History sponsored studies on state economic policy. Promising young scholars like the political scientist Louis Hartz and the historian Oscar Handlin wrote influential monographs.

These studies amplify the broad picture Frank Bourgin had sketched some years before. But they do not render his own analysis obsolete or superfluous. His approach, while focused on the national government, has a broad perspective that includes the implications of the Constitution and the planning ideas of Hamilton, Jefferson, Gallatin, and J. Q. Adams. Though one may disagree with nuances of his argument, Frank Bourgin clearly proves the affirmative role the national government played in the years before the laissez-faire myth gripped the national mind.

His book, elegant in formulation, clear and cogent in presentation, remains in my view, even after forty-five years, a fresh contribution to the political and economic history of the early republic. And it represents an act of intellectual liberation from the laissez-faire myth so long cherished and propagated by those who profit from laissez-faire policies. It enriches our national traditions by reminding us of the long-established role of government as an instrument to promote the welfare of the people.

In an almost unprecented gesture of academic contrition, the Chicago department of political science in 1988 reconsidered its 1945 decision and rectified its error. Professor Pritchett, finally reading the manuscript after forty years, wrote Professor Joseph Cropsey, "In my judgment this is not only an acceptable doctoral dissertation by University of Chicago standards; it is a major research effort which successfully supports the author's thesis that the American founders believed in and practiced 'affirmative government.' . . . This is a massive scholarly production, organized around a significant theme with findings powerfully supported by the data."

On 10 June 1988 the University of Chicago conferred a Ph.D. degree on Frank Bourgin.

Arthur Schlesinger, Jr.

PART I

THE CONSTITUTION MAKERS: THE FEDERAL CONVENTION AND THE CONSTITUTION

CHAPTER I

Introduction:

Clearing the Mind of

Cobwebs

A new country in a new world had declared in its Declaration of Independence that it was a self-evident truth that among the inalienable rights with which the Creator endowed man are "Life, Liberty and the Pursuit of Happiness." It was a unique theory, so emphatically proclaimed: One of the essential functions of government is to create an environment that enables people to live better.[1]

This belief has always prevailed in America. No formal declaration was needed for men to believe it. It is one of our earliest and best-established traditions, lingering, persistent, and powerful in its inspiration. The poet Archibald MacLeish has lately recalled this tradition and its millennial hope in his lines:

> *America was promises to whom?*
> *East were the*
> *Dead kings and the remembered sepulchres:*
> *West was the grass.*
>
> *America was always promises.*
> *From the first voyage and the first ship there*
> *were promises.*[2]

It matters little by what phrase this national hope be called. Herbert Croly has called it "The Promise of American Life."[3] To the Puritans, this hope figured as a mission to escape the religious disabilities and persecutions in England, and to found here a land of freedom for religious worship.[4] To many who fought in the American Revolution, it appeared as the opportunity to redress the balance of political power and to establish for all time equality and self-government. "The decree has gone forth," said John Adams in 1776, "and cannot be recalled, that a more equal liberty than has prevailed in other parts of the earth, must be established in America."[5] To Thomas Jefferson and the masses of people whose hopes and wishes he voiced, America was to be the opportunity to encourage in practice all that was good and beautiful in human nature, free from the senility and decay and despotisms of the Old World. To John Quincy Adams and James Monroe, who framed the Monroe Doctrine, there lay basic to their system the belief that America must continue free from European ambitions and imperialisms, to work out its own policies and its own destiny. Back of the phrase "manifest destiny" lurks also the faith that some unique force working for the good governs the development of our society. To the countless millions who poured through our gates for a whole century in never-ending hordes, mainly in search of a larger portion of familiar benefits, America beckoned them on as the Land of Opportunity.

The tradition has continued as a powerful force through our country's first two centuries in raising and maintaining human expectations that the future will be better. The phrases have changed from time to time, but the longer-term vision has not. In the earliest years, the term "pursuit of happiness" applied; at another, Roosevelt's "Four Freedoms"; after World War II, the "American standard of living"; and later still, just "the American dream." To the sophisticate, they may have seemed farfetched and unwarranted. But there is no doubt that they have exerted a major force throughout our history.

The aim of the present study is to show how the government of the United States in its early years, from 1787 to 1829, contributed through national planning to making the American dream possible.

This study was begun in the 1940s as a doctoral dissertation in political science at the University of Chicago. The idea of my writing it originated with Professor Charles E. Merriam who proposed it so that we might learn more about our early national policies. During the first decade of the New Deal, until the coming of World War II, the idea of national planning was often proposed as a practical means of getting us out of the Depression and guiding the nation to a better future. Dr.

Merriam, a member of the National Resource Planning Board, had written extensively on American politics and political theory. He hoped that my dissertation would aid in understanding our early national traditions.

In the course of my research, I explored every avenue of policy that I could reasonably conceive of as "national planning." In order to differentiate national planning from transient political policy, I defined it as having the following characteristics: 1. long-term rather than short-term projections, ruling out transitory political policies; 2. some systematic study and research utilizing existing scientific knowledge and state of the arts; 3. certain defined goals or national objectives, rationalized as necessary to achieve or enhance the national well-being. It was assumed that the Founding Fathers and their successors in the national government were not acquainted with the term "national planning." My task was to find if there existed any political projects or phenomena that fitted this description, and to evaluate their influence or role in our history.

I began my research with the recognition that I was almost certain not to find any new or undiscovered materials. In the years since 1787, historical scholarship had already mined the data that were available. As I combed through book after book, I had some anxious days and nights wondering if I would be able to produce a dissertation that was not just rehash. I wanted very much to make a contribution to the knowledge of that period. Yet the odds hardly favored it. There seemed to be little to say about the Constitutional Convention, or Hamilton or Jefferson's writings, that had not already been said many times.

Dr. Merriam exerted a peculiar magic on his students to make them push forward the frontiers. He had done this often, and with new ideas had opened new doors and new perspectives. Many months later—I am not sure just when it happened—I began to be able to brush the cobwebs from my mind.

My problem—the cobwebs—was that I was continuing to see the latter part of the eighteenth century through the lens of my own scholastic upbringing. It took a long time before I was able to begin to think in terms of the meanings of the words of the people whose ideas I was studying. I was aware that the writing of history is a selective process, and that historians at any given time are prone to pick and choose their facts in terms of what they currently regard as important. And more, they are inclined to interpret the facts in light of their own cultural and social values. So instead of viewing the ideas and projects of leaders of the late eighteenth century as they viewed them, their meanings came filtered down to us in terms of how later generations of historians understood them.

The cobwebs were of long-standing; since childhood, in fact. I had never forgotten how often my high school civics teacher repeated Thomas Paine's maxim, "That government which governs least, governs best." In my college years, too, there were variations on the same theme expressed in more sophisticated language. But they all amounted to the same thing—from the beginning of our national history, our political and economic tradition was strongly laissez-faire, with the attitude of suspicion and distrust of government and a preference for private enterprise.

There was never any question in my mind about the role of laissez-faire in our national policy after Andrew Jackson assumed the presidency, when laissez-faire appeared in the garb of states' rights. Jackson was absolutely clear in his own mind that "our internal affairs" were "to be left where the Convention found it—in the state governments . . . in leaving individuals and State as much as possible to themselves . . . not in binding the States more closely to the center, but leaving each unobstructed to its proper orbit."

I knew enough of American history to know that there was a solid difference between Jackson's ideas of the 1830s and those that had existed before. I made up my mind to try to make an exhaustive study of the economic background of the period to understand how political policies were shaped by the economic environment and problems.

If I were going to identify the role of laissez-faire as it affected or did not affect our early national policies, it required a clear definition. Webster defined laissez-faire as "a doctrine opposing governmental interference in economic affairs beyond the minimum necessary for the maintenance of peace and property rights." For futher specificity: "1: A respect by government for the legal rights of property—that these rights will not be disrupted or interfered with. 2: A complete reliance upon private risk capital and its availability with little or no assistance from government to augment its availability. 3: Abstention from economic activity on the part of government and also to maintain a free market to avoid regulation or granting of favors to individuals or groups. 4: There is presupposed a condition of free competition between buyers and sellers in which each may seek the competitive advantage through the use of one's capital and labor."

For almost fifty years after completing my study, from 1942 to 1987,

I wondered whether my conclusion regarding the absence of laissez-faire in this early period was correct. My facts seemed to me to be incontrovertible. Yet I wondered why I had never found the same ideas expressed elsewhere. How was that possible? And then, in May 1987, I discovered that Professor Arthur M. Schlesinger, Jr., Pulitzer Prize–winning historian, in his *Cycles of American History* (1986) presented the same conclusion, and for the same reasons, in his Chapter 9, "Affirmative Government in the American Economy."

Schlesinger argues that it is a "cherished national myth" that "ascribes the economic development of the United States to the operations of unfettered individual enterprise" as though it "had sprung from the loins of Adam Smith." The coincidence of *The Wealth of Nations* and the Declaration of Independence both occurring in 1776 "encouraged the notion that the stars of laissez-faire and of the American republic rose in unison." On the contrary, says Schlesinger, it was "a good deal more complicated than that." The colonies had become accustomed to governmental intervention by the British, who followed the policies of mercantilism. When independence was achieved, given their lack of capital and a later start in manufacturing, it was hardly a surprise that their leaders would use the resources of government to promote economic development. "For the Hamiltonians, the national government was the grand instrument by which to transform a pastoral economy into a booming industrial nation." And again, "The Founding Fathers had no doctrinal commitment to the unregulated marketplace. They were not proponents of laissez-faire. Their legacy was rather that blend of public and private initiative known in our day as the mixed economy."[6]

Whether I had actually pioneered in opening up this line of thinking on this period of our history, I must leave to others to decide. But no one can doubt the importance of challenging the myth of laissez-faire that has hung over our national credo and has so distorted our understanding of much that took place. It will be seen in the chapters that follow that the rejection of the laissez-faire premise results in a different view of governmental policy during those years.

During the past year, having renewed my attention to the study, I became acquainted with the stream of research studies of this era that have been published since the 1940s, all of which in one way or another have affirmed my conclusions: the works of Leonard D. White (my teacher at the University of Chicago), W. W. Crosskey, Dumas Malone, Daniel Elazar, and Carter Goodrich. My research is indeed modest by comparison with some of these. But it should be remembered that some of these authors spent a lifetime researching their work, while at the time I was writing, I was guided principally by hunch that I was on the right path. I refer to these more recent works in the appropriate chapters.

Throughout the chapters that follow, it will be evident that there were certain influences, both intellectual and economic, that played major roles in shaping national planning during the period 1787–1829. (These will be more thoroughly explained later.)

Mercantilism. Although the mercantilist philosophy was already in decline in Europe, it offered strong attractions to the newly freed colonies on this side of the Atlantic. Once a strong central government had been organized, it gave the merchant, trading, and financial classes leverage to use the power of government to improve their economic status. Government intervention at this stage of our economic development was accepted as a matter of fact and on the basis of pragmatic results. Adam Smith's *The Wealth of Nations* was published in this country in 1789. A number of decades would pass before its philosophy permeated the public mind, and then it appeared as a rationalization of states' rights. In the meantime, statesmen with the vision of Hamilton worked aggressively to utilize the new authorities of the federal government to speed the transformation from a pastoral economy to an industrial state.

Lack of Private Capital. It was easy for later historians to confuse the abundance and availability of capital of the later years with its relative absence at the beginning. Had there been ready capital when the national government was first organized, there would have been no need for private enterprise to rely on the financial structure created by Hamilton. At the beginning, ours was an impoverished agrarian economy, owing large delinquent debts both here and abroad, and with no credit status for borrowing. It was not until well after the War of 1812 that financiers in Europe were willing to finance enterprises in the United States.

Value of the Public Lands. It is a bit mystifying to try to understand why historians have failed to appraise the value of the public lands owned by the United States government in their true relation to the rest of the economy. In probably no other economy in history has the government stood as the undisputed owner of the millions of square miles of the uninhabited territory that extended (after the Louisiana Purchase) to the Pacific Ocean. It would be impossible to place any realistic dollar value on these lands at the early period in relation to all the accumulated wealth of private entrepreneurship to that time. Yet it is apparent that the value of the public lands must have greatly exceeded that of the entire private sector, and the government as owner acted in the capacity of private landlord in making disposition of them. Nor should it be forgotten that it was the government that set the terms: the free market did not set the price; the public acres could not be sold without being first surveyed and then sold by platted location and at prices specified by law. As will be shown, during the early period many of the national leaders regarded the public lands as the great national resource that with wise management would provide a treasure for future settlers for decades to come. But even beyond this, they were aware that by investment in roads and canals, the value of the lands contiguous to these improvements would appreciate greatly in value, from which the national treasury itself could benefit. The public lands, managed so frugally and carefully during the early period, after Jackson began to be given away with unabashed prodigality for the subsidization of building the railroads. The speed with which our early rail system was built owed much to government land subsidy. It is clear that the United States in these respects was not a classic example of laissez-faire economic policy.

Influence of the Enlightenment. The philosophy of the eighteenth-century Enlightenment already pervaded the air during these years when our government was being established. The spirit of social change influenced persons of all social rank to greater or lesser degree, even though most were probably not fully conscious of the philosophical basis of the new ideology. The spread of the new doctrines led to a conflict between the new liberalism and the old conservatism. The conservative philosophy favored a passive acceptance of the present structure of society and looked benignly on the past. Liberalism, on the other hand, viewed man's nature optimistically, based on his essential rationality, perfectibility, and continued improvement. It will be seen from statements made by members of the Constitutional Convention, that they viewed their responsibilities with optimism, as an unparalleled opportunity for social amelioration.

It was no accident, therefore, that during the early era of our national government the governmental policies leaned in an affirmative direction: positive and active rather than negative and passive, which followed later.

Part I of this study looks at how the United States Constitution was developed with a view to establishing federal supremacy, but also to creating a government capable of assuming an affirmative role in developing the national economy. Part II discusses how the national leaders of that period extended governmental action into different sectors of the economy: Hamilton, Jefferson, Gallatin, and John Quincy Adams.

CHAPTER II

The Federal Convention

Assembles

It was an appropriate place to begin my research—the United States Constitution. My charter was to study what precedents existed in our early history for national planning. And as Charles Merriam had emphasized both in his writing and lectures, no nation on earth had begun its history with such celebrated planning as the Constitution.

Since the launching of our federal government, thousands of books have poured forth from scholars of American history on every phase and wrinkle of the Constitution. I had to ask myself what new ideas I could offer in a dissertation that had not already been told many times. I decided to concentrate on how the Constitution evolved as an integral plan. I would focus also on the background that the standard histories might have slighted or that may have slipped through the cracks, hoping thereby to be able to offer a fresh persepctive. The reader will find some of my material hackneyed by historical repetition, yet it is necessary to the story of how the Constitution came into being. Where possible, I have tried to present aspects that have not been stereotyped.

There is no single authentic way of viewing the Constitution. I am reminded of the parable of two people viewing the same glass of water: one sees it as half empty; the other as half full. In the past, where historians have viewed our history through the lens of laissez-faire philosophy, they focused on those features of our government that emphasized its negative aspects which limit political power, such as the separation of powers, checks and balances, or that the authority of Congress was limited to the expressly delegated powers, the Bill of Rights, etc. These are not to be minimized; they are assuredly in the Constitution.

But I have chosen instead to concentrate on how I thought the framers of the Constitution viewed the affirmative side of government, and how and why they designed a government both capable and ready to deal with the issues of the day and far beyond into the future.

As they assembled in May 1787 in Philadelphia to begin their deliberations, no one could have anticipated that this was the beginning of one of the great events of human history. A similar meeting had been held in Annapolis the previous September, and only five states had sent delegates. Its only accomplishment was a report drawn by Hamilton proposing that all thirteen states choose delegates to a convention to meet the following year. It urged the need to "devise such provisions necessary to render the constitution of the federal government to be adequate to the exigencies of the Union." The Congress took notice in February 1787 and invited the states to send delegates in May, "for the sole and express purpose of revising the Articles of Confederation adequate to the exigencies of government and the preservation of the Union."

For four months, until they had completed a new constitution, there were bitter debates among the delegates. Not until near the very end, when they had forged an instrument based on give and take, was there any real agreement. Every interest represented demanded a voice: the small states against the large, the agrarian interest against the financial/trading, the debtor versus the creditor, the newly settled Western areas against the established Eastern seaboard, the North against the South, and so on. But although it would take four months to hammer out the details of what they were *for*, from the start they were in agreement on what they were *against*: They were against revising the Articles of Confederation—their single appointed mission. A new constitution was needed. The leaders of the convention—Madison, Edmund Randolph, and others—came prepared to offer an alternative: no mere revision, but instead a plan that would supplant the Articles. The fact that from the first day all members were sworn to secrecy and they worked through a long hot summer with the windows closed to prevent eavesdropping is proof that there was near unanimity about their mission. From this we may assume that if successful, there would emerge a new plan of government. Within four days of the convention's opening, on May 29 Randolph of Virginia presented what became known as the Virginia Plan representing the views of the large states—but not at all compatible with the Articles.

Some historians have pictured the decade under the Articles—from their adoption in November 1777—as ominous and portentous. John Fiske portrayed it as "the critical period in American history," as sweeping toward an abyss from which it was rescued in the nick of time by the heroic framers of the Constitution.[1] This was hardly true.

In certain areas, very great progress had been made. Indeed, some of the landmarks of American legislation were written then, such as the Land Ordinance of 1785 and the Northwest Ordinance of 1787. Worth noting is the fact that although Congress was timorous in all other matters, it was assertive as proprietor of the public lands in making long-range plans that looked forward to the ultimate settlement of these vast areas.

While one could point to some short-term amelioration of economic conditions, it was clear that without substantial changes in the instrument of government, the economy would go on drifting. Under the Articles, Congress had no power to lay and collect taxes. It could ask for requisitions of the states, but these were generally ignored. Committees of Congress were formed to serve as executive departments—such as foreign affairs, finance, and post office—but they met with little success. The problems that confronted Congress were legion, and it was powerless to deal with them, especially problems with England and its hostile actions taking advantage of Congress's weakness. There were domestic problems of all sorts: stronger Eastern states levying tariffs against weaker Western states, boundary disputes, disagreements over the use of the Mississippi River. But most urgent of all were those arising from debtor-creditor relations, which threatened the property interest. In later years, James Madison said he believed these "contributed more to that uneasiness which produced the Constitution and prepared the mind for a general reform" than any political inadequacies of the Articles. The public credit was gone, due to inability to pay foreign bankers and debts owed to the demobilized army officers. As conditions worsened, debtors pressed the state legislators for relief to pay off their debts in cheap paper money. In the autumn of 1786, there had occurred in Massachusetts the uprising of farmers and others demanding that further judgment for debts be suspended. It was this so-called Shays's Rebellion and the issuance of unfunded paper money by seven states in 1786 that more than anything else helped crystallize public opinion that a new system of government was necessary.

Over the past two centuries, many books have been written to explain why the Constitution took its present form.[2] There has always existed the temptation to read into past events whatever present interest seems to prevail. For example, Supreme Court Justice Thurgood Marshall recently chose to find that document reactionary because under Article I, Section

IX it accepted the continuation of slavery until 1808, and (Section II) black persons would be counted as only three-fifths of a "free person."[3] The facts of his allegation are unquestioned. But how is the Constitution to be regarded—by the standards of our time or those of the late eighteenth century?

Earlier in this century, when populist politics were more the order of the day, there were other attacks on the Constitution as reactionary. In his famous *Economic Interpretation of the Constitution*, Charles A. Beard showed that the wealthy and financial property interests were disproportionately represented at the convention and that they stood to gain personally and directly by its adoption. J. Allen Smith regarded the replacement of the Articles as a kind of capitalist conspiracy to establish the wealthy in control. W. E. Dodd even went so far as to compare the Constitution to the treaty of the Congress of Vienna in 1815 for its reactionary qualities.[4] And on a much milder side, the conservative historian Andrew A. McLaughlin viewed its formation as a continuation, a slow accretion of experience rather than a break with the past.[5]

There is clearly no one way to view the Constitution. Each generation sees it differently. Nor is there any way one can even know how all of the Founding Fathers viewed their mission in Philadelphia. Some offered comments; others did not. But for those whose thoughts are on record, there can be no doubt that they fully understood the meaning and significance of what was happening in those fateful summer months.

Several principal ideas stand out as we read statements made at the time: 1. The immensity of their feeling of responsibility that in Madison's words, they were framing an instrument of government that "is intended to last for ages." 2. They were breaking with the past. Even though there was at that time no clear recognition of democratic government as we now know it, theirs was a rejection of governmental despotism practiced in the Old World. 3. By the time the convention met to frame a new constitution, there existed a sufficient science of politics by which with innovation they would be guided to produce an enduring new framework of government.

Here are a few excerpts:

From James Wilson of Pennsylvania:

> The magnitude of the object is indeed embarrassing. The great system of Henry the IV of France . . . is small when compared to the fabric we are now about to erect. In laying the stone amiss,

we may injure the superstructure; and what will be the consequence if the cornerstone should be loosely placed?[6]

From George Mason of Virginia:

The eyes of the United States are turned upon this assembly and their expectations raised to a very anxious degree. May God grant that we may be able to gratify them by establishing a wise and just government. For my part, I never before felt myself in such a situation, and declare, I would not, upon pecuniary motives, serve in this convention for a thousand pounds a day.[7]

From a North Carolina delegate:

A very large field presents to our view without a single straight or eligible road that has been trodden by the feet of Nations. A Union of Sovereign States, preserving Civil Liberties and connected together by such Tyes . . . is a system not described, it is a circumstance which has not occurred in the History of men.[8]

From George Washington:

The foundation of our empire was not laid in the gloomy age of ignorance and superstition; but at an epoch when the rights of mankind were better understood and clearly defined, than at any other period. The researches of the human mind after social happiness . . . the treasures of knowledge . . . are laid open for our use and their collected wisdom may be happily applied in the establishment of our form of government.[9]

From Thomas Jefferson:

Happy for us that abuses have not yet become patrimonies; . . . That we are yet able to send our wise and good men together to talk over our form of government, discuss its weaknesses and establish its remedies with the same *sang-froid* as they would a subject of agriculture. The example we have given to the world is single, that of changing our form of government under the authority of reason only, without bloodshed.[10]

From Alexander Hamilton:

> The science of politics, however, like most other sciences, has received great improvement. The efficiency of various principles is now well understood, which were either not known at all, or imperfectly known to the ancients.[11]

From James Madison:

> Happily for America, happily we trust, for the whole human race, they pursued a new and noble course. They accomplished a revolution which has no parallel in the annals of human society. They reared the fabrics of government which have no model on the face of the globe. They formed the design of a great Confederacy, which it is incumbent on their successors to improve and perpetuate.[12]

It is fair to observe that some of the quoted statements were made after the Constitution was written, and were presented—as in *The Federalist*—to move the states to ratify it. It is probable that although some of the leaders of the convention were consciously radical innovators, most members were pragmatists rather than conscious inventors of a new kind of government. The most important single goal that influenced the convention was to ensure that their final product be approved and ratified.

The extent to which the convention violated the canons of accepted credibility can probably be best understood if we examine how the Constitution was received abroad. It should be remembered that in both England and France, the governments were products of slow organic growth, an unbroken continuum built on the foundations of ancient traditions. When the French Revolution broke out in 1789, conservatives reacted with horror, not only at its violence and pillage, but at its rejection of its own splendid past. This was best reflected in Edmund Burke's impassioned pleas voicing the sentiments of conservatives throughout the world in his *Reflections on the Revolution in France* (1790) and *Appeal from the New to the Old Whigs* (1791).[13]

The reception accorded our finished Constitution on the Continent offers proof of its radical character from the world's point of view. Liberal Frenchmen were delighted that it gave them encouragement and inspiration to renovate their own system of government. In England, it gave solace to the radicals by furnishing them with a concrete example of creating a republican government and of mixing liberty with order. We know much of how the Constitution was received in England from an excellent monograph by Leon Fraser. Fraser found that the Constitution's chief effect on English thought was that on the one hand it inspired radicals with its example, and on the other hand it caused conservatives to search for more ways to defend their views. Fraser believed that as a side effect, it created "a great impetus" for Parliamentary reform. The English clergy, however, were especially outraged, feeling that a system of government based on reason alone was an affront to the Almighty. As an example, one sermon said, "We hear nothing in the Scriptures about Republics." Another took affront that it tried "to substitute a creature of its own reason for the fabrication of *God's wisdom*" and regarded it as a "fantastical theory . . . to violate the primogenial law of nature by . . . venturing upon the bold innovation of creating a Republic."[14]

While the Constitution helped foment division in England between liberals and conservatives, its effect here was to solidify thinking favorable to its success. There were two major influences, both of them closely interrelated. The first was what became known as the Age of Enlightenment; the second was the influence of a growing nationalism inseparable from preserving the gains of the Revolution.

Economist Alvin H. Hansen clearly delineated the importance of the Enlightenment on public thinking during this period. It was an age of great dreams and expanding hopes. Enlightened men seriously believed in human progress as destined and assured, and this would be reflected in all aspects of society—the sciences and the arts, social morality, and economic amelioration.

> In the eighteenth century the idea dominated that if a scientific evaluation and direction of effort were instituted, it would be possible to realize an indefinite progress of mankind. . . . [T]hrough the progress of invention and discovery, man had come into a body of materials that might be used for the gaining of incalculably superior materials for the achievement of societal welfare.[15]

The growth of nationalism, though difficult to identify or to quantify, found expression in the convening of the convention. In some ways, the convention was the successful culmination of practically a decade of agitation and proposal for the revision of the Articles. The existing system of government, emphasizing the sovereignty and independence of the states, gave inadequate expression to the common cause and witnessed now the petty bickering of faction and class. If Shays's Rebellion was decisive in leading to trimming the powers of the state legislatures, the growing sentiment of nationality was even more significant in endowing the national government with positive powers for the new affirmative government.

Madison played to rising sentiment of nationalism in this clarion call: "Harken not to the unnatural voice which tells you that the people of America, knit together as they are by so many cords of affection, can no longer live together as members of the same family . . . can no longer be fellow citizens of the one great, respectable and flourishing empire."[16]

While the growing consciousness of a common nationality was a powerful force in knitting together the people politically, tied to it was the desire to preserve the gains of the Revolution. In the words of Hansen, the Revolution had not "purchased a final good as a simple result."[17] Political freedom was a beginning, not an end, an opportunity to erect on Amercian soil new social institutions based on republican, humanitarian principles. Noah Webster had expressed this view: "A fundamental mistake of the Americans has been, that they considered the revolution as completed when it has just begun." In a pamphlet issued in 1787 to affect the ratification of the Constitution, Benjamin Rush had written,

> The American war is over, but this is far from being the case of the American Revolution. On the contrary, nothing but the great drama is closed. It remains yet to establish and perfect our form of government, and to prepare the principles, morals and manners of our citizens for these forms of government after they are established and brought to perfection.[18]

Fate and fortune had determined that it was to be on this small strip of English settlement in America that the unique social experiment was to be made. The settlements were still, except in the most densely populated areas, relatively isolated and poorly connected with one another. By all existing standards, they were exceedingly young, lacking a distinctive character. If a distinctively American culture existed, it was chiefly in aspiration, at best in embryo. Cultural ideals were just beginning to emerge, and they were only a thin veneer that became thinner as one traveled westward. The diversity and variety in America were great, being at once a promise, a threat, and a challenge. The size of the country, with the imperative need of binding it together, would be either our great opportunity or our peril. How could we weld together the discordant elements of America—the merchants of the Eastern cities, the German and Scotch-Irish settlers beyond the Alleghenies, the agrarian aristocrats from the South, the artisans and mechanics, and the other national and racial elements beginning to appear along the seaboard and in isolated Western communities? How could we create a national unity and a harmony of interests out of these dissonant and clashing groups? Some common interest lying deeper than that of accidental residence or the enjoyment of a common freedom would have to be devised. Programs of economic development would have to be undertaken to increase and expand the scope of these interests; means of transportation and communication would have to be established and extended to link the scattered settlements; the great socializing forces of education and self-government would have to be expanded to fuse the population of the country so that they might respond to the common stimuli and harness the energies of the nation to furthering the ultimate purposes of the American Revolution.

In a lecture series at the University of Chicago in 1931, Charles E. Merriam dealt with the view, dominant at that time, that the delegates at the convention were overwhelmingly conservative in their views of government. His opinion to the contrary is worth quoting.

> Our Constitution-makers were, when judged by the standards of their time, decided revolutionists. From the point of view of contemporary America, some have thought that the Constitution was conservative, even reactionary in its tendencies. . . . If we look at the field from the world point of view, the Constitution was in reality a revolutionary document of the most disturbing character, and its makers were fully aware of this. . . . They were venturesome, experimental, inventive, eager to adjust the forms and procedures of government to actual forces and facts of their time. They were not unmindful of the business advantage of having a Constitution, but they were willing to work out this new government in terms of experiment and innovation.[19]

In the final analysis, the Founding Fathers were met with the great challenge of using power in both a negative and an affirmative way. Their immediate goal was to design the new instrument of government—the

Constitution—and see to its acceptance and ratification. They sought to impose a system of checks and balances, separation of powers, and other limitations of government as safeguards against future tyrannies. But an even greater challenge consisted in creating a new government endowed with positive powers over a loose system of federated states, a government which would foster national unity and generate economic growth by developing the great resources of the common lands.

CHAPTER III

Mercantilist Influences in Designing Our Constitution

When I began my research into the motivations of the framers of the Constitution, I would not have guessed that mercantilism was involved in any way, shape, or form. From my superficial knowledge, I had identified mercantilism as entirely a European practice, and having overthrown the yoke of economic bondage to England, I assumed that our leaders would have preferred to stay free of mercantilist practices. I accepted the current mythology that Adam Smith's *Wealth of Nations*, published in 1776, was somehow identified and commingled with our Declaration of Independence. It was not until a while afterward that I began to understand the role of mercantilism in affecting the design of our Constitution. This chapter aims to explain its influence.

The doctrine of laissez-faire was hardly known to the framers of the Constitution.[1] It was not until a number of decades later that our national public policy came to terms with its doctrine. By that time, the impetus of national planning activity was pretty much spent on the rapid growth of states' rights philosophy, which in effect was laissez-faire.

It may fairly be assumed that even if laissez-faire, in its later sense as a system of mechanical postulates for determining agenda and nonagenda of government, was known, it is extremely unlikely that the framers of the Constitution would have adopted it. Laissez-faire did not fit the purposes of the Constitution makers, for it was against the laissez-faire policy of the confederation that the Constitution was struck. In the words of James

Wilson, one of the leaders of the convention, "the great fault of the existing Confederacy is its inactivity. It has never been a complaint against Congress that they have governed overmuch. The complaint has been that they governed too little. To remedy this defect, we were sent here."[2] The manner in which the detailed powers of the national government were written into the Constitution, their number, their phrasing, and the circumstances attending thereto—all this indicates that the convention members were fairly of one mind to create a vigorous instrument of government capable of standing beside any foreign power in unity, stability, and power. In all America at this time, there was no one who better understood the need of nascent commerce and industry relying on the resources and aid of a powerful government than Alexander Hamilton, as will be shown in a later chapter. Despite Hamilton's disappointment that the convention would not completely deprive the states of their powers, the finished Constitution corresponded fairly closely to the system he had earlier envisaged in the impressive list of powers it gave the federal government. Had the Constitution makers really favored laissez-faire, it is difficult to see why they should have desired any change from the inactive policy of the Confederation.

I have said that the Constitution framers were endeavoring primarily to create an efficient instrument for the effective administration of government. Considering the diversity of views and interests represented in the convention, it is unlikely that they were trying deliberately to institute a specific social and economic program. It is more probable that they were trying to fashion an instrument for general purposes and capable of adjusting to many uses. The common emphasis during the convention was that the Constitution must be made "to last for ages."

In shaping the new instrument of government, it seems hardly likely that the framers of the Constitution could have escaped the influence of mercantilist doctrines and practices on their own thinking. The prevalent interest in the Lockeian doctrines emphasizing the restraints on government and the sanctity of private property has probably obscured the full significance of the influence of mercantilism in shaping the contours of our federal Constitution.[3]

I am not saying that the Constitution embodies the philosophy and the practices of mercantilism. I am saying only that the precepts of mercantilism were the raw stuff of the social experience of the men who wrote the Constitution, and that mercantilism was an important ingredient in their thinking. At the time of the convention, mercantilism was in a state of decline, both as theory and practice. Yet it formed a body of social experience from which the Constitution makers could draw in case of necessity; more important, it was part of the background of thought that molded their attitudes toward the state. Even though mercantilism was not in high repute among the former colonists who had revolted from the British uses of it, nonetheless, the Constitution framers could hardly have failed to recognize that it offered an arsenal of practices and policies that suited the needs of a new republic aspiring to commercial and industrial rank.

Eighteenth-century mercantilist practices presented models of commercial policy that implied a view of the state as a positive instrument for the shaping of national economic policy. It was no longer necessary that all enterprise be fitted into the pattern of mercantilist policy, as in the more dominant phases of mercantilism. Yet there remained this view of the political state that left an enlarged scope for governmental activity. In making possible the attainment of desired objectives, the government was expected to assume an active role and bring to the fore all its resources in aid of private enterprise. These preconceptions were part of the thought processes that were commonly entertained, and they certainly entered into the making of the Constitution. Hamilton and Adair, who have carefully examined the *Records of the Convention* for evidence of mercantilist precepts, found mercantilist ideas a common ingredient in the Constitution's formation. They describe the eighteenth-century conception of the state that it embodied:

> The state was the thing. In the Eighteenth Century, it was "no brooding omnipresence in the skies," an abstraction outside of and above the realities which made it up. . . . It was an affair of groups and interests whose concerns must be promoted through its policies and whose aspirations must be trimmed to the requirements of "the general welfare." Hence, no sharp line was to be drawn between the political and economic order. The state had the dominant role in the matters of commerce, and a political economy of mercantilistic economics of principles.[4]

Influenced by the mercantilist philosophy of the state, in which it was anticipated that the government would assume an important role in directing the economic activities of the nation, the Constitution makers were therefore not miserly in the manner in which they carved the portions of political power to be borne by the national government. It seems probable that in detailing the powers of the national government, the enumerated list was intended to be viewed as a whole, and liberally, rather than strictly and as separate powers. Their purpose, in the final analysis, was to create an effective instrument of government, not a written corpus for the later exegesis of courts and constitutional lawyers. The idea that a government constructed as they framed it could still be technically knocked out on the ground that it was proven before a court that one of the enumerated powers was inefficacious, in all probability never entered their minds. The state was conceived functioning as a unit, not as a heap of separate powers.

That the men who framed the Constitution placed far less emphasis on the specific enumeration as a careful delimitation of the powers to be exercised by the federal government seems likely on the evidence available. They seemed to be interested primarily in the enumerations as a conveyance of power rather than as a limitation of power. They seem to have looked at the powers of the government as a whole, as an effectively functioning instrument comparable to foreign states, rather than as a composite of separate powers. As Hamilton and Adair state their views: "to the Fathers, the 'grants' were not so many distinct powers, each with its separate domain and specified use. Instead, they were so many weapons which might be used singly or in concert as political occasion demanded. . . . Here was an arsenal, equipped with all the techniques essential to the power to govern."[5]

Madison's explanation of the nature of the federal authority confirms this view. He said that "though the general government is not to be charged with the whole power of making and administering laws," he added significantly, "its jurisdiction is limited to certain enumerated objects, which concern all the members of the republic, but which are not to be attained by the separate provisions of any."[6] That the framers of the Constitution gave little or no attention to the enumeration as a careful limitation of the powers of the federal government is also borne out by the circumstances attending the construction of the enumerated list and by the general loose construction of their meaning during this early period of affirmative government.

If it were intended that we regard the enumerated powers as the courts have since interpreted them, as a deliberate attempt to fix the federal authority within carefully defined limits, it seems hardly likely that so little care and debate would have been allotted to their construction. It should be noted that the separate powers were constructed almost in toto by the Committee on Detail—as though they were a mere detail! When the committee reported its list of powers that it chose to include in the Constitution, the convention accepted the list practically as it was offered, refusing only to entertain the power of Congress to pass "a navigation act" even with a two-thirds majority.[7] There was practically no further debate on what subjects should be included within the scope of the federal power. Moreover, it seems more probable that many regarded the list of powers in such broad terms as to include lesser subjects that some of the members would have made more explicit.

Even while admitting that the members of the convention were impatient to adjourn, there is a good reason to believe that this was not the reason they did not entertain debate on the proposed inclusion of other subjects. For example, Madison and Pinckney in separate resolutions proposed to add the following powers to those already listed by the Committee on Detail as given to Congress:

To dispose of the unappropriated lands of the United States.
To institute temporary Governments for the New States arising therein.
To regulate affairs with the Indians as well within as without the limits of the United States.

To grant charters of incorporation in cases where the Public good may require them, and the authority of a single State may be incompetent.
To secure to literary authors their copyrights for a limited time.
To establish an university.
To encourage by premiums and provisions, the advancement of useful knowledge and discoveries.

To fix and permanently establish the seat of Government of the U.S. in which they shall possess the exclusive right of soil and jurisdiction.
To establish seminaries for the promotion of literature and the arts and sciences.
To grant patents for useful inventions.
To grant public institutions, rewards and immunities for the promotion of agriculture, commerce, trades and manufactures.

To secure the payment of the public debt.

To grant letters of marque and reprisal.

To regulate Stages on the post roads.[8]

Again, the Committee on Detail was entrusted with the power to decide whether this long list of powers were "to be added to the General Legislature." Some of them, as we know, were added to the text of the Constitution in another verbal form. Other powers the committee did not see fit to include: to grant charters of incorporations; to establish a university and seminaries; to grant public institutions rewards and immunities for the promotion of agriculture, commerce, etc; to regulate stages on post roads. Yet it is significant that Madison, who was such a formidable debater for things he believed in, did not once feel compelled to argue further the merits of including these powers in the Constitution.

The reason for this is not that he did not feel them worth insisting on, or that the convention would certainly reject them. It is more probable that he believed that they could be included within the federal power as incident to the other powers already granted Congress. The truth of this is borne out by a letter Madison wrote some forty-five years later, in 1832, when he had already swung to the states' rights and strict constructionist point of view. Nevertheless, he avowed that the failure to include specifically some of his suggestions did not imply their rejection, but on the contrary, their implicit inclusion. His statement is worth quoting in its entirety:

> Attempts have been made, to show from the journal of the Convention of 1787, that it was intended to withhold from Congress, a power to protect manufactures by commercial regulations. The intention is inferred from the rejection or not adopting of particular propositions which embraced a power to encourage them. But without knowing the reasons for the votes in those cases, no such inference can be sustained. The propositions might be disapproved because they were in bad form or not in order; because they blended other powers with the particular power in question; or because the object had been, or would be, elsewhere provided for. No one acquainted with the proceedings of deliberative bodies can have failed to notice the frequent

uncertainty of inferences from a record of naked votes. It has been with some surprise, that a failure or final omission of a proposition "to establish public institutions, rewards and immunities for the promotion of agriculture, commerce and manufactures" should have led to the conclusion that the Convention meant to exclude from the federal power over commerce regulations encouraging domestic manufactures. . . . In expounding the Constitution and deducing the intention of its framers, it should never be forgotten that the great object of the Convention was to provide, by a new Constitution, a remedy for the defects of the existing one; that among these defects was that of a power to regulate foreign commerce; that in all nations this regulating power embraced the protection of domestic manufacturers by duties and restrictions on imports; that the States had tried in vain to make use of the power, while it remained with them; and that, if taken from them, and transferred to the Federal Government, with an exception of the power to encourage domestic manufactures, the American people, let it be repeated, present the solitary and strange spectacle of a nation disarming itself of a power exercised by every nation as a shield against the effect of the power as used by other nations. Who will say that such considerations as these are not among the best keys that can be applied to the text of the Constitution? and infinitely better keys than unexplained votes cited from the records of the Convention.[9]

Without other facts to corroborate this statement, it might seem possible that Madison was rationalizing after the fact to win legal support for the specific policy of encouraging manufactures. That this is not true is shown by other events that took place both during the convention and afterward. The reasons the convention did not feel impelled to include in explicit form other detailed powers of Congress are that 1. many members felt that it was unnecessary to do so, inasmuch as these lesser powers were already included as incidents of greater and more inclusive powers; 2. their specific inclusion, by creating fears of the excessive powers of Congress, might jeopardize the acceptance and ratification of the Constitution. An incident that took place in the convention is an example of this. At one point in the discussion, Benjamin Franklin moved to include the power "to provide for the cutting of canals where deemed necessary" after the words "post roads."[10] When this motion was ultimately voted on, it lost by a vote of eight to three. On the face of the record, it would seem a plausible inference that the convention rejected the power in any form, explicit or implicit. Yet a closer examination of the convention's record casts some doubt on this conclusion. Immediately following Franklin's motion, Madison moved to enlarge it to include the power "to grant charters of incorporation where the interest of the U.S. might require and the legislative provisions of individual States might be incompetent." He explained that "his primary object was however to secure an easy communication between the States which the free intercourse now to be opened, seemed to call for."[11]

Madison's motion immediately precipitated a discussion of granting "mercantile monopolies," an issue loaded with political dynamite. Did Madison's general proposition imply that Congress, by having the power to grant charters of incorporation, could grant "mercantile monopolies"?[12] A bitter fight had been fought in Philadelphia and New York, recalled Rufus King, a delegate from the latter state, and he had no desire to jeopardize the acceptance of the Constitution by raising the issue again. King stated, furthermore, that it was unnecessary to include the power of granting charters of incorporation separately since he regarded it as being included within the powers already granted "to regulate commerce." Thus, when the convention voted against Franklin's motion "to include the power to provide for the cutting of canals where deemed necessary," it was not so much rejecting the power as avoiding having to make an explicit statement on a delicate subject, the desired result to be better attained by silence.

It is worth noticing that the failure to include these subjects in the completed Constitution was not regarded by some of its most important makers as implying a rejection of the necessary powers. Surely Madison, popularly regarded as "the Father of the Constitution," should have been in the most authoritative position to interpret the will of the convention. He argued that the adoption of the Constitution would result in improving communications and intercourse throughout the Union.

> Roads will everywhere be shortened, and be kept in better order
> . . . an interior navigation on our eastern side will be opened
> throughout, or nearly throughout, the whole extent of the thir-

teen States . . . the communication between the Western and Atlantic districts, and between different parts of each, will be rendered more easy by those numerous canals with which the beneficence of nature has intersected our country, and which art finds it so little difficult to connect and complete.[13]

Although the written Constitution being presented to the people for ratification did not specifically include the power of Congress to construct roads and canals, Madison nonetheless felt that its adoption would in some manner facilitate their construction. In spite of the fact that it was not included because of "an apprehension . . . that it might prove an obstacle to the adoption of the Constitution,"[14] Madison was nonetheless willing to use the roads and canals argument in winning support for ratification.

No final answer can be given to the question of what the framers of the Constitution intended to include within the scope of the enumerated powers. As we have seen, it is a subject on which the evidence leaves something to conjecture. Yet, as we shall see, during the early period of affirmative government, it seems to have been assumed by a number of persons in high political authority that powers such as those over roads and canals, granting charters of incorporation, encouraging agriculture and manufactures, and establishing seminaries and schools were well within the scope of federal authority.

Some light on the question of the intended scope of federal authority may be revealed by examining the meaning of the term *commerce*, included within the enumerated powers. It is possible, as a number of scholars have argued, that a generality of purposes was intended to be served by the use of this term.[15] In their careful study of the contemporary uses of the term *commerce*, Hamilton and Adair come to the conclusion that *commerce* was chosen advisedly as having the most comprehensive meaning of any of the alternative terms; *commerce* served the catholicity of uses that would be forced on it.

Thus in issue, incident, and implication the concern over commerce runs throughout the debates. Commerce proposals invite difference of opinion. Although detail may be avoided, there is no unanimity as to the concretions which are to be set down in the document. Yet there is everywhere in evidence an intent to endow the general government with the power to formulate a policy for the national economy, a power which is to extend to trade, manufactures, the staples of agriculture, internal improvements, and the creation of corporations. A broad grant of power was to be given to Congress in a clean-cut clause of the utmost brevity. If possible, a single key word must here—as elsewhere in the Constitution—be made to tell the story. It was of no avail to bother with manufacture or production, words of such narrow confine, even if set down in clusters, could only have made up an irregular verbal fragment. A more comprehensive term—such as business or industry—was not for many decades to become available. The choice was narrowed to traffic, trade and commerce. Traffic would not do; it was lowly in origin and clearly headed for vulgar verbal company. Trade was too specialized in meaning and too barren in larger implications to serve the occasion. Commerce excelled in the larger breadth and range, the greater dignity and prestige which attached to it. And commerce alone had competency for so high a verbal duty.[16]

They go on to say that the word selected to mark the intended grant of power had to describe "a most inclusive range of activities." It had to do triple duty for dealings with "foreign nations, among the several States and with the Indian tribes." Three distinct provinces were involved, and three separate domains for public policy. That the same term sufficed to extend equally to foreign commerce, trade with the Indians, and regulation among the states brings it within an orbit of power comparable to the war and treaty-making powers. Say Hamilton and Adair, "The ease with which it could be accommodated to such a trio of national purposes attests the catholic character of commerce."

Substantially the same conclusions are reached by D. W. Brown, although his are based on a more traditional approach. Brown examines the intentions concerning the scope of the commerce power prior to and during the Constitutional Convention and shows that the convention of 1787 was only the culmination of a number of efforts to establish a uniform system of commercial regulations and to create in the federal government a more adequate instrument for the promotion of commerce. The movement for an enlargement of the commerce power began as early as 1778 when a memorial of the New Jersey legislature urged it. Then in 1781 John Witherspoon, the noted liberal head of the College of New Jersey, presented a resolution to the New Jersey legislature stating that "It is indispensably necessary that the United States in Congress assembled should be vested with a right of superintending the commercial regulations of every state, that none may take place that shall be partial or contrary to the common interests." The Annapolis convention that immediately preceded the Philadelphia convention was merely the climax of a growing and deep-seated feeling that it was impossible to establish commerce throughout the United States on a secure footing without such a power in the possession of the general government. Brown concludes with the opinion that the grant of power in the Constitution "to regulate commerce ... among the several States and with the Indian tribes" was intended to convey a power equivalent to its power "to regulate commerce with foreign nations."[17] Like the latter, the former was intended to be plenary.[18]

The same line of argument was pursued more recently by W. W. Crosskey of the University of Chicago Law School, who spent a lifetime studying the Constitution. He accepts Hamilton and Adair's interpretation of the comprehensive meaning attached to *commerce* as understood in that period, and especially during the first decade after the federal government was organized. It was only after judicial interpretation that the original meaning was obfuscated and lost. Crosskey derides the "stock argument" that the regulation of commerce was intended to be replaced by states' rights. In his opinion, instead of being synonymous with liberty, when the Constitution was drawn, states' rights stood for "vested rights" of a small and vociferous group of local politicians.[19]

Thus a new instrument of government was forged out of the counsels of the Philadelphia convention, designed in the hope that it would endure for the indefinite future. Powers were detailed and enumerated, but written into the Constitution in the broadest manner that they might continue adequate. To these was added the general clause, the last of Section VIII, Article I, empowering Congress "to make all laws which shall be necessary and proper for carrying into execution the foregoing powers." This idea was conceived by the Committee on Detail in its fourth draft of the Constitution, and was adopted by the convention without debate.[20] Here was provided a general formula by which the Constitution could be accommodated to future exigency. The framers wisely refrained from fitting the government of the future into a narrow framework of powers that suited only their own interest and experience. In designing the constitutional edifice to last for ages to come, they realized that permanency implies not changelessness, but the capacity to adjust to the unceasing stream of social change. In the words of Hamilton and Adair:

> The Fathers . . . created no august and inflexible corpus of constitutional law. . . . Instead they wrote the briefest sort of document. They laid down a structure for a state and endowed the Federal Government with the most general powers. . . . They were concerned to list matters of national importance and to point the direction for public policy. They were content to leave its detailed formulation to their descendants who would be better able to shape remedies to their own necessities. In this declaration of political faith in posterity they created a purposive and inflexible instrument which allowed a gracious accommodation of government to the changing needs of future decades.[21]

Finally, they included in the construction a specific provision for its own amendment. Lest even the broad phrasing of the powers and a liberal interpretation of them prove eventually inadequate, the Constitution was made to provide for its own alteration. Thus, by providing in advance a regular procedure for legal change, the framers made possible a system of orderly change.[22]

CHAPTER IV

The Convention Designs

a Strong Executive Office

The office of the presidency has been subject to a greater variety of interpretations than any other.[1] The differences are in part due to the remarkable variety of characters and talents who have held that office. But only in part. No office in our national government has beat so closely to the rhythm of the times as the presidency. In calm and in crisis, under states' rights and under extreme nationalism, the executive office shaped and was shaped by political events. In every great political crisis in our history, it has seemed almost natural to turn to the presidency. The office of the president has been big enough—and small enough—for all occupants. Question: What kind of office did the framers of the Constitution intend it to be?

The answer was not clear to me when in the fall of 1940 I was struggling to get from Farrand's *Records* a clear picture of their design in creating the presidency. From their finished product as described in Article II, it was clear that the new executive office was "the boldest feature of the new Constitution."[2] Yet in relation to my study of national planning, it was most important for me to understand *why* they created such a strong executive, and what role they expected the president to have in developing national policies.

By accident, the answer came to me quickly and with definitive impact. It was during the presidential election campaign when Franklin Roosevelt was running for reelection for an unprecedented third term. My teacher, Charles Merriam, as an adviser to the president, had been in Washington where the issue of the third term was being discussed. Knowing that I had been studying Farrand's *Records*, Merriam called me into his office one day and asked if I could prepare a short research report. The question he posed was, Would the Founding Fathers have favored or opposed reelection of the president for a third or successive term?

I had been studying the *Records* very intensively, and in a few days I was able to give to Dr. Merriam a ten-page report. The Founding Fathers, of course, did not consider that specific question, but they did debate many corollary issues. It was not until I had compiled my report on the basis of the pros and cons that I realized with absolute clarity what the framers of the Constitution had in mind when they constructed the presidency. Their greatest fear was not that the chief executive would become too strong,[3] but that the office would be too weak and succumb, as under the Articles, to being a creature of the Congress.

To make sure that this did not happen, they designed the office so that the presidency also derived its authority directly from the Constitution—to be elected independently of Congress, for a fixed term and eligible for reelection, removal only for cause. The convention's debates on how and why they reached their conclusions will follow in this chapter. The design for the presidential office closely followed the design for achieving federal supremacy. They envisaged an activist and affirmative role.

The kind of government the Founding Fathers were trying to set up was the opposite of that obtaining under the Articles. Congress under the Articles was synonymous with laissez-faire, with local popular sovereignty, lackadaisical government lacking in energy. Congress had no real powers, and for its purposes, needed none. But the Constitution involved an altogether different conception: a close-knit Union, endowed with large comprehensive powers that its makers wanted to be used toward promoting national economic development. Toward augmenting the forces of cohesion, they provided too for a separate federal judiciary whose main purpose was to preserve the principle of national supremacy against state separatists or particularistic tendencies. Does it seem even faintly possible that such a system of government as they were establishing would be equipped with a weak executive branch? The answer is, obviously not.

The experience under the Articles was in fact a long and costly lesson in having a weak executive. Article II of the Constitution was conversely an application of the knowledge of that lesson. The creation of a separate and independent strong executive was in every way a departure from the absence of an executive under the Articles and the weak executives existing in almost all of the states. In fact, not until one has compared the president under Article II and the state governors of the period does the contrast of the two stand out in stark relief.

When the Revolution occurred, there seemed nothing to do but to oust the royal governors and have the representative legislature assume their former executive powers. This happened not so much by design, as fortuitously. There developed out of this conjuncture the practice of legislative supremacy, reinforced as it came to be by the doctrine of popular sovereignty. With the exception of New York, and partially in Massachusetts, the supremacy of the legislative department was made the rule in all state constitutions. The governor—such he continued to be called—was made a "cypher."[4] Whatever powers he possessed were what the legislature chose to give him, and here, it is true, the "fear of executive despotism" was responsible for stripping the governor of his authority. The term was reduced, his veto and appointive powers were taken away, he could not adjourn the legislature, and what few powers were left him had to be shared by an executive council. The legislatures ruled virtually unrestrained, and in most of the states possessed even the powers of changing the constitutions, either by ordinary legislative process or modifications to it.

The actual omnipotence of the legislature was obscured by the rendering of pious lip service to the current intellectual vogue of the "separation of powers" theory. Massachusetts paid Montesquieu homage by incorporating his theory in its classic form into its constitution. A thorough examination into the practices of the separation of powers theory reveals that, although it commanded the most devout obeisances in theory, in practice there existed the greatest confusion as to how strictly it ought to be applied. Among state constitution makers, faced with the pressing need of enacting new instruments of government, it was a convenient tool for dividing governmental functions into the three traditional categories, but hardly much more. William Bondy, historian of the separation of powers theory, says that they were "familiar with the theory of Montesquieu," but were "unfamiliar with any supposed possibility of classifying powers according to their intrinsic nature. That no separation of powers, based upon the nature of the different governmental powers was ever intended to be inserted into our organic law, would convincingly appear from a most cursory perusal of the debates in the constitutional conventions."[5] In practice, therefore, in the revolutionary state governments, the separation of powers meant instead the virtually omnipotent rule of the legislative branch. Few persons were deceived thereby, and even a liberal like Thomas Jefferson commented in his *Notes on Virginia*: "The concentrating of these in the same hands is precisely the definition of despotic government. It will be no alleviation that these powers will be exercised by a plurality of hands, and not by a single one. One hundred and seventy-three despots would surely be as oppressive as one."[6]

It was not long thereafter that there developed a demand that a strong executive be erected as a counterpoise to the overbearing legislature. The movement was especially strong among the conservatives, who were shocked by the states' populist excesses. The later Constitutional Convention of 1787, evidencing a desire to strip the states of many of their powers, was part of the same tendency. Legislative disregard of constitutional principles soon urged on the conservatives the need of substituting a more balanced form of government by giving the executive independent powers. On the scale of conservative esteem, authority seemed preferable to liberty, and correspondingly, liberty was identified with legislative majorities and authority with a strong executive.[7] Madison summed up his thought on the matter in a letter to Jefferson:

> Wherever the real power in a government lies, there is the danger of oppression. In our Governments the real power lies in a majority of the community, and the invasion of private rights is *chiefly* to be apprehended, not from acts of Government contrary to the sense of its constituents, but from acts in which the Government is the mere instrument of the major number of the Constituents. This is a truth of great importance, but not yet sufficiently attended to, and is probably more strongly impressed on my mind by facts and reflections suggested by them than on yours, which has contemplated abuses of power issuing from a very different quarter. Wherever there is an interest and a power to do wrong, wrong will generally be done, and not less readily by a powerful and interested prince.[8]

The issue involving an independent executive was more complex, however, than simply the desire for a check on populist legislative majorities. The need for a functional redistribution of authority was becoming more and more apparent both in the states and before Congress. The experience of Congress with the use of legislative committees to perform executive tasks was anything but commendable. As early as July 1775, Washington predicted "the Inconvenience that must unavoidably ensue from dependence on a number of Persons for supplies" and he submitted "it to the Consideration of the Congress whether the publick Service will not be best promoted by appointing a Commissary General for these purposes."[9] Others soon shared his views. Robert Morris of Pennsylvania believed that "If Congress means to succeed in this contest, they must pay some good executive men to do their business as it ought to be done."[10] "The want of method and energy in the administration" was likewise noted by Hamilton. "Congress have kept the power too much in their own hands, and have meddled too much with details of every sort," he said. "Congress is, properly, a deliberative corps, and it forgets itself when it attempts to play the executive. It is impossible such a body, numerous as it is, and constantly fluctuating, can ever act with sufficient decision or with system" (1: 209–10). These criticisms were hardly too severe. The record of Congress's vain experiments with legislative committees and so-called boards was "pathetic."[11] Before finally succumbing to the necessity of establishing separate executive departments in war, finance, and marine and foreign affairs,[12] Congress had experimented with a variety of multiheaded executive expedients, and found satisfaction in none. The conclusion seemed obvious: "executive energy and responsibility are inversely proportional to executive size; that consequently, the one-man executive is best."[13]

As great an improvement as the creation of separate executive departments proved to be, however, there was no way of preventing Congress from meddling in the details of administration. Though a personal separation of functions had been achieved, the executive departments, being strictly creatures of Congress, were inherently and unavoidably subordinate to it. Jefferson's proposed scheme of enlarging the orbit of authority of the Committee of the States, had it been successful, would have created a multiheaded general "superintending administrative agency standing between the departments and Congress." In the absence of such an agency, Congress as a whole continued to try to exercise nonlegislative powers in such matters as appointments, finance, and foreign affairs, and succeeded by 1787 in thoroughly discrediting itself.[14] Under these circumstances, it is understandable that the theories of Montesquieu and Blackstone, emphasizing that confusion of powers in the same hands is tyranny, exerted an especial appeal. The theory of the separation of powers was a useful tool in paving the way for a strong, independent, and coordinated executive branch in the new national government. The dogma of the separation of powers described a relationship between the several branches of government that the contemporary "political science" accepted as ideal. As the existing state constitutions and the Articles of Confederation were based on a theory that also had a strong popular appeal, viz., the virtual identity of popular sovereignty and legislative supremacy, it is easy to see why Montesquieu's authority was so frequently appealed to and his arguments so eagerly seized on to controvert the exisiting practices as unscientific and contrary to political freedom. As Thach puts it, "The truth is that the Fathers used the theorists as sources from which to draw arguments rather than specific conclusions." Or, to state the matter in another form, the influences of the separation of powers doctrine, though predetermining, "were not the determining influences."[15]

The necessities of the case promoted the decision for a strong and independent executive, but the model was furnished neither by the British Constitution nor by Montesquieu's celebrated doctrine. The model was the government of the state of New York, defined in its constitution of 1777. Of all the state constitutions, it alone furnished an example of strong executive leadership under a constitution in which the constitution controlled the three departments of government.[16] The long tenure of George Clinton, who held the governorship from 1777 to 1795, exposed the possibilities of a strong and vigorous executive. Clinton's rule, combining vigor and independence, compelled the admiration even of his staunchest political opponents. The New York constitution provided that the governor, in whom was vested "the supreme executive power and authority of the State," was to be elected by a constitutionally defined electorate for a three-year term without limitations as to reeligibility. He possessed the important powers of qualified appointment and qualified veto. His was the power to convene the legislature and to prorogue it for a period of sixty days. His office made him the "general and commander in chief of all the militia." He was expected to furnish legislative leadership, for the constitution made it his duty "to inform the legislature at every session of the condition of the state so far as may concern his department; to recommend such matters to their concern as shall appear to him to concern its good government, welfare and prosperity."[17] Upon him too devolved the duties of conducting the state's relations with the Continental Congress and other states. He was in fact the real head of the state administration. He was "to transact all necessary business with the officers of government, civil and military; to take care that the laws are executed . . . ; and to expedite all such matters as may be resolved upon by the legislature."[18] The important fact is that all these powers stemmed not from the legislature, but from the same source from which the legislative branch received its powers.

Such was the background of the executive under the confederation and the states when the Philadelphia convention began its discussions on the framing of a proper executive branch. This was a commonly felt need, since the Virginia, New Jersey, Pinckney, and Hamilton plans all recommended a separate executive. The Virginia and the New Jersey plans intended a multiple executive elected by the Congress and ineligible for reelection; the Pinckney and Hamilton plans favored a single and powerful executive, as far as possible divorced from the control of Congress.[19] Pinckney made no mention of how the president was to be elected, though he would be reeligible. Hamilton would have the president elected by Congress, and his term to extend for life during good behavior. Neither the Virginia nor the New Jersey plan gave the president a veto over legislative acts, though the former described a council of revision composed of "the executive and a convenient number of National Judiciary" that would have an absolute veto over legislative acts. Pinckney gave the president a qualified legislative veto, and described in detail the executive's other powers, similar in content and form to those the president now enjoys. Hamilton endowed the president with an absolute veto, and with a plenitude of power that made him virtually a king.

The inspiration and the driving power to create a presidency as the Constitution finally defined the office came from none of these proposals. It came from James Wilson of Pennsylvania, the one man who came to the convention with a clear-sighted vision of the type of an executive that would be needed—and obtained. Later, as he assumed the leadership in the determination of the executive form, he won the services of Pinckney, Hamilton, Gouverneur Morris, Madison, and others. "A nationalist of nationalists, as he conceived the executive as a part of the governmental whole, which, deriving its powers from the general body of the nation, would supplant separatism, and reduce the States to a position of practical and legal subordination to the nation."[20]

Whereas Madison seems to have dominated the convention in formulating the principles on which the federal government would be constructed, he seems not to have had a clear perception of what was needed in the case of the executive. He sensed the defects under the Articles, but saw no remedy.[21] The form of the executive he offered in his Virginia Plan was a personal separation from the legislative branch, but in all other respects the design was the same as in the Articles: a multiheaded agency subordinate in powers to Congress and elected by it. Instead of obtaining executive autonomy by an independent election, and by extending the length of the term of office, Madison provided against making the executive reeligible. Reeligibility under conditions of election by Congress was regarded as the certain way of making the executive the legislative puppet. Wilson, on the other hand, saw the defects of the existing system and also perceived the remedy. On the first day that the convention considered Randolph's introductory Resolution 7, Wilson immediately moved that the executive "consist of a single person."[22] Sherman, arch defender of the existing system, countered at once that he considered

> the Executive magistracy as nothing more than institution for carrying the will of the Legislature into effect, that the person or persons ought to be appointed by and accountable to the Legislature only, which was the repository of the supreme will of Society. As they were the best judges of the business which ought to be done by the Executive department . . . the legislature should be at liberty to appoint one or more as experience might dictate. . . .
>
> An independence of the Executive on the supreme Legislative, was in his opinion the very essence of tyranny if there was any such thing.[23]

Not a single principle implied in Sherman's statement was incorporated into the final draft of the Constitution: neither legislative supremacy, nor executive dependence, nor a plural executive. The final provisions in the Constitution incorporated, to the degree that was possible, Wilson's view of what the executive should be.

> Mr. Wilson preferred a single magistrate, as giving most energy dispatch and responsibility to the office. He did not consider the Prerogatives of the British Monarchy as a proper guide in defining Executive powers. . . .
>
> Mr. Wilson said that Unity in the Executive instead of being the fetus of Monarchy would be the best safeguard against tyranny.

The executive power as he conceived it should be shorn of its legislative and judicial powers, and "the only powers he conceived strictly Executive were those of executing the laws and appointing officers, not (appertaining to and) appointed by the Legislature."[24] But later he restated his view:

> If the Legislative, Executive and Judiciary ought to be distinct and independent, the Executive ought to have an absolute negative. Without such a self-defense the Legislature can at any moment sink it into non-existence. He was for varying the proposition in such a manner as to give the Executive and Judiciary jointly an absolute negative.[25]

Wilson also supported executive appointment of the judiciary, as opposed to their appointment by the national legislature as Randolph's resolutions proposed.[26] As a member of the Committee on Detail, Wilson was influential in shaping the draft on the executive powers to conform to his ideas.[27] Wherever possible he lent his aid to strengthening the presidential office. When it was proposed to deprive the Senate of its sole power to make treaties and appoint ambassadors and justices of the Supreme Court, in return for the powers of impeachment, and to make these executive powers, Wilson and his coterie of nationalists—Madison, Morris, Pinckney, etc.—fought the issue to a successful conclusion.[28] It is not implied here that Wilson was solely responsible for formulating the terms of the second article of the Constitution. As we have seen, his leadership depended on the aid of others whom he had brought around to his point of view. Article II as finally completed did not include a number of provisions that he felt were inseparable from a properly organized executive. Wilson was, in fact, the only member of the convention who spoke in favor of a popularly elected executive. Yet, in spite of the fact that a number of his ideas failed to find their way into the finished instrument, the terms in which the presidency was ultimately defined owed their form and content to Wilson's initiative and determination.

The problem that vexed the convention more than any other—and certainly the problem on which it expended the most time and effort—was defining the relationship of the executive to the legislative branch.[29] The particular powers of the president that I have enumerated—such as his veto, his appointive and treaty-making powers—were readily soluble once this matter was decided. In a word, the problem was that of preventing the president from falling under the domination of Congress. The importance that the convention attached to maintaining executive independence and leadership is measured by the time and care it gave to it. The discussions that entered into the making of the provision deciding the mode of the president's election show how concerned the delegates were that any check on the president might result in the loss of his independence.

It will be remembered that the Virginia and New Jersey plans provided against the reeligibility of the executive. It might be imagined that the reason for this provision was a "fear of executive despotism." The exact contrary is the case: In view of the never-ending encroachments of the legislative branch on the executive powers, both in Congress under the confederation and in almost all of the states, the convention members were almost desperate in trying to construct an executive that would escape domination of the legislative branch. This fear found frequent expression during the convention. As Madison expressed his view:

> Experience has proved a tendency in our governments to throw all power into the Legislative vortex. The Executives of the States are in general little more than Cyphers; the legislatures omnipotent. If no effectual check be devised for restraining the instability and encroachments of the latter, a revolution of some kind or other would be inevitable.[30]

Gouverneur Morris stated:

> Our great object of the Executive is to control the Legislature. The Legislature will continually seek to aggrandize and perpetuate themselves; and will seize those critical moments produced by war, invasion or convulsion for that purpose. It is necessary that the Executive Magistrate should be the guardian of the people.

He believed especially that the size of the country necessitated a strong executive:

> It has been a maxim in political Science that Republican Government is not adapted to a large extent of Country because the

energy of the Executive Magistracy cannot reach the extreme parts of it. Our Country is an extensive one. We must either then renounce the blessings of the Union, or provide an Executive with sufficient vigor to pervade every part of it.[31]

Morris anticipated little danger from an overpowerful executive. Instead:

Much has been said of the intrigues that will be practiced by the Executive to get into office. Nothing has been said on the other side of the intrigues to get him out of office. Some leader will always covet his seat, will perplex his administration, will cabal with Legislature, till he succeeds in supplanting him.[32]

But how was one to obtain the kind of executive that was needed? The mode of his election was intimately related to the question of his eligibility for reelection, the length of his term of office, and his powers. Wilson's suggestion that the president be elected by the people[33] seemed to command practically no support. Until Elbridge Gerry of Massachusetts and Oliver Ellsworth of Connecticut offered the plan of indirect election by means of a separate electoral college,[34] there seemed no alternative to accepting the mode of his election by the legislature or else circumventing the legislature's control of the presidency by providing against his reelection altogether. The hopelessness of the expedient is obvious, but it suggests also the despair the members must have felt for failure to find some better method. It was not lost on the delegates that preventing the legislature from electing the same puppet twice was hardly an effective means of ensuring an independent and vigorous executive. This is, as we shall see, the only explanation for the convention's early preference for maintaining the ineligibility of the president for reelection.[35] The expressions of anxiety that eligibility for reelection would weaken the executive by encouraging his dependence on the legislature were frequently made. Madison, in arguing that the established principle of independence for the judiciary applied no less to the executive, said at one stage of the controversy:

This could not be if he was to be made appointable from time to time by the Legislature. It was not clear that an appointment in the 1st instance [even] with an ineligibility afterwards would not establish an improper connection between the two departments. Certain it was that the appointment would be attended by intrigues and contention that ought not to be unnecessarily admitted. He was disposed for these reasons to refer the appointment to some other source.[36]

Gerry said likewise: "If the Executive is to be elected by the Legislature, he certainly ought not to be reeligible. This would make him absolutely dependent."[37] Randolph spoke in favor of Luther Martin's motion to make the president ineligible for a second term because he believed that "If he ought to be independent, he should not be left under a temptation to court reappointment. If he should be reappointable by the Legislature, he will be no check on it. His revisionary power would be of no avail."[38]

A variety of conclusions were drawn with reference to the length of the president's term of office and a provision concerning his eligibility for reelection. But all of them point indisputably to the fear that whatever method they devised, the president might fall under the legislature's influence. For example, Broom of Delaware was of the opinion that since the convention (in one of its many changes of mind) had just previously rejected the provision of the president's ineligibility for reelection, a shorter term than seven years was desirable. "Had he remained ineligible a second time, he should be preferred a longer term."[39] McClurg of Virginia drew the opposite conclusion from the same facts: "By striking out the words declaring him not reeligible, he was put into a situation that would keep him dependent forever on the Legislature; and he conceived the independence of the Executive to be equally essential with that of the Judiciary department." McClurg therefore moved to change the term of the executive's office from seven years to "during good behaviour."[40] Gouverneur Morris thereupon seconded the motion and "expressed great pleasure in hearing it. This was the way to get good Government. His fear that so valuable an ingredient would not be attained had led him to take the part he had done. He was indifferent how the executive should be chosen, provided he held his place by this tenure." In other words, Morris believed that a permanent tenure would ensure a strong and independent executive regardless of how he was chosen. Strangely, at this juncture, Broom, who had just before announced his choice for a shorter term if the president was not to be ineligible for reelection, now rose to say that he "highly approved the motion. It obviated all his difficulties."[41] John

Rutledge of South Carolina was, on the other hand, one of the few delegates who were satisfied with the appointment of the president by the national legislature. But here, too, he conditioned the president's term with the provision of ineligibility for reelection to assure that "he will be sufficiently independent."[42]

The delegates were not interested in establishing a monarch in the executive office. Certain animadversions were made on monarchy, yet it cannot be denied that sentiment prevailing for a strong executive was willing to go a long way toward "monarchy" in ensuring a powerful executive. L. B. Dunbar has concluded that "The existence of monarchical purposes in the Continental Convention is largely a matter of definition."[43]

A certain few of the members seemed to be pronouncedly in favor of a monarchy. John Dickinson of Delaware believed "A limited monarchy . . . one of the best Governments in the world. It was not certain that equal blessings were derivable from any other form."[44] Franklin, on the other hand, who was no lover of monarchy, nevertheless wondered whether "there is a natural inclination to Kingly Government" and seemed on the whole pessimistic about it being eventually averted even in America.[45] Madison, however, made the issue of monarchy before the convention perfectly clear. He asked the convention to give serious consideration to McClurg's proposal that the executive serve "during good behaviour" lest they construct another weak executive—like those in the states, "little more than Cyphers"—in which case "a revolution of some kind or other would be inevitable. "The preservation of Republican Government therefore required some expedient for the purpose, but required, evidently at the same time that in devising it, the genuine principles of that form should be kept in view."[46]

The leaders of the convention were so cognizant of the need for strength and independence in the executive that they were willing to extend his term of office to a length that seems shocking to conceptions of democracy in our generation. Gerry thought that the longer the president's term of office, the less will be his dependence on the legislature. "It will be better for him to continue 10, 15 or even 20 years and be ineligible afterwards." Luther Martin was for an eleven-year term, and Rufus King for a term of twenty years, saying, "This is the medium life of princes."[47] The value of the experience gained by the president in office was likewise emphasized in determining the length of his term. Both Wilson and

Gouverneur Morris were apprehensive that the term of office be made too short, or that his continuance be cut off by a provision of ineligibility. Wilson said:

> If the Executive should come into office at 35 years of age, which he presumes may happen and his continuance should be fixed at 15 years, at the age of 50, in the very prime of life, and with all the aid of experience, he must be cast aside like a useless hulk.[48]

Morris maintained similarly,

> If a good government should not now be formed, if a good organization of the Executive should not be provided, he doubted whether we should not have something worse than a limited monarchy. In order to get rid of the dependence of the Executive on the Legislature, the expedient of making him ineligible a second time had been devised. This was as much as to say we should give him the benefit of experience and then deprive ourselves of the use of it.[49]

It may be observed, too, that those who desired a long term for the president, or shorter terms under condition of reeligibility, relied heavily on impeachment to check the president.[50] Such importance did they give to this power of the legislature over the executive that it was feared that it might become a too powerful whip over the president. Gouverneur Morris urged that the causes of impeachment be defined, and King was of the opinion that the president should "not be impeachable unless he hold his office during good behaviour,"[51] and in no case should the legislature be allowed to have this power.[52]

The proposal that the president be neither elected by the national legislature nor by the people but instead by a college of electors was offered to break the deadlock that for many weeks had prevented the convention from coming to a decision. It must be abundantly clear by now, from the evidence adduced, that the issue of the executive's term of office, his reeligibility, and his powers reflected a strong fear that the presidential office might be constructed too weak, rather than too strong. Following Gerry's animadversion on his plan,[53] earlier rejected, of having the national executive elected by the state executive officers, Ellsworth offered his plan of indirect election—the president would be chosen by electors appointed by the state legislators. In explanation, be it noted, Ellsworth "supposed any persons might be appointed Electors, excepting solely members of the national Legislature."[54] The problem of determining a mode of election of the executive was not so easily solved, although Ellsworth's proposition commanded a heavy majority. Opinion was strongly divided as to method, although the fear of legislative influence on the executive was well nigh unanimous, to greater or lesser degree. Ellsworth was himself a marginal case: He was in favor of allowing the president "to be reelected if his conduct proved him worthy of it," but he believed "the most eminent characters will be more willing to accept the trust under this condition, than if they foresee a necessary degradation at a fixed period."[55] He was therefore disinclined to reinstate the terms of ineligibility. But the convention was completely at odds with itself, debating without end the proper term of office, reeligibility, and the mode of election. Ellsworth tried to resolve the impasse by suggesting that the national legislature make the appointment of the executive in the first instance, and have a college of electors appointed by the state legislatures determine his reelection.[56] Neither was this acceptable. The issue was debated many times on the floor and in the Committee on Detail (judging by the changes in the successive drafts), and finally committed to the Committee of Eleven to be determined, along with other vexing and seemingly insolvable problems relating to the executive.[57]

The report of the committee was a compromise, embodying Ellsworth's method of indirect election, adopting a four-year term, and maintaining silence on the issue of reeligibility. But it will be recalled, the report settled also the issue of the disputed powers of treaty making and appointment by giving them to the executive, though leaving the impeachment powers with the Senate. On the whole, the report was a distinct victory for a strong and independent executive. The principles of a balanced government were preserved, but the executive as finally created was a far cry from any conception of a national executive that had existed before. Unity, responsibility, and discretion[58] were lodged with the president, who would act in his own right. Though numerous suggestions were offered for the creation of an executive council,[59] the convention decided to make the president his own chief of the administration. To avoid any misunderstanding, they added Gouverneur Morris's final embellishment to the document: "The executive power shall be vested in a President of the United States of America."[60]

Readers may wonder at this point, having waded through such a mass of proposals and argumentation, why they have been burdened with so much detail. There are several reasons. In our historical tradition of explaining the Constitution, the emphasis has been on how governmental power was limited by such devices as the separation of powers, checks and balances, etc. No one can deny their importance. But it is clear that the Founding Fathers were surely intent on creating a strong executive office—which they did. What were their reasons? Obviously not merely to balance power against the legislature to resist possible tyranny in the negative sense. It is clear that they expected the president to perform a positive role with initiatives of his own and thus they endowed the office with sufficient independence and authority.

Perhaps the best way to understand what the Founding Fathers had in mind is by studying how the early national leaders used the presidential powers. If we compare the authority exercised by the presidents from 1789 to 1829 to the period after Jackson, the contrast is evident. One can hardly dispute the fact that Hamilton, in his drive to create an industrial state, having participated in helping to design the Constitution, knew where the levers of power were and how to use them.

PART II

THE NATIONAL

PLANNERS

CHAPTER V

Alexander Hamilton:

Credit and Finance

Hamilton's Role in National Planning

In the brief period of five years that Alexander Hamilton served as George Washington's secretary of the treasury, he was able to mold and influence the character of our government to a degree that has seldom, if ever, been equaled.[1] To his planning genius, perhaps more than to any other cause, do we owe the direction and form taken initially by our national government. Hamilton's leadership imparted definite meaning to the new federal Constitution—until then, a mere outline on paper. As secretary of the treasury, he assumed the task of organizing the administration and shaping its policies toward the goal of establishing a powerful centralized capitalist state. Within a few years, Hamilton's principles were stamped indelibly on the features of the new national economy, even though he failed to accomplish his whole program.

Why was Hamilton so successful? Why was he able, in only five years, to leave so great a mark on our history? Why were his financial arrangements of so enduring an effect? Why has Hamiltonianism persisted through the years?

One reason, no doubt, is that Hamilton profoundly grasped the meaning of the economic forces and trends of his time. He understood clearly the significance of such trends as the development of credit and the growth of factory production. He had watched the Industrial Revolution taking place in England, and he became passionately interested in the promotion of industry in the United States. Hamilton felt certain that the economic society of the future would rest heavily on the twin pillars of credit and industry. His vision was of a capitalist industrialized state aiding and assisting private enterprise by means of large-scale, continuous programs of national planning.

Without having to analyze Hamilton's other dynamic qualities of political leadership, there is no doubt that he owed much of his success to the system and care with which he formulated the elements of his national policy. His clear and orderly mind functioned in terms of coherent plans and integrated programs of action.[2] Hamilton disliked shifty and unbusinesslike methods, and he left little to chance. He was superbly equipped intellectually for the task of secretary of the treasury. He had thought deeply and long on the fiscal problems of the nation. It is true that the scope of his intellectual interests was limited, and he was lacking the qualities of sensitivity, curiosity, and depth. Nevertheless, what he lacked in these areas, he compensated for with a clear vision of what he wanted to achieve and a resolute determination to achieve it. He seems to have developed every main principle of his political and economic philosophy before his twenty-fifth year. As early as 1780, at the age of twenty-three, he had submitted to Robert Morris, superintendent of finance, a plan for a national bank. Simultaneously he was working on plans for permanent funds as a means of restoring public credit and for a new political and commercial system under which a national system of manufactures would be promoted by the government's "general superintendence of trade."[3]

Hamilton was bound by few of the emotional attachments and sectional prejudices that hampered the native-born American. An Anglo-French West Indian by birth and early training, he was able to survey American policy with the imperialistic outlook of an Englishman. During the confederation, as a member of Congress he complained that "despite the good intentions in the majority of Congress . . . there is a fatal opposition to Continental views" (11: 313). Hamilton espoused commercialism and industrialism instead of agrarianism, but not because he had any special affection for them as a way of life. To him, commerce and industry represented the trend of the future; agriculture represented the past. He foresaw an industrial future for the United States if the proper steps were taken. With vast quantities of cheap land available, he believed that agriculture could take care of itself. But in a world in which each national state acted by measures of subsidy and protection to promote its own manufactures, he realized that domestic manufactures in the United States would be condemned to failure without at least equal measures of protection and support.

The first step necessary was the strengthening of the political state. The Constitutional Convention had not seen fit to accept the model of autocratic government that Hamilton had proposed. He had had doubts concerning the ultimate efficacy of the Constitution as it was finally completed, but he accepted it as the best that could be obtained. Now that he was in a strategic position to strengthen it and give it life and purpose, he set for himself the task of making the government a proper instrument of his larger national policy. In his view, the security of the Union was far from being achieved by the acceptance of the Constitution and the establishment of the machinery of government. It was a good start, but nothing more. The Union might still suffer a gradual disintegration if the national government's authority were not consolidated.[4] The strength of the Constitution would depend on its works, not its words. A positive policy was needed to win to the support of the government those classes in society that could give it strength and stability.

Hamilton's class predilections coincided with the objects of his policy. He accepted the twin principles of class domination and exploitation as inevitable, and with them, the maxim that political power rests on the control of property. The political state could be strong only if it commanded the support of property interest. Hamilton acknowledged that the adoption of the Constitution was made possible by the fact that it commanded the confidence of men of wealth.

> The public creditors, who consisted of various descriptions of men, a large proportion of them very meritorious and very influential, had had a considerable agency in promoting the adoption of the new Constitution, for this peculiar reason, among the many weighty reasons which were common to them as citizens and as proprietors, that it exhibited the prospect of a government able to do justice to their claims. . . . There was also another class of men, and a very weighty one, who had had great share in the establishment of the Constitution, who though not personally interested in the debt, considered maxims of credit as of the essence of good government, as intimately connected by the analogy and sympathy of principles with the security of property in general, and as forming an inseparable portion of the great system of political order. (7: 418)

That a policy's adoption could be assured by having a vested interest to support it was no new discovery in the art of governing. Hamilton had himself in 1783 recommended that the influence of the army be united with the other interests to demand a restoration of the public credit.[5]

As secretary of the treasury, however, Hamilton intended to go much beyond uniting all groups in favor of his policies. He aimed not merely at invigorating existing property groups by having the national government extend them benefits. That government policy always benefited some and sometimes penalized others was obvious. But here Hamilton proposed nothing less than the creation of a new strong and permanent class throughout the country as a result of his policies. This class would be bound to the government and his administration by the strongest of all possible ties—direct and immediate personal interest. He proposed in this new working alliance between government and property to create those conditions that would facilitate an early and rapid industrialization of society. He therefore chose as his allies men of personality and fluid capital, whose relative position he correspondingly improved, hoping thereby to promote investments into industrial channels. That the erection of such a moneyed interest would antagonize the persons of real property and bonded slave property, Hamilton knew. But he trusted in the wisdom of his policies that it was safer to insure the enmity of the agrarian interest than of the commercial and manufacturing interests. Hamilton felt certain that the forces of the future were on his side.

Hamilton had hardly been appointed as Washington's secretary of the treasury when he was called on to formulate his program for funding the public debt and reviving the public credit. The first session of Congress had devoted its effort toward fashioning the administrative and judicial structures, passing the measures for obtaining immediate revenue, and considering the first ten amendments to the Constitution. It had done nothing on the public debt except to pass a declaratory resolution to the effect that a provision for the public creditors was necessary and that it should be considered during the next session. Only ten days following his appointment, the House passed a resolution directing that the secretary of the treasury prepare a plan for the support of the public credit and report it to the House at its next meeting.[6]

Less than four months later, in January 1790, when Congress assembled for its second session, Hamilton announced that his Report on the Public Credit was ready for publication (2: 227, 291).[7] Hamilton was anxious to present his report in person, but the House compelled him to communicate it in writing. It was laid before the House on January 14, and a fortnight later was taken up for consideration.

In this first of his monumental reports, Hamilton laid the foundations for the building of a capitalistic economy.[8] He proposed to deal with the debt not merely as a heavy financial obligation of the struggling new republic, but as an instrument of reviving the financial life of the nation. A proper funding of the debt, by its consolidation and capitalization, would turn a national liability into a great public asset. Instead of treating the problem piecemeal, or even as a separate problem in itself, the funding of the debt was part of a comprehensive, clearly conceived financial scheme, and only the first step proposed toward it. In a succession of masterly reports, Hamilton would presently offer to Congress plans that would go beyond immediate urgencies of the national and state debts. Their objects would be additional national revenue, the establisment of a national bank, a system of national coinage, and a program for fostering and promoting national manufactures. Taken together, his reports constituted a unified and integrated program of planning on such a grand scale that even today it would appear as a magnificent conception of an economy directed and controlled toward socially chosen objectives.

Plan for Improvement of Public Credit

In his Report on the Public Credit, Hamilton proceeded in systematic fashion to lay his financial program before Congress. He introduced the report by observing the truth in the House resolution that "an adequate provision for the support of the public credit is a matter of high importance to the honor and prosperity of the United States." The establishment of the nation's credit must be set on the soundest principles. A future exigency may necessitate resort to borrowing, which is "an indispensable resource even to the wealthiest at times." The nation's credit standing will depend on its "good faith" and its "punctual performance of contracts. . . . States, like individuals, who observe their engagements are respected and trusted, while the reverse is the fate of those who pursue the opposite conduct. . . . Every breach of public engagements, whether by choice or necessity, is in different degrees hurtful to public credit" (2: 229). It is on grounds of self-interest that the observance of our debts was urged. A "general belief prevails," he said, "that the credit of the United States will quickly be established on the firm foundation of an effectual provision for the existing debt." He went on to urge that "the time for doing so is now, since the embarrassments of a defective

Constitution which defeated this laudable effort have ceased" (2: 231). Hamilton advanced his cause both on grounds of general policy and of particular benefits to be gained from it. The "general considerations" on which he based his argument were: the enhanced "respectability of the American Name," the assurance of justice, furnishing new resources both to agriculture and commence, cementing the union of the states, adding to the security against attack, and establishing public order on the basis of an upright and liberal policy. In addition, he argued that "it will procure, to every class of the community some important advantages, and remove some no less important disadvantages" (2: 232). The benefit to the public creditors is obvious—"from the increased value of that part of their property which constitutes the public debt" (2: 233).[9]

> But there is a consequence of this, less obvious, though not less true, in which every other citizen is interested. It is a well known fact, that, in countries in which the national debt is properly funded, and an object of established confidence, it answers most of the purposes of money. Transfers of stock or public debt are their equivalent to payments in specie; or in other words, stock and the principal transactions of business, passes current as specie. The same thing would, in all probability, happen here under the like circumstances.

As a result, he argued, "trade is extended by it, because there is a larger capital to carry it on; . . . agriculture and manufactures are promoted by it, for the like reason, that more capital can be commanded to be employed in both." Finally, he maintained, "the interest of money will be lowered by it" because of the increased quantity of money. This would help materially in reducing our deficiency of capital resources, and would "enable both the public and individuals to borrow on easier and cheaper terms" (2: 233–34).

Hamilton was insistent that it would be "unjust and impolitic" to force a discrimination "between the original holders of the public securities and the present possessors, by purchase." The latter should be treated on equal terms with the former, for it would also be "ruinous to public credit" (2: 238, 241) for the government to breach its contracts. That many had suffered the loss of their equities through forced sale he did not deny. But it would be impairing the effectiveness of his remedy for the public credit as well as violating the Constitution to insist on a discriminatory honoring of the debt. As if what he had already proposed were not drastic enough, Hamilton now boldly recommended that the national government assume all the state debts, too. He believed that this would "contribute, in an eminent degree, to an orderly, stable and satisfactory arrangement of the national finances." It could be "more conveniently and effectually made" in one plan "than by different plans originating in different authorities." He wanted to avoid a "competition for resources" (2: 244–45) between the national and state governments, which would perforce drive up money rates. He wanted to eliminate the danger of disgruntled state creditors uniting to sabotage the success of his whole program. Hamilton knew full well that to carry through the rest of the program maturing in his mind, he would need the aid and support of every interest. As he rationalized it, "if all the public creditors receive their dues from one source, distributed with an equal hand, their interest will be the same. And, having the same interests, they will be united in the support of the fiscal arrangements of the Government" (1: 246).

Let us stop for a moment and ponder what Hamilton was proposing here. He was recommending that the national government immediately assume a burden of upward of $70 million of debt. This would include not only the national government's foreign and domestic debt, but also the indebtedness of the states, to be funded and redeemed in full, without discrimination and without discount.

It is difficult for a generation whose thinking has become inured to annual expenditures of hundreds of billions of dollars to feel awed by the sum of $70 million. Yet the relative resources must be considered. The government was new and untested. Its population was only four million, of whom one-sixth were Negroes, mostly slaves. Industry was still undeveloped and agriculture was relatively primitive. Writing in 1941, Alvin Hansen said "the federal debt was larger at the end of the Washington Administration than it is at the present moment," the relative fiscal capacity being considered.[10]

The debt could be divided into three categories: foreign debt, domestic debt, and states' debt. The foreign debt, including principal and interest, amounted to $11,710,000 (2: 254–55).[11] On it the government was from four to six years delinquent in its interest payment, and it had met none of the installments of the principal that began to be due in 1787. The domestic debt, representing a variety of accrued credit obligations, was $40,414,000, of which a little over $13 million was in arrears of interest. The sale of the public lands had helped liquidate a fraction of the principal, but interest arrearages had continued until the interest due represented one-third of the total. By recommending the assumption of the states' debt, Hamilton proposed to add approximately $20 million to the debt of the new republic.

The government could probably have settled its obligations honorably with a far smaller load of debt than Hamilton wished to impose on it. Why did he propose a greater debt than was either legally or morally necessary? He could, for example, have driven a hard bargain with the public creditors and won certain concessions, by way of discounts and low interest rates. He might have planned the restoration of the public credit after the manner of a thrifty merchant, by reducing all expenses to the barest necessities and applying all savings toward the payment of the debt, hoping that eventually it would be paid off.

Hamilton was indeed frequently charged with trying to maintain a perpetual debt on the shoulders of the people for the special benefit of a select class of creditors. Indeed, Jefferson attacked him on precisely this ground. In a letter written to President Washington in 1792, he said, "This exactly marks the difference between Colonel Hamilton's views and mine, that I wish the debt paid tomorrow; he wishes it never to be paid, but always a thing wherewith to corrupt and manage the legislature" (2: 464). Hamilton had too keen a mind to be befuddled by the argument of the Jeffersonians that he was trying to impose a perpetual debt and interest burden on posterity. He wanted to achieve certain goals for the new government and toward effecting an economic policy, which under the circumstances was impossible without incurring a large public debt. He did not shrink from doing so, for he was confident of the correctness of his views. Politically, from his point of view, his debt policy was indispensable. It would have the effect of enhancing the government's stability. But political reasons alone are not sufficient to explain Hamilton's debt policy.

The conception of an economic balance is basic to Hamilton's policies. This is not immediately apparent in his writings. He seems at first glance to favor trade and industry at the expense of agriculture. The reason, in short, is that there was a preponderance of agriculture compared to industry. He believed that a proper balance between these economic forces should be established, and this could come about only by acts of public policy, not by automatic economic forces. The exact point at which balance was to result would be determined by the specific facts of the situation—that is, by careful investigation and watching of trends. Hamilton may be criticized on the grounds that he was too solicitous of one interest and not solicitous enough of another. This is a matter of opinion. It cannot be maintained, however, that he was indifferent to or unconcerned with the welfare of any important segment of the economy. The idea of achieving an economic balance is implicit in his whole scheme of planning.

Hamilton's debt policy aimed also to effect a balance between the level of debt and the national capacity to pay, based on a plan of using the debt to augment the nation's supply of circulating capital.[12] The debt was always to be kept in appropriate limits, and measures were to be taken with a view to the debt's ultimate redemption. The object of the debt, however, was to convert the depreciated bonds into credit instruments that could pass for additional capital for the expansion of industry. Hamilton's debt policy was intended to synchronize with his policy of industrial expansion. America's need for additional capital was apparent. The funding policy aimed at expanding commercial and industrial credit in order to increase national productive capacity. Others might be timid or afraid of so large a national debt. Hamilton had optimistically gauged its size by his calculations of future national income.

Hamilton felt his optimism warranted by his estimated trends of the nation's prospective economic development. Although existing economic knowledge did not permit exact figures, he had reckoned fairly accurately on the course of our economic growth. As early as 1781 he voiced this confidence in our economic future in a letter to Robert Morris:

> Speaking within moderate bounds, our population will be doubled in thirty years; there will be a confluence of emigrants from all parts of the world, our commerce will have a proportionate progress and of course our wealth and capacity for revenue. It will be a matter of choice if we are not out of debt in twenty years, without at all encumbering the people. (3: 387)

He felt convinced that his policy would eventually redound to the advantage of the government itself, however oppressive it might seem to some now. In his Report on the Public Credit he stated, "The Secretary conceives that there is a good reason to believe, if effectual measures are taken to establish public credit, that the Government rate of interest in the

United States will in a very short time, fall at least as low as five per cent" (2: 258). Hamilton did not believe that in general "public debts are public benefits," a position that he said was "inviting to prodigality and liable to dangerous abuse" (2: 283). But he believed that under certain circumstances "a national debt, if it is not excessive, will be to us a national blessing" (3: 387). He feared not debt in itself, as that debt would be invited by government through extravagance and expenditures incurred for frivolous reasons.[13] Nor did he think that public debt should be incurred without provision being made for its repayment. For example, in his Report on the Public Credit, he recommended "extension of taxation to a degree" (2: 256), offering a detailed program for obtaining revenue. (See pages 83–85.) His political enemies may have had valid reasons for opposing Hamilton's measures for obtaining revenue. But no one can charge the secretary of the treasury with evading his responsibility of recommending ways and means of obtaining the necessary funds. He told Congress that he "ardently wishes to see it incorporated as a fundamental maxim in the system of public credit of the United States that the creation of debt should always be accompanied with the means of extinguishment. This he regards as the true secret for rendering public credit immortal" (2: 283).

Hamilton believed that his program would be certain to improve the nation's borrowing power, with the result that "no country will be able to borrow of foreigners upon better terms than the United States, because none can, perhaps, afford so good security" (2: 258). The acceptance of his plan would be accompanied by an "increase of the moneyed capital of the nation by the funding of the debt" with the consequent fall in the interest rate to the public and private borrower alike. A public debt, now a liability, would be rendered an asset to the nation, helping thereby to create a strong industrial commonwealth. Charles A. Beard summarizes the usefulness of Hamilton's public credit scheme:

> The upshot of the whole procedure, from an economic point of view was the transformation of well nigh worthless public paper into substantial fluid capital to be employed in commerce, manufacturing, and the development of Western lands. It was not merely the payment of the debt that Hamilton had in mind; on the contrary, the sharp stimulation of capitalism, banking, commerce, and manufactures—was an equally fundamental part of his system.[14]

Plan for a National Bank

When Congress met again in December 1790 after the passage of the funding and the assumption measures, Hamilton brought forth his great Report on the Establishment of a National Bank. Like the first, this report was in response to the order of the House calling for a further provision the secretary might consider necessary for establishing the public credit. The fact that the treasury was faced with an immediate deficiency of $826,624 as shown by his accompanying report on the public credit (2: 337) gave the subject of a national bank extreme urgency.

Hamilton had long been convinced of the need to establish a national bank. He had carefully explored the subject in 1781, proposing the idea to Robert Morris who was then superintendent of finance (3: 319–41, 342–87). The earlier and later plans were essentially the same. He was already thinking of the national bank when he gave Congress the Report on the Public Credit almost a year earlier (2: 286). But he wisely refrained from mentioning it until his funding scheme was accepted.

When Jefferson aided in passing the act of assumption he could hardly have known that Hamilton stood ready, like the magician pulling rabbits out of a hat, to bring forth not one, but a series of financial measures.[15] As soon as one act was passed, Hamilton was ready to present another. Jefferson belonged definitely to the placid world of eighteenth-century country life; Hamilton saw with a modern eye the possibilities inherent in credit agencies and instruments. Where one was content to allow the world to move along at its leisurely gait, the other was for pushing ahead the growth of commerce and industry with all the system and energy that he could muster. While Hamilton's plan for a bank was visibly influenced by the example of the Bank of England, it embodied remarkably the conception of our own Federal Reserve banking system. Hamilton saw it as a necessary agency to the maintenance of the paper edifice that had resulted from his first report. He conceived of a national bank as more than a depository for the safekeeping of government funds, or even as a source for governmental borrowing.[16] Although the bank was designed to benefit the commercial and financial classes, Hamilton regarded it primarily as "a political machine of the greatest importance to the State" (3: 424). It could render service to the treasury by helping it collect and transfer its moneys, in addition to making it loans. But far more important, a strong and well-managed national bank, through its power to issue notes and make loans, could augment the supply of fluid capital, provide a system of uniform bank currency (and yet eliminate the dangers of government paper money), and control and direct the use of credit in the national economy.

Hamilton had vision; he could see that society was rapidly advancing into an age of credit media and credit institutions. At a time when Jefferson and many other agrarians saw no utility in banks and banking other than as a device for speculation and financial jugglery,[17] Hamilton saw that banks were rapidly becoming necessary for the transaction of everyday business.

The question, then, was not whether we would have banks, but what kind of banks, and on what kind of a system. Hamilton chose to have the government create a bank under its own auspices and under its own conditions, rather than have note-issuing banks mushroom without system and order. He was not worried about the possible dangers of financial monoply; he regarded the absence of adequate credit institutions as a greater danger to the national security. He was prepared to offer some safeguards against irresponsible banking practices—and if need be, also against a too powerful banking monopoly.[18] He felt fully confident in the power of the government to rectify a situation of this kind.

Much of Hamilton's Report on a National Bank was concerned with simple explanation of the function of banks in a credit economy, how they work, and their advantages. Hamilton was acting as a schoolmaster to Congress and the nation. He discussed in detail many problems that are today common knowledge. Chiefly, he was interested in showing that banks should not be condemned simply because they were liable to abuses.

> If the abuses of a beneficial thing are to determine its condemnation, there is scarcely a source of public prosperity which will not speedily be closed. In every case, the evil is to be compared with the good; and in the present case such a comparison will issue in this, that the new and increased energies derived to commercial enterprise, from the aid of banks, are a source of general profit and advantage, which greatly outweigh the partial ills. (3: 402)

Hamilton wanted especially to convince Congress of the benefit of a well-conducted national bank in producing "an augmentation of the active or productive capital of a country." He argued that gold and silver, when used only for exchange, are "dead stock." When deposited in banks and becoming the basis of a paper circulation, "they then acquire life" and take on "an active and productive quality." The problem in the United States—long on natural resources and short on capital—was maximum utilization of its limited liquid capital resources. If it could stretch the uses of its existing gold and silver supply by making them the basis of increasing its total circulation, there was every reason for doing so. Banks "in good credit," Hamilton carefully explained, "can circulate a far greater sum than the actual quantum of their capital in gold and silver . . . performing in every stage the office of money" (3: 391). The employment given to money by a bank becomes" to all purposes of trade and industry an absolute increase of capital" (3: 393).[19] Other advantages to be obtained from a bank were: "the greater facility to the government in obtaining pecuniary funds, especially in sudden emergencies"; facilitating the paying of taxes through the assistance of bank loans; and eliminating the need of, and expense entailed in, shipping specie to enable the making of tax payments. Hamilton denied that banks diminish the national supply of precious metals by causing the export of specie. In countries like the United States that produce no gold of their own, the gold supply must ultimately depend on the "exchange of the products of its labor and industry" for goods of other countries. "Hence, the state of its agriculture and its manufactures, the quantity and quality of its labor and industry, must, in the main, influence and determine the increase and decrease of its gold and silver" (3: 405). (This argument, as Hamilton makes clear, is dependent, of course, on a number of other circumstances.) The credit and currency problem, though not even primary and certainly not alone in affecting the national prosperity, if handled advantageously was one means by which our existing disadvantages could be remedied and our existing resources augmented.

Having established the general desirability of banking, Hamilton went on to examine the peculiar needs of the United States that might recommend the establishment of a national bank. The "deficiency of circulating medium" was a subject with which everyone was familiar. This was especially noticeable "in the more interior districts of the country." The settlement of these "vast tracts of waste land" (3: 411) constituted, furthermore, a continual drain on the existing supply. Every section of the country—not merely the commercial centers—would benefit by the additional amount of banknotes and bank credit that would be available from a national bank. Uniform banknotes having a "general currency, equivalent to gold and silver" would avoid the waste attendant to accumulation, suspension from circulation, and expense involved in shipping of specie to the distant places.

Hamilton's plan for a national bank was therefore part of his larger program of expanding the limited credit facilities and financial resources of the United States by means of government action. Since there was no bank in existence that he considered capable of assuming these great public responsibilities, he recommended that one be created.[20] The bank should be erected primarily on the basis of performing a public utility rather than rendering a profit to its organizers. "Public utility is more truly the object of public banks than private profit," he said (3: 419). Yet he was opposed to making it completely a public institution, wholly under government control. Hamilton had no prejudices against the government participating in banking per se, but in this case he feared that it would be "liable to being too much influenced by *public necessity*" (3: 424). He felt that in the case of banks, "the keen, steady, as it were, magnetic sense of their own interest as proprietors, in the directors of the bank . . . is the only security that can always be relied upon for a careful and prudent administration" (3: 428). The government might too easily yield "to the temptations of monetary exigency . . . should the credit of the bank be at the disposal of the government. . . . What nation was ever blessed with a constant succession of upright and wise administrators?" he asked. Hamilton feared that, under governmental pressure, the bank might become "an immediate instrument of loans to the proprietors of land." He held that "land is alone, an unfit fund for bank circulation" and bank loans issued on land as bank security "would amount to nothing more than a repetition of the paper emissions" (3: 425). Hamilton's warnings seem prophetic in the light of early-nineteenth-century wildcat banking experience when land speculations formed the state banks' stock in trade.

Having decided that the government should not own all the stock of the national bank, Hamilton went to say, "It will not follow . . . that the state may not be a holder of part of the stock of the bank, and consequently a sharer in the profits of it. It will only follow that it ought not to desire any participation in the direction of it, and therefore, ought not to own the whole or a principal part of the stock" (3: 430). As the bank was to be primarily a public utility, certain precautions must be taken to protect the interest of the public in its management. 1. The government was to be represented on the governing board of the bank, to the extent of its ownership of the total shares of the bank.[21] The bank would have a total capitalization of $10 million, divided into twenty-five thousand shares, to which the government would subscribe $2 million in stock.[22] 2. The bank's charter was to contain certain precise limitations on its power and terms under which it could do business. For example, its total real estate could never exceed $15 million in value; its maximum debts should never be allowed to exceed its capital stock; it could trade only in bills of exchange, gold and silver bullion, and the sale of goods pledged as rent; it could not charge more than 6 percent interest on its loans and discounts. 3. Its charter was to extend for a period of twenty years, during which time Congress could charter no similar institution. Since the bank would have to depend on the goodwill of the federal government for a renewal of its charter, Hamilton felt that "it will not be likely to feel a disposition to render itself, by its conduct, unworthy of public patronage" (3: 430). 4. Finally, the public interest was to be secured by a regular and periodic inspection by the Treasury Department of the condition of the bank, and by its securing a statement of the bank's finances as often as it required. In Hamilton's words, "the Government owed to itself and the community . . . to reserve to itself a right of ascertaining, as often as may be necessary, the state of the bank" (3: 430).

Plan for Currency and Coinage

While Congress was divided in bitter debate on the question of the national bank,[23] Hamilton communicated to it his Report on the Establishment of a Mint (4: 3–58). Here, in what A. B. Hepburn calls "his justly celebrated report,"[24] Hamilton again revealed his talent for systematically considering a problem in all its aspects and formulating a long-range plan for its achievement. The investiture in the new national government of powers to coin money and regulate its value, and of the corresponding denial to the states of the same power, made it incumbent upon the secretary to obtain the needed changes at the earliest opportunity. The provision of a stable, convenient, and uniform coinage and currency in ample amounts was an important means of facilitating exchange and the transaction of business. It was but another part of Hamilton's program of implementing the existing economy by public policy. Characteristically, Hamilton did not undertake the improvement of the nation's money piecemeal. He waited until he had had an opportunity to examine the problem in all its relations, and then presented Congress with a definite plan of action.

Others had preceded Hamilton in making plans for coinage. Robert Morris in 1782, then superintendent of finance, had presented to Congress a comprehensive report on the subject in which he recommended the establishment of a mint and the coinage of the pieces he proposed. He pointed out the need of having uniformity of coinage, and of legal tender provisions as well. Morris proposed a money unit that would be 1/1400th part of a dollar, as the fraction into which the several state currencies were directly divisible. Jefferson, as secretary of state, suggested the use of the decimal system to divide the currency, and he offered a substitute plan in which the Spanish dollar would be adopted as the unit, divisible by multiples of ten (4: 297–313).[25] The substance of Jefferson's report was accepted by Congress, which by a series of acts laid the basis for the decimal system of coinage. In 1785 Congress established the dollar as the monetary unit, divisible in the decimal ratio. In 1786 two acts were passed: one decided the relationship of weight and fineness that was to exist between the metals constituting the dollar; the other authorized the establishment of a mint. These acts, Hepburn writes, "never became fully operative,"[26] and only copper coins were actually minted. A diversity of coins, mostly of foreign origin (chiefly Spanish), continued in circulation. When the national government was established, no system of coinage actually existed. The time was ripe for a complete overhaul of the problem.

Hamilton's report called attention to the "immense disorder which actually reigns in so delicate and important a concern, and the still greater disorder which is every moment possible" (4: 5). The dollar established by statute had depreciated fully 5 percent with scarcely an effort made to repair the disparity. There was still a great dissimilarity in the kinds of money used in different parts of the Union, and even the same coins, in different places, had unequal values.

The problem of deciding what should be the unit of money in the United States was further complicated by inconsistency and ambiguity of the two previous resolutions of Congress in 1786. After a detailed examination of all the problems involved, Hamilton arrived at the same conclusions as Morris and Jefferson in their previous reports: A bimetallic system offered advantages over having the money unit attached exclusively to either one of the precious metals. Although his preference would have been a single gold standard, he felt that this would result in reducing the utility of the supply of silver. Again, his criterion was facilitating the maximum utilization of the existing resources. Hamilton went on to consider all the problems and details of organizing a currency and a minting system, such as the advantages of free coinage over seigniorage, the number of units of pure metal that the money unit should comprise, the ratio by weight between them, the number of coins that would be required, and the cost of the mint's operation. Within the limits of estimate and forecast, as little as possible was left to chance. Hamilton had presented to Congress an exact, comprehensive, long-range plan for the facilitation of exchange and for the maximum utilization of its credit and currency resources.

Detailed Analysis of Hamilton's Funding Scheme

The details of Hamilton's funding scheme and his plan for obtaining of revenue are of historical interest only, but are relevant to a full under-standing of his system of fiscal planning. Hamilton's methods of funding were not original. He relied largely on English and Dutch precedents, the subject being too grave and intricate "to allow him to travel freely beyond the line of tried and known expedients."[27] Hamilton admits this in his report (2: 276). The system of funding he worked out was exceedingly complex. He offered the creditors six different options with varying rates of interest, varying terms of redemption, conversion in whole or in part into annuities of several kinds, including also public land grants in part payment of twenty cents per acre. This was so complicated a scheme that few could fully understand it. Its complexity exposed Hamilton to the charge that its purpose was to enable him to juggle the treasury funds without detection. Actually, of course, Hamilton wanted to offer the creditors the largest number of alternatives. As Dunbar says, "With a domestic money market as yet untried and with the public credit still to be created, it may well have appeared dangerous to Hamilton at the end of 1789 to stake his success upon the possible popularity of any single form of investment."[28] His tontine scheme, fashioned after the British tontine of 1789, involved a system of rights of annual payments to survivors, the annuities therefrom becoming the means of creating a permanent invest-ment class. Dunbar, however, explains Hamilton's willingness to leave the term of redemption open and his scheme of a permanent sinking fund not to his unwillingness to see the debt finally paid off, but as better suited to the needs of a government whose future revenues were undetermined and unascertained. Hamilton's first proposition, he says, was "for a security perpetual—having no fixed time for maturity, but redeemable whenever the government might find redemption convenient—temporary or perpetual therefore according to the financial strength of the debtor.[29]

Hamilton estimated the annual charge of interest on the domestic debt as $2,239,163, to which he added $600,000 as the estimated cost of the governmental services, making a total annual estimated expenditures of $2,839,163 (2: 271–72). How did he propose to raise this amount? To avoid an immediate drain of cash, which the United States "could illy bear" now, he proposed that the installments of the foreign debt be paid by new loans abroad. Since the exact amount of the states' debts was undetermined, and since the consent of the state security holders must be first obtained, he argued that for the present "an actual provision would be premature" (2: 270–71, 286–87). Hamilton proposed the sale of Western lands at twenty cents an acre for the discharge of the debt as one of the options offered the creditors. In Hamilton's view, the public lands were regarded almost exclusively as a financial asset, and the receipts from their sale could be pledged to discharge the public debt. He expected further that the proposed reorganization of the post office would afford a surplus that could readily be applied to payment of the debt. He offered Congress a detailed program of taxes, which in addition to "the present duties of imports and tonnage . . . which, without any possible disadvantage, either to trade or agriculture" (2: 272), would bring in an estimated annual revenue of $1,703,400 (2: 281). This was to come from new duties on wines, spirits (including those distilled in the United States), tea, and coffee. He argued that these articles were, for the most part, luxuries of foreign origin, and a tax on them would occasion no suffering. In any case, should the tax result in a decrease of their consumption, "the effect would be in every respect desirable." (Hamilton did not overlook efficient enforcement of this act to eliminate customs evasion.)

For his fiscal edifice, Hamilton erected a sinking fund that was to be in the charge of a group of commissioners to consist of the vice president, speaker of the house, the chief justice, secretary of the treasury, and attorney general. This body was to be authorized to borrow $12 million on the government's credit, and with this, in addition to other sums (as from the post office), they were to make payments on the interest and installments of the foreign debt and to make payments of any deficiencies that might occur, to effect if possible a lowering of interest.

Finally, the commission would have authority to purchase and redeem government securities in the market "at a price . . . while it continues below its true value" (2: 284–85).

CHAPTER VI

Alexander Hamilton:

Industrial Development

Plan for Industrial Development

Hamilton's plan for establishing the funding system and the national bank was only part of the total system of planning that he envisaged for the future. Although separate objectives in themselves, they constituted the first step in his larger financial program. They were integrally related to his plan for the ultimate industrialization of the United States, which, I believe, was the focal point of his whole program. They were to furnish the means of expanding America's fluid capital resources and in turn to attract this additional capital into channels of domestic manufactures and industrial production. Industry was to be deliberately and systematically encouraged by means of a long-range and far-reaching plan.

No prophetic gifts were needed to see at this time that industrial progress was the road of the future. Manifestations of growing industry were to be seen everywhere; a trend toward manufactures was apparent even before the Revolution. The frustrations of American manufacturers working under the prohibitive and restrictive rules of British mercantilism had, in fact, contributed materially and explosively to the impetus that resulted in the Revolution. In the period after the Revolution, American manufacturers encountered many obstacles in the path of their continued progress. England was exacting her price for the freedom that had been won; she imposed conditions on her foreign trade to hamper American industrialism at every turn. Markets formerly available to American trade were withdrawn. Fine hopes prevailing immediately after the Treaty of Paris that international trade would be soon restored on a parity basis were to be rudely dispelled.[1]

86

Prior to the ratification of the Constitution, those engaging in manufactures keenly appreciated the need for a strong political organization. The lack of a uniform market and a uniform currency, the presence of interstate trade barriers and conflicts, and foreign disparagement of our export trade fostered discontent among manufacturing enterprises. Dissatisfaction had about reached a turning point when the Philadelphia convention was convened. The desire of the manufacturing interest to establish domestic industry on a sound basis was a powerful support for the ratification of the new federal Constitution.

Hamilton certainly was not alone in wishing to give permanence to the American industrial structure. Others had likewise awakened to the possibilities of establishing manufacturing in the United States. The progress being made by industry in Europe was fully appreciated by many in America. Washington's attitude may be regarded as typical of those who favored the growth of industry if it could be accomplished without detriment to agriculture. He believed that in the improvement of manufactures would be found a way to increase national wealth and prosperity. On the eve of assuming the presidency, he wrote his friend the Marquis de LaFayette: "Certain, it is, great savings are already made in articles of apparel, furniture and consumption. Equally certain it is, that no diminution of agriculture has taken place, at the time when greater and more substantial improvements in manufactures were making, than were ever known before in America."[2]

The expansion of commerce and industry was believed also to be the means of strengthening the ties of human brotherhood between the countries. As foreign trade developed, mankind might become, in Washington's opinion, "connective like one great family in fraternal ties." He could not "avoid reflecting with pleasure on the probable influence that commerce may hereafter have on the human manners and society." For a time, in common with many other leaders in American political life, he believed in the virtues of free trade. In 1786, when American hopes were highest that Europeans would trade with this country without discrimination, Washington wrote LaFayette that in his opinion "the period is not very remote when the benefits of a liberal and free commerce will pretty generally succeed to the devastations and horrors of war" (9: 194).[3]

Washington's hope that foreign trade relationships would remain free expressed the view predominant among American statesmen until fairly late in the 1780s. As the decade drew to its close, many began to perceive that the hope was a delusion. No European country gave any evidence of changing its discriminatory policy by treating the new American republic as an equal in trade. The belief that the newly organized national government should assume a share in protecting the industrial interest had its adherents in the first Congress. According to Hill, the first revenue act passed by Congress in 1789, although ostensibly a revenue measure, was tinged with the protectionist viewpoint.

Alexander Hamilton's views on the development of manufactures would be worthy of little consideration if they were merely arguments in behalf of a protectionist tariff. His Report on Manufactures became the Bible of protectionists during the nineteenth century when the tariff controversy was revived. In consequence, Hamilton became known chiefly as a protectionist, not as a planner for industrial development.

Hamilton was not interested simply in protecting manufactures. He planned to do more than perpetuate America's present development of industry. He aimed at developing manufactures as a whole, in short, in industrializing the United States. His views did not develop because of our experience with European discriminatory trade policies. Hamilton had never been an internationalist. He did not share the optimism of Washington and others that European treatment of American trade was temporary, preceding a revival of the international trade. Had the European countries behaved in a more brotherly manner, in all probability Hamilton would still have favored his broad policy of planning for our industrial development. He favored it not because the Europeans allowed us no other course, but because he believed that in industry lay our great national destiny. He believed in industry for its own sake, for the benefits it wrought. As early as 1774, he voiced his confidence in America's industrial future: "If . . . manufactures should once . . . take root among us, they will pave the way still more to the future grandeur and glory of America."[4] The growth of a favorable protectionist sentiment beginning in the late 1780s and early 1790s gave Hamilton the opportunity for which he had long been waiting.

The main outline of his plan was the product of slow maturation. His scheme to expand credit facilities by means of the funding proposal and the establishment of a national bank, although separate objects in themselves, served also to promote his plan for a systematic development of industry. Hamilton's political purposes must never be forgotten in evaluating his policies. Morison, Commager, and Leuchtenburg have gone so far as to say, "Instead of his political policy having an economic object, his economic policy had a political object."[5] These views, in my opinion, overstate the importance that Hamilton attached to the political results of his policy. There can be no disputing, however, that in Beard's phrase, Hamilton's industrial program would serve "to draw another allied group of interest to the aid of the security and bank stockholders in maintaining the new government."[6] The need of strengthening the manufacturing interest and adding its support to the newly founded government explains, in part, why Hamilton seemed so desperately eager to push his industrial program into effect.

Hamilton's views concerning the planned development of industry were derived from his acceptance of current mercantilist practices.[7] He seems hardly to have questioned the propriety of governmental regulations of trade. He felt that an energetic policy of encouraging commerce and industry had proven its merits in actual practice. In the "Continentalist" paper written in 1781–82, he cited the fact that "trade may be said to have taken its rise in England under the auspices of Elizabeth." Its "rapid progress" was "in great measure to be ascribed to the fostering care of government in that and succeeding reigns." Likewise, in his opinion, France owed much of "her prosperous conditions . . . to the abilities and indefatigable endeavors of the great Colbert" who he believed laid the foundation of French commerce and taught his successors to enlarge and improve it (1: 267, 270). So far as European countries were concerned, mercantilism was already in a stage of decline. Hamilton, however, viewed some of the methods of mercantilism as the efficient means of combating European trade discrimination, and to an even greater extent, of planning the growth of American industry.

Hamilton was sufficiently a student of political economy to understand the "fixed principles according to which it must be regulated." He realized that "if these are understood and observed, it will be promoted by the attention of government; if unknown, or violated, it will be injured." He was opposed to "the injudicious attempts made at different times to effect a regulation of prices." Trade "had its fundamental laws, agreeable to which its general operations must be directed, and . . . any violent attempt in opposition to those would miscarry." But this proposition should not be confused with the view that "trade will regulate itself, and is not to be benefited by the encouragements or restraints of government . . . . Such persons," he said, "imagine that there is no need of a common directing power."

In his opinion, "vesting Congress with power of regulating trade . . . is as necessary for the purposes of commerce as of revenue." He believed that this was in consonance with "the uniform practice and sense of the most enlightened nations." Hamilton accounted himself a follower of David Hume's ideas on foreign trade. Hume's essay, "Of the Balance of Trade," did not intend to imply "that trade will hold a certain unvariable course independent of said protection or concern of government" even though "it will in the main, depend upon the comparative industry more and physical advantages of nations" by which trade will ultimately return to its proper level. This much may be taken for granted. "But," says Hamilton, "it was no part of Hume's design to insinuate that the regulating hand of government was either useless or hurtful." The preservation of a nation's "balance of trade . . . ought to be a leading aim to its policy." He believed that pains ought to be "taken to cultivate particular branches of trade" and "to discourage others." It was the duty of government to explore the "possibility of opening new sources" of trade. In certain cases, "great difficulties" often attend initial efforts to develop new trade channels. "The undertaking may often exceed the influence and capitals of individuals and may require no small assistance, as well as from the revenue as from the authority of the state." Hamilton believed the state ought to interfere and he was certain that the improvements in commerce would "amply repay the trouble and expense of bringing them to perfection."

Hamilton's views expressed as a private citizen in the "Continentalist" in 1781 had not changed when he became secretary of the treasury in 1789. He never believed in laissez-faire so far as the promotion of trade and industry was concerned. His new official position gave him an opportunity to make his views those of the Washington administration. He saw his chance when, in reply to Washington's first annual address, the House of Representatives requested that the secretary prepare a plan by which the United States may become "independent of other nations for essential, particularly for military supplies." Hamilton immediately began to assemble the data, relying on his own extensive knowledge and the experience of his many associates and friends in industry.[8]

Within less than a year, the Report on Manufactures was ready to be presented to Congress, being communicated to the House of Representatives on December 5, 1791. The time must have seemed opportune for launching domestic manufactures on a large scale. The recent and deliberate embarrassments to our trade by England inclined many to the acceptance of retaliatory measures. Protectionist sentiment was now ready to urge a long-range program of industrial development. Unsettled conditions in Europe might also assist in advancing industry by furnishing a supply of skilled labor. In Hamilton's opinion, "the disturbed state of Europe" made it possible for "the requisite workmen to be more easily acquired than at another time" (4: 82–83). During such times, there would be increased opportunities for this country beginning its own industrial career.

The greatest single obstacle to the growth of manufactures in America, in Hamilton's opinion, was the opposition of the agrarian interest. The Report on Manufactures shows clearly Hamilton's understanding of the prejudice and suspicion held by the American farmer. Unless this distrust and antagonism could be removed, there was little hope of establishing a concerted effort in Congress in favor of planning industrial development. Much of the report is devoted to proving that there existed between agriculture and industry a mutual interest that was to the advantage of both to promote. He pleaded the cause of industry with every argument and rhetorical device at his command. Time was to show how right he was in stressing the need of overcoming agriculture's prejudices against manufacturing. It was in fact the ingrained dislike for manufactures by Jefferson's agrarian party that more than anything else explains Congress's rejection of Hamilton's plan.

With what discretion and prudence Hamilton began his courtship of the agricultural interest! He assured Congress that he was not trying to prove "that manufacturing industry is more productive than agriculture." His object was only to show "that the reverse of this proposition is not ascertained" and that "the establishment and diffusion of manufactures have the effect of rendering the total mass of useful and productive labor in a community greater than it would otherwise be" (4: 139). With patient logic and disarming reasonableness, he tried to prove that although the interests of agriculture and manufactures were different, they were not repugnant. On the contrary, each interest could gain from the other. With extreme care, he examined the basis of the arguments of those "unfriendly to the encouragement of manufactures." It was not true that 1. "agriculture is the most beneficial and productive objects of human industry"; nor does this apply "with peculiar emphasis to the United States on account of their immense tracts of fertile territory, uninhabited and unimproved" (4: 71–72). "To endeavor by the extraordinary patronage of the government, to accelerate the growth of manufactures, is in fact" 2. not "to endeavor by force and art, to transfer the natural current of industry from a more to a less beneficial channel." Nor was it any more true that 3. the prosecution of manufactures is unsuited to the United States at that time. It was unnecessary to wait for redundancy of population after all the land had become settled. Certain adverse conditions existed, and these could be admitted without affecting the essential practicability of manufactures. There existed "a scarcity of hands of manufacturing occupation"; there was undoubtedly "a deficiency of pecuniary capital." The "constant allurements to emigration . . . to the unsettled parts of the country" would make the establishments of manufacturing difficult. The "prospect of successful competition with the manufactures of Europe" was likewise cheering. Yet in Hamilton's view, none of these arguments singly or taken together was conclusive that the plea for the establishment of manufactures ought not to be seriously considered.

Having considered the practicability of manufactures, and having shown them to be compatible with a healthy condition of agriculture, Hamilton proceeded to enumerate the positive advantages of an industrial development, both for the farmer and the nation as a whole.

He listed what he called "principal circumstances from which it may be inferred that manufacturing establishments not only occasion a positive augmentation of the produce and revenue of the society, but that they contribute essentially to rendering them greater than they could possibly be without such establishments." These circumstances are:

1. The division of labor.
2. An extension of the use of machinery.
3. Additional employment to classes of the community not ordinarily engaged in the business.
4. The promoting of emigration from foreign countries.
5. The furnishing of greater scope for the diversity of talents and dispositions, which discriminate men from each other.
6. The affording a more ample and varied field for enterprise.
7. The creating, in some instances, a new, and securing, in all, a more certain and steady demand for the surplus produce of the soil. (4: 86–88)

His strongest appeal consisted, of course, not in proving the economic advantages of manufactures in the abstract, but in citing the specific benefits that the growth of manufactures would produce for the farmer. How would agriculture gain by the development of industry?

He cited first the fact that "it is a primary object of the policy of nations, to be able to supply themselves with subsistence from their own soils." No one would dispute the apparent "unwillingness" of other nations "to permit the agricultural countries to enjoy the advantages of theirs, and sacrifice the interests of a mutually beneficial intercourse to the vain project of selling everything and buying nothing" (4: 96). Moreover, even when there was a foreign market, it was generally unreliable. It gave the farmer little assurance that it would absorb his surplus produce at a price that would cover his costs. In Hamilton's words, it was "rather casual and occasional, than certain or constant."

There was no rational reason why American agriculture must remain in this condition of abject dependence on undependable foreign markets. The growth of domestic manufactures would absorb the agricultural surplus.

> The idea of an extensive domestic market for the surplus produce of the soil, is of the first consequence. It is, of all things, that which most effectually conduces to a flourishing state of agriculture. . . .
>
> To secure such a market there is no other expedient than to promote manufacturing establishments. Manufacturers, who constitute the most numerous class, after cultivators of the land, are for that reason the principal consumers of the surplus of their labor.
>
> . . . The multiplication of manufactories not only furnishes a market for those articles which have been accustomed to be produced in abundance in a country, but it likewise creates a demand for such as were either unknown or produced in inconsiderable quantities. (4: 97–99)

He appealed to the agricultural interest to accept these alternatives. The diversification of "industrious pursuits" and "the establishment of manufactures is calculated not only to increase the general stock of useful and productive labor, but even to improve the state of agriculture in particular—certainly to advance the interests of those who are engaged in it" (4: 97–99). The expansion of manufacturing would certainly offer an additional market for the products of the soil. He offered the farmer the prospect of an increased demand for his flax, cotton, hemp, wool, raw silk and indigo (4: 140–41). Hamilton pleaded for an understanding by the agricultural section of the grounds on which it could enter into a partnership with industry profitable to both.

> Ideas of a contrariety of interests between the Northern and Southern regions of the Union are, in the main, as unfounded as they are mischievous. The diversity of circumstances, on which such contrariety is usually predicated, authorizes a strictly contrary conclusion. Mutual wants constitute one of the strongest links of political connection; and the extent of these bears on natural proportion to the diversity in the means of mutual supply. (4: 139)

Hamilton cleverly turned one of the arguments of his opponents to his own advantage. It had been maintained that manufactures could not develop in the United States as long as the new Western settlements offered a superior attraction. Persons would prefer to settle the land than to work as factory laborers. Hamilton sought to show that delay in the establishment of manufactures would work to agriculture's own peril. The prosperity of the farmer did not permit its postponement until population became redundant. "Considering how fast and how much the progress of new settlements in the United States must increase the surplus produce of the soil" (4: 97–99), the agrarian interest was left to choose between a dependency on the fickle and arbitrary trade policies of the Europeans and building up a domestic market for its surplus produce.

Hamilton's views toward agriculture have been considerably distorted as a result of partisan interpretation. His protectionist policy has occasionally been identified with the tariff policies of the 1920s that almost spelled the doom of American agriculture. Hamilton would certainly have been a fool if he had tried to establish industry in the first place over agriculture. The great majority of American citizens still made their living from the land. Hamilton was certainly no fool; he planned only a moderately paced development of industry. Also, our national economy had not awakened to the great possibilities presented by the technology of the Industrial Revolution. Manufactures offered a most promising field for enterprise in the United States. The secretary prophetically discerned the importance of steam power: "substituting the agency of fire and water" (4: 108). Although he was confident that manufactures could be successfully established in the United States, he was firmly of the opinion that this could not be done effectively without artificial aid by the government. The odds against such a possibility were too great. Meanwhile, the American economy was seriously out of line: Agricultural surpluses would continue to grow without being assured of a dependable foreign market. There was no chance of foreign nations renouncing their own trade advantages. If the United States wanted to effect a stable economic balance, the government would have to institute a deliberate public policy.[9]

The need of military security and national defense was also forcefully argued to support the development of manufactures. It will be recalled that the resolution of the House of Representatives had requested the preparation of a plan that would "tend to render the United States independent of other nations for essential, particularly for military supplies." Hamilton certainly presented the military argument in the most persuasive terms. He argued from the assumption that the independence and security of a nation depend on its possessing within itself "all the essentials of a national supply. These comprise the means of subsistence, habitation, clothing and defense." It will be seen that Hamilton was taking a very broad view of the terms of the House's request. The "extreme embarrassments during the late war," he believed, should have taught us to avoid a repetition of these dangers in the future. The provision of these essential supplies must be "the next great work to be accomplished." The distance from European supplies, the high freight tolls, "the want of a navy of our own," and above all the "precarious reliance for the supply of essential articlès upon foreign nations must have served to strengthen prodigiously the arguments in favor of manufactures" (4: 135–36). Hamilton indicated even more strongly

> the improvidence in leaving these essential supplies of national defense to the casual speculations of individual adventure—a resource which can less be relied upon, in this case, than in most others. . . . As a general rule, manufactories on the immediate account of government are to be avoided; but this seems to be one of the few exceptions which that rule admits, depending on very special reasons.

He recommended that Congress consider "whether manufactories of all the necessary weapons of war ought not to be established on account of the government itself" (4: 168).

Could a system of domestic manufactures flourish without government support and direction? Hamilton was emphatically certain that it could not. It was not true "that industry, if left to itself, will naturally find its way to the most useful and profitable employment. Whence it is inferred that manufactures, without the aid of the government, will grow up as soon or as fast as the natural state of things and the interest of the community may require." He cited as powerful obstacles to a successful development of manufactures the influence of inertia, the fear of failure in untried fields, and the intrinsic difficulties of competing with those "who have previously attained to perfection in the business to be attempted." But the most important of all obstacles and deterrents to entering manufacturing enterprise in this country were the "bounties, premiums, and other artifical encouragements with which foreign nations second the exertions of their own citizens, in the branches in which they are to be rivalled" (4: 104). Without similar aids, Hamilton failed to perceive how infant industries in the United States could compete and survive.

> Whatever room there may be for an expectation that the industry of a people, under the direction of private interest, will upon equal terms, find out the most beneficial employment for itself, there is none for a reliance that it will struggle against the force of unequal terms, or will, of itself, surmount all the adventitious barriers to a successful competition which may have been erected, either by the advantages naturally acquired from practice and previous possessions of the ground, and by those which may have sprung from positive regulations and an artificial policy. (4: 107)

What he was saying was "not made in the spirit of complaint. It is for the nations whose regulations are alluded to, to judge for themselves" (4: 102) the wisdom of their policy. But he was convinced that it was sheer folly to try to compete with industrially advanced nations on other than approximately equal terms.

Could the United States overcome the weaknesses arising from its inferior industrial position? In Hamilton's mind, there was no doubt whatever that it could. The United States was destined to become industrialized. European countries had merely achieved an early start. They pursued a policy of subsidizing and encouraging their industrial growth. These were temporary advantages that could be overcome if this country pursued a siimilar policy according to a well-laid plan.

Three basic objections were commonly argued against the practicability of manufactures in America: "scarcity of hands, dearness of labor, want of capital" (4: 107). Although these obstacles might seriously retard the growth of domestic manufactures, they were not beyond remedy. Hamilton's original financial program of funding the public debt and establishing the national bank was aimed at reducing the difficulties of obtaining adequate supplies of capital. He hoped also that the redemption of the public credit would result in attracting additional foreign capital to the United States. If industry became profitable in the United States, higher interest rates would appeal effectively enough to European investors. The shortage of manpower and the resulting "dearness of labor" were also not to be ignored; but neither were they an argument for inaction. An aggressive government could contribute to its solution. First, the nation should make the most effective use of its existing supplies of labor. The labor of men could be augmented by "the great use that can be made of women and children." The losses occasioned by seasonal variations in employment might be reduced. Second, the government should systematically encourage European workmen and artisans to emigrate to this country. In industries of extraordinary importance, the expenses of emigration could be borne by the government. Skilled workers would need little persuasion to remove themselves from the disturbances and unsettled conditions resulting from the European wars. Third, the introduction of machinery and the improvement of industrial techniques would have the same effect of enlarging the national labor supply. The use of labor-saving machines would enable the country to accomplish more production with the same labor resources.

The cynic might suppose that Hamilton was more interested in fostering a political interest dependent on his policies than he was in establishing industry on a sound economic basis. If Hamilton's statements are to be trusted, there seems to be no reason to believe that this was the case. He was not interested in breeding lusty but unsound "war babies," but rather in creating a long-range healthy growth.[10] He was no more trying to perpetuate vested interests resulting from the Revolutionary War than he was attempting to form an industrial monopoly for a few. He admitted the danger inherent in his program: "measures which serve to abridge the free competition of foreign articles, have a tendency to occasion an enhancement of prices" (4: 129–130). Although he was honest enough to admit that industrial monopoly might result from a policy of encouragement, this need not necessarily happen. The "fact does not always correspond with the theory," he said. On the contrary, the consumer would gain by a reduction in the price of the goods in the long run. The "reverse of what might have been expected did often happen: A reduction of prices has, in several instances, immediately succeeded the establishment of a domestic manufacture" (4: 129–130). The increase in size of our industrial production would be more likely to lead to a lowering of the price than create a private monopoly.

As proof of the practicability of his long-range plan for industrial development, Hamilton pointed to the nation's own industrial trends of production. What better proof was needed than to survey the rapid rise of industry during the past two decades? Manufactures plainly showed their vitality by the increase in the number and size of new productions. He presented to Congress a list of seventeen articles of manufacture that supported his thesis: skins, iron, wood, flax and hemp, bricks and tiles, spirits and malt liquors, paper, hats, sugar, soils, copper, tin, carriages, and tobacco, and in addition, "the vast scene of household manufacturing" (4: 127–28).

So far this analysis has shown the general arguments that Hamilton presented in support of the advantages and practicability of establishing manufactures in the United States. His case was so thoroughly prepared that the report, for a century afterward, established itself as the standard treatise and source for protectionist arguments. The fine mastery with which he marshaled his arguments and facts to prove the general usefulness and feasibility of manufactures compel alike the admiration of friend and foe.

The Report on Manufactures had a definite and specific objective: Hamilton had come prepared not to convince Congress of his industrial *thesis*, but to persuade it to enact a specific industrial *plan*. Before offering the measures that he hoped would be adopted, he listed the means "which have been employed in other countries in order to provide a better judgment of the means proper to be resorted to by the United States."

1. Protecting duties—or duties on those foreign articles which are the rivals of the domestic ones intended to be encouraged.
2. Prohibitions of rival articles, or duties equivalent to prohibitions.
3. Prohibition of the exportation of the materials of manufactures.
4. Pecuniary bounties.

5. Premiums.
6. The exemption of material of manufacture from duty.
7. Drawbacks of the duties which are imposed on the material of manufacture.
8. The encouragement of new inventions and discoveries at home, and of the introduction into the United States of such as may have been made in other countries; particularly those which relate to machinery.
9. Judicious regulations for the inspection of manufactured commodities.
10. The facilitating of pecuniary remittances from place to place.
11. The facilitating of the transportation of commodities.

Having shown Congress the progress that had already been made in specific lines of industry, Hamilton then proceeded to enumerate those specific products whose records had demonstrated their practicability and need for further systematic encouragement. He chose certain manufactures as worthy of promotion by the national government, and in each case he offered a specific procedure, outlining in a general way his ultimate objective. The following products were selected as the first to be encouraged by his plan: iron, copper, lead, coal, wood, skins, grain, flax and hemp, cotton, wool, silk, glass, gunpowder, paper, printed books, refined sugars, and chocolate (4: 164ff). This list included many of the items in which his report recorded considerable progress already having been made. Here, his action may be interpreted as projecting existing industrial trends toward desirable production levels. But on what grounds did he exclude spirits and malt liquors, brick and tile, tobacco, oil, sugar, tin, carriages, and hats? What was his rationale in choosing the products to be systematically fostered? Hamilton offered Congress the following criteria—what he called the "five circumstances"—by which the objects were "entitled to particular attentions":

(1) the capacity of the country to furnish the raw material; (2) the degree in which the nature of the manufacture admits of a substitute for manual labor in machinery; (3) the facility of execution; (4) the extensiveness of the uses to which the article can be applied; (5) its subserviency to other interests, particularly the great one of national defense. (4: 163–64)

The report did not elucidate the relative importance of these five standards, nor did it offer a means by which they could be measured. Yet the criteria offered an excellent beginning for industrial planning, however crude. Experiment and practice would demonstrate the practicability or the impracticability of developing the industries listed. Later, others could be added; those shown to be impractical, or those having attained a stature capable of sustaining themselves, would then be excluded from the list.

Hamilton was under no illusion that such a program could be administered by the legislative enactment of declared benefits. It is unfortunate that he did not leave a systematic record of his ideas on public administration.[11] One can glean here and there a few stray fragments on how he proposed to have his plans administered. It is certain, however, that Hamilton entertained no very high opinion of the legislative branch. Undoubtedly he would have regarded it an inadequate and clumsy instrument to execute his scheme of industrial planning. The report proposed no single measure to be executed in one fell swoop, but a continuing program administered by a regulative body. For this purpose he recommended the establishment of a "board" for promoting arts, agriculture, manufactures, and commerce. It should be noted that objects other than manufactures were included; arts, agriculture, and commerce were also to be the board's interest. Washington also had suggested creating a board for agriculture. By incorporating within the same body authority to plan for agriculture, Hamilton hoped to win the support of the farming interest. He recommended that a special fund be made available to be administered by the board. He anticipated that, in time, additional funds would be forthcoming from the "increase of national industry and wealth" as well as from the increased tariff duties. Some of the money would be used to pay "bounties which shall have been decreed."[12] The remainder would be used to

> defray the expenses of the emigration of artists and manufactures in particular branches of extraordinary importance; to induce the prosecution and introduction of useful discoveries, inventions and improvements by proportionate rewards, judiciously held out and applied; to encourage premiums, both honorable and lucrative, and exertions of individuals and of classes . . . and to afford such other aids to those objects as may be generously designated by law. (4: 196)

Hamilton wisely refrained from describing in detail the system of administration his plan would have involved. Congress was suspicious enough of his intentions without adding fuel to the flames. The report described only briefly how the board would function. The fact that Congress immediately dropped the consideration of the Report on Manufactures deprived Hamilton of any opportunity to elucidate his scheme of administration. It seems fairly clear that he did not intend simply a legislative enactment of tariff duties for the encouragement of domestic manufactures. Several references in the report indicate that detailed adjustments would be necessary from time to time in administering the plan. Such a function could hardly be performed by Congress; it would have to be done by a body continuously engaged in surveying industrial trends and progress. He foresaw the necessity of implementing the original legislation with administrative adjustments as needed. For example, in suggesting the importation of iron free from duty and its probable effect of stimulating manufacture here, he wrote: "But caution nevertheless in a matter of this kind is advisable. The measure suggested ought, perhaps, rather to be contemplated subject to the lights of further experience, than immediately adopted" (4: 169). Again, concerning the improbability of a successful manufacture in the United States of distilled grain spirits, he wrote, "Experiments could perhaps, alone decide with certainty the justness of the suggestions which are made" (4: 177). On the encouragement of cotton manufacture, his opinion was:

Those circumstances conspire to indicate the expediency of removing any obstructions which may happen to exist, to the advantageous prosecution of the manufactories in question, and of adding such encouragment as may appear necessary and proper. . . .

When a sufficient progress shall have been made, the drawback may be abrogated, and by that time the domestic supplies of the articles to be printed or stained will have been extended. (4: 182, 185)

Periodic adjustments of the kind suggested here would probably require some kind of an administrative apparatus, at least for the purpose of continuously gathering data.

In summary, if Hamilton's scheme for industrial planning is viewed as a whole, it is apparent that he proposed not merely a policy of high protective duties to encourage infant industries. He recommended not a general policy of protection but a specific program with a definite object and method for its achievement. His program was drawn to fit the long-term needs of industry at that particular stage of American industry.[13]

His plan stated not only a direction for national policy, but offered the means for its execution. He pointed out the need of creating balance between interests in our economy. As long as agriculture was so predominant, the country would always be faced with a continuing farm surplus, for whose absorption a foreign market would be needed. The growth of manufactures would offer a more reliable market for these surpluses. The national economy would gain in balance and stability. He surveyed the changing industrial scene and showed that the steady growth of our industrial production was the best proof of the practicability of his thesis. Although much progress had indeed been made, its continuance depended on a forthright and aggressive policy of planning and encouragement. Without a protective market to foster its growth, American infant industries could not expect to overcome the advantages of subsidy and systematic support that manufacturers received abroad. The government could redress the unequal struggle and assume an active role in directing the progress of industry.[14]

Hamilton presented the criteria by which industries to be encouraged would be selected. As an initial exercise in planning, it was a practical beginning. He also listed the separate industries and products of which the United States stood especially in need. He showed that the record of these industries justified a belief in their continued progress. In each case, he analyzed what should be done and the method that should be employed. The Report on Manufactures was only a preliminary stage of industrial planning. No production goals were stated and no date fixed for their ultimate realization. The important fact is that industrial planning was based not on hope but on proven production trends.

Hamilton's report was planning on a comprehensive scale. It was not merely a recommendation for an indiscriminate bestowal of legislative favors. It aimed to change the face of the American economy by systematically inducing a change toward industrial and large-scale enterprise. An administrative board would promote not only manufactures, but also "arts, agriculture and commerce." It would be vested with power and financial resources to carry out its long-range program. It would use means other than the tariff—such as premiums and bounties—in effecting its purpose of encouraging manufactures. It would also take steps to promote manufactures by encouraging skillful artisans and mechanics living abroad to emigrate to this country. Not less important, plans would be formulated for improving the means of transportation in order to facilitate the marketing of products. In all this, the government was to play the leading and directing role.

The Society of Useful Manufactures

Hamilton's broad plan for the development of American industry comprehended not only the Report on Manufactures but also the Society of Useful Manufactures, more commonly known as the S.U.M. The S.U.M. figures in both the inception and defeat of the report. Although not nearly as well known as the report, and frequently misinterpreted as being a scheme of stock-jobbing, a more candid analysis shows how far ahead of his time Hamilton was in his idea of the promotion of large-scale industry.

The S.U.M. was the child of Hamilton's brain. He conceived it and guided its growth so far as this was consistent with his position as secretary of the treasury. The Society of Useful Manufactures—"New Jersey's first contribution to the galaxy of American business corporations" (1: 349)—was chartered by the legislature of New Jersey on November 21, 1791. It was promoted as an experiment in large-scale organization and production, and had the support of many of America's largest fortunes. Its authorized capital was $1 million, as large as the fifty largest manufacturing firms in Europe (1: 447). Only one other enterprise in the United States was as large—the Bank of the United States, also a Hamilton enterprise (1: 410). Special inducements were necessary to assemble so much financial resource, and the legislature of New Jersey was willing to assist. The launching of the S.U.M. was contemporaneous with the Report on Manufactures, which was introduced a fortnight later, on December 5, 1791. There is no doubt that Hamilton intended it to be of "real public importance," not the speculative stock adventure it eventually became. Hamilton hoped to prove by its success that business interests in the United States could successfully emulate large-scale factory production abroad. The S.U.M. would share in the financial benefits suggested by the report.[15] In assembling the data for his report, Hamilton had become keenly aware of the disadvantages under which American manufacture labored. The dearth of individual large fortunes would be remedied by investments joined in a single large corporation. With the aid of his assistant, Tench Coxe, Hamilton persuaded a number of leading capitalists and financiers to organize America's first million-dollar manufacturing firm.

The life of the S.U.M. as a manufacturing enterprise was as brief as it was tumultuous. It had hardly selected its location in Paterson, New Jersey, when the speculative debacle of 1792 swept a number of its leading promoters, including its "Governor," William Duer, to financial ruin. The financial crash that resulted not only discredited the S.U.M. in the eyes of many, it resulted in many stockholders being unable to pay the balance of their stock subscriptions.

The S.U.M. was begun, in truth, without a clear idea of what it was going to produce. Hamilton advised its management to concentrate authority in one competent person and to specialize in its production. The corporation was without adequate leadership. Hamilton soon realized that he could not, in addition to his official duties, guide its fortunes from Philadelphia. A thousand and one problems confronted factory production at this stage of American industry: Factory wages could not compete with the attractions of relatively free land; management was lacking in both experience and skill necessary to handle the problem of organizing a firm of this size; the problem of marketing a large volume of manufactured goods would still need to be solved even assuming that production could be satisfactorily organized.

The adverse reaction of the public to the launching of the S.U.M. helps to explain why Hamilton's Report of Manufactures received so little support. People were clearly not yet prepared to accept a regime of large-scale manufacturing enterprise, especially if subsidy and special privileges were involved. Agricultural interests were not disposed to accept large-scale manufactures as even a junior partner in contemplating America's economic future.

When the S.U.M. was first announced in 1791, it received a relatively good press. Conservative mercantile newspapers were especially favorable and regarded the new project as of national importance.[16] Agrarian leaders like Jefferson were at first noncommittal concerning certain enterprises. Then, gradually, letters and columns began to appear that criticized aspects of the corporation's organization. Condemnation centered on the exclusive privileges that its critics said were "well calculated to aggrandize and increase the influence of the few at the expense of the many."[17]

After the financial crash of 1792, the S.U.M. in the views of many was limited with the current rage of speculation, rather than a plan for industrial production. Gradually it was brought into the vortex of political controversy. After Hamilton's identification with the suppression of the Whiskey Rebellion, both his plans for industrial development served as media for waging partisan warfare. The S.U.M. was identified in the popular mind as a "political engine"[18] rather than as a scheme for constructive enterprise. Appeals were made, too, to the small manufacturer, who was warned that he would be unable to compete with this new colossus. All this was part of the background into which the Report on Manufactures was received. Following the furious and bitter controversy over the establishment of the national bank, it is hardly surprising that the proposal to organize industrial production on so far-reaching a plan met with an organized and determined opposition.

For decades thereafter, the attitude of agrarian leaders toward industrial planning was largely colored by animosities engendered in the partisan conflicts with Hamilton's party. Projects in any way connected with Hamiltonian policies were regarded by agriculturists as tainted. Not only did this lead to a failure to integrate and harmonize industrial development with agriculture, it created in the minds of agrarian leaders an attitude of hostility and fear of government itself. So far as Jefferson's party was concerned, the federal government had incurred a bad name. Centralizing policies were to be avoided; policies perpetuating state authority were to be extolled.

Hamilton was too thoroughly identified with the financial interests to have made much of an impression on the agricultural bloc by his plea that he was sincerely interested in the prosperity of agriculture. Former members in Congress distrusted his dialectics, and his arguments for a balanced agriculture and a stable home market carried little appeal. Hamilton's past was against him. When he made his report to Congress on land policy in 1790, he had an opportunity to demonstrate his interest in behalf of the average small landowner. Instead, he presented recommendations that to the agrarian bloc seemed like a bold proposal to enrich the moneyed speculators at the expense of the small, land-hungry farmer.[19] Agricultural interests were accordingly disinclined to take Hamilton's protestations seriously when he approached them with his plan for aiding them. Even less were the agrarians willing to enter a partnership with him under his leadership.

This chapter has furnished a view of the psychological milieu that lay behind the scheme to advance industrial planning during this period. Instead of an integration of interests between agriculture and industry, each drifted its own way. Instead of planning the future of each on some common ground, their leaders looked on each other with suspicion and hostility. The initial proposal for industrial planning was bred of that distrust which followed the establishment of the national bank. Aid for manufacture was deemed by agriculture a species of special privilege, mulcted from agriculture alone. Agriculture therefore refused to further a plan for what Hamilton conceived as a systematic, controlled, and directed development of manufacturing enterprise.

CHAPTER VII

Thomas Jefferson:

Public Land Policies

The Democratic Goals of Jeffersonian Planning

The life of Thomas Jefferson is so rich and variegated that his biographer must often feel unsure which character was the real Jefferson. The range of his interests was enormous; only Franklin could approach him in this respect. In private life he was a planter managing his own estate. He engaged in agricultural experiments, such as growing rare plants and developing wine making and olive growing in Virginia. He prepared scientific papers in such various fields as horticulture, anthropology, and geography. For several decades he served as president of the American Philosophical Society. He wrote *Notes on Virginia*, a treatise on the geography, social economy, and politics of his state. He personally organized the University of Virginia, even designing its first buildings. He was the architect also of our first Western land policy. For many decades thereafter, until the West was settled, the national land laws were based largely on his plans and ideas. He was the lawyer-statesman who drafted the Declaration of Independence, a standing challenge to tyranny and an affirmation of the rights of men.

Jefferson's achievements in national politics are no less numerous and varied. There were in fact few fields in which he did not make a contribution. In scope they included, for example, a report recommending the general use of the decimal system, a far-sighted formulation of neutrality policy in foreign affairs, a plan for financing public education by means of grants of public lands, the Louisiana Purchase, the preparation of a gigantic program of public works aiming to develop a national network of transportation and communications (roads and canals). His statesmanship was no less matched by his talents for political leadership and party organization. He was a realist in politics, and an opportunist who never divorced himself from the sentiments and opinions of the people. Although he would compromise on specific issues to win half a loaf rather than obtain none, he never would compromise on matters involving the democratic principle.

It is hardly to be expected that one so catholic in his interests should be narrow and dogmatic in his views. All his life, Jefferson's mind was open to new ideas and influences. Unlike Hamilton, he had no preconceived formula for America's future. Having been raised on the Western frontier, he grew up in the belief that America's abundant land resources constituted our best promise of freedom and opportunity. As the growth of commerce and industry revealed their potentialities of an improved standard of living, Jefferson came to recognize the need for promoting domestic and household manufactures. He did not rate consistency as the most important of political virtues. When he became president he preached economy as a means of liquidating the country's heavy indebtedness. Once the national debt was on its way to becoming extinguished, he did not propose a reduction of taxation (which bore principally on luxury imports), but instead offered a program of spending to improve the country's transportation. Jefferson did not hesitate to change his mind when he believed it warranted, and especially if the underlying conditions had changed. In fact, there are few issues on which he maintained an unchanging single view.

Yet there runs through Jefferson's life and work a thread of continuity and consistency—his essential belief in democracy and democratic values. He believed in the people and in the dignity and work of the common man. He waged unrelenting war on special privilege, on ignorance, and on tyranny in whatever form, whether by the church, land jobbers, bankers, the entrenched aristocracy, or the government. Jefferson believed in America as a place where mankind could start anew. The country was young, with vigor and abundant resources, and without the inbred old-world tyrannies. Freedom for the common man was his goal, freedom not as an abstraction but as those social conditions which would assure the pursuit of happiness. Jefferson's experience in the use of governmental power shows that he was cognizant not only of its possible abuse, but also of its practical uses. Freedom he conceived not as a void or as freedom from evil, but as a positive condition in human society that might sustain continued social improvement and would afford expression of man's best nature. Jefferson's life demonstrated not only that he hoped for these things, but that he planned for them, and, to some degree, achieved them.

National Land Policy

The Homestead Principle

A year before the Declaration of Independence, Jefferson flatly presented the case of the Western settler in his "Address to Lord Dunmore from the House of Representatives," later published as *A Summary View of the Rights of British America.* "Our ancestors . . . who migrated hither, were farmers, not lawyers" (1: 443). He denied "the fictitious principle that all lands belonged originally to the King." Long before the Norman Conquest, "Our Saxon ancestors held their lands, as they did their personal property, in absolute dominion, disencumbered with any superior, answering nearly to the nature of those possessions which the feudalists term allodial." The practice of the king extorting double the previous price of the land was rendering "the acquisition of lands . . . difficult" and checking the growth of "the population of the country. . . . It is time, therefore, for us to lay this matter open before his Majesty, and to declare that he has no right to grant lands of himself." The lands belong not to the king, but to the people organized collectively, and they should be made available to those who would occupy them. From the following, there can be no doubting the direct purpose of Jefferson's argument:

> From the nature and purpose of civil institutions, all the lands within the limits which any particular society has circumscribed around itself are assumed by that society, and subject to their allotment only. This may be done by themselves assembled collectively, or by their legislature, to whom they may have delegated sovereign authority and if they are allotted in either of these ways, each individual of the society may appropriate to himself such lands as he finds vacant, and occupancy will give him title. (1: 445–46)

The object of his argument was a free land policy of donating Western lands to encourage settlement. As long as fiscal exigencies could allow a generous program of land donations, Jefferson was for it.

I am against selling the lands at all. The people who will migrate to the Westward and whether they form part of the old, or of a new colony will be subject to their proportion of the Continental debt then unpaid. They ought not to be subject to more. They will be a people little able to pay taxes . . . they will settle the lands in spite of everybody. I am at the same time clear that they should be appropriated in small quantities. (2: 239–40)[1]

In order to encourage settlement on the frontier, Jefferson added a proposal that instead of making "wealthy foreigners pay in money . . . for liberty . . . provided for them," they be required to "bring a settler for every 100, or 200 acres of land" granted them.

Jefferson sought to incorporate his "homestead" provision into the new Virginia constitution. His draft included this paragraph: "Every person of full age neither owning nor having owned 50 acres of land, shall be entitled to an appropriation of 50 acres or to so much as shall make what he owns or has owned 50 acres in full and absolute dominion. And no person shall be capable of taking an appropriation"(1: 25–26).[2] The Virginia convention refused to incorporate the free land grant principle into the constitution. Defeated in this attempt, Jefferson energetically promoted the passage of land legislation of even greater importance to our national landholding policies.

Abolishing Feudal Land Tenures

Few played a more important role than Jefferson in destroying the economic foundations of the "pseudo-aristocracy" that had grown up during the Colonial period. Recalling his own activities during the period of the Revolution, Jefferson wrote to John Adams:

At the first session of our legislature after the Declaration of Independence, we passed a law abolishing entails. And this was followed by abolishing the privilege of primogeniture, and dividing the lands of intestates equally among all their children or other representatives. These laws, drawn by myself, laid the axe to the root of pseudo-aristocracy.[3]

During the 165 years beginning with the grant of the Virginia charter by King James I, there had been transplanted into the New World the English feudal land institutions. The English aristocracy was given land grants numbering thousands of acres, creating in America principalities like those in the old country. These princely grants were to be kept intact by the feudal land rules of primogeniture and entail, which became incorporated into the body of American Colonial law. The system of quitrents preserved for the grantees a perpetual toll on the labor of the settler, thus preventing him from obtaining freehold on the land he improved. While settlers were prohibited by the Quebec Act from moving across the Allegheny Mountains, speculative land companies made up of royal officials and their cronies were gambling millions of acres on the future destinies of the Ohio Valley.

Land for Use, Not for Trade

No less important than the abolition of feudal land tenures for America's democratic land system was the establishment of a system of land disposal avoiding the dangers of large-scale land speculation. Few persons today realize the dangers that existed at the close of the Revolution threatening our whole land policy. Researches of Abernethy, Jensen, and others reveal how serious this threat actually was.[4]

For years prior to the Revolution, speculative land companies consisted of some of the most influential persons both in England and America. They engaged in intrigues at the royal court to obtain grants of land in the Ohio Valley amounting to millions of acres. Following the breach with England, the scene of conflict for land grabbing shifted from the royal court to the new state legislatures.[5] The extent of the speculators' power may be judged by the fact that through their control over certain legislatures, they were able to delay for over three years the ratification of the Articles of Confederation. Had they been successful, it is possible that the vast territory of the Northwest would have been organized into great baronial estates rather than a multiplicity of small landholdings.[6] Had the land speculators been able to seize the territory of the Ohio Valley in a few great tracts, Congress would probably have been precluded from launching its constructive land surveys and territorial policies. The evils that Congress was able to avoid by circumventing the rapacity of the speculators may be appreciated by surveying the follies of the landed states that succumbed to their influence.[7]

As a landowning gentleman, cultivating his own acres, Jefferson had a healthy dislike for the practices of the land jobbers. He disdained to adventure in land speculations (4: 369), readily appreciating that it was completely at odds with his own policy of saving the land for actual settlers. He was not slow in acting to make sure that the land speculators would get no more of Virginia's western lands than was unavoidable.

The chief objective of the land speculators was to obtain a confirmation of their spurious Indian treaties and purchases. They hoped to win for their claims the sanction of Virginia, the chief landholding state. Jefferson must have understood their motive well when he succeeded in getting incorporated into the Virginia constitution the provision stipulating that the state's western and northern boundaries remain as fixed by the charter of King James I in the year 1609, "unless by act of this Legislature one or more governments be established westward of the Allegheny Mountains." Jefferson's constitutional provisions also excluded recognition of any purchase of lands "made of the Indian Natives but on behalf of the public by authority of the General Assembly."[8] As long as Virginia refused to yield these two principles, the land speculators were stymied. But for virtually the next three years the land jobbers held up ratification of the Articles of Confederation. Maryland, strongly under the influence of these groups, refrained from entering the Union as long as the land-owning states refused to cede their lands.[9] The land company promoters evolved the theory that the Continental Congress had inherited the sovereignty of the British government, and particularly, the power of disposing of the Western lands. They attempted to insert into the Dickinson draft of the Articles of Confederation a clause whereby Congress might determine Indian boundaries by treaty and thereby implicitly control the remaining lands once the state boundaries were established. Jefferson, who was then a member of Congress, saw no need for Dickinson's Article 14, since he regarded the boundaries of the Southern colonies as already fixed. He countered with another proposition, which had as its object the extension of Congress's powers to acquire new lands. He proposed to prohibit "purchases to be made by the individual States or Persons, of lands on this continent not within the boundaries of any of these United States." He added a further provision that lands purchased by Congress "shall be given freely to those who may be permitted to seat them."[10] Imbued with the idea of agricultural imperialism, Jefferson was already apparently thinking of the extension of the Western territory that later culminated in his great Louisiana Purchase. He took action to prevent the cession of Virginia's lands until he could be assured that Congress would dispose of them according to an approved plan. When Virginia did finally cede its Western lands—by an act of cession prepared by Jefferson's hand—it was given repeated assurance by Congress that the land would be disposed of for the common benefit of the United States. Congress had to pledge that the territory would be formed into distinct republican states, which would become members of the federal Union, and have the same rights of sovereignty, freedom, and independence as the other states.[11]

Orderly Settlement: The Land Surveys

Jefferson grew up on the frontier of Virginia when it was still virtually a wilderness. His sympathies lay always with the humble frontiersman who struggled to make an independent livelihood from cultivating the soil. His own experience was with conditions prevailing in the South, where land was plentiful. The practice of selling land according to careful surveys based on discriminate locations was little known. Only in New England (and later extended into the middle Atlantic states) did the system of prior surveys prevail. Considering the plentifulness of land, the great cost of making surveys, the necessity of strengthening the frontier, and, above all, the desire for untrammeled land selection, it is easy to understand the widespread practice of locating lands and fixing land titles by the use of warrants and indiscriminate locations.

Jefferson's sense of order and system revolted at the irregularities of the Southern land usages. In 1776 he expressed his opinion: "The idea of Congress selling out unlocated lands has been sometime dropped, but we have always met the hint with such determined opposition that I believe it will never be proposed" (2: 239–40). He perceived readily that the use of indiscriminate locations caused little difficulty as long as the frontier was sparsely settled. Once an area began to become more thickly populated, however, difficulties multiplied, and the frequency of land litigations developed a lawyer's paradise. The New Jersey congressman Elias Boudinot early in the national era cited the effects of the system in his state: "more money had been spent at law, in disputes arising from that mode of settlement . . . than would have been necessary to purchase all the land of the State."[12] Jefferson could hardly have looked favorably on the mad scramble for land, mineral, and forest wealth that prevailed later in the nineteenth century. He regarded orderly settlement of the land necessary to a progressive and sound growth of agriculture in the West. For example, in 1803, in considering the policy for the newly acquired territory of Louisiana, he proposed to settle gradually the states east of the Mississippi tier by tier, going westward by degrees as the Eastern sections became inhabited.

The best use we can make of the country for some time, will be
to give establishment in it to the Indians on the East side of the
Mississippi, in exchange for their present country, and open
land offices in the last, and thus make this acquisition the means
of filling up the Eastern side, instead of drawing off its population. When we shall be full on this side, we may lay off a range
of States on the Western bank from the head to the mouth, and
so, range after range, advancing compactly as we multiply.
(10: 5–7)[13]

In 1784, as a member of Congress, Jefferson offered a contribution to
the solution of the land problem in the shape of a draft of "An Ordinance
Establishing a Land Office for the United States" (4: 334–35). At this
time he was experimenting with the possibilities of the decimal system,
which he was trying to apply to the national system of coinage
(4:297–313). He attempted to utilize the decimal arrangements for land
measurement. He proposed that the land "Shall be divided into Hundreds
of ten geographical mile squares each mile containing 6,086 feet and four
tenths of a rod, by lines to be run and marked due North and South, and
others crossing these at right angles, the first of which lines, each way,
shall be at ten miles distance from one of the corners of the state within
which they shall be" (4: 334–45). He also recommended a modified
system of using warrants for locating land, but according to a discriminate location determined by prior surveys.

The principles embodied in his draft ordinance were not entirely
new. Land practices throughout the colonies were so varied that there
existed precedents in some form for almost any new legislation that was
proposed.[14] The Congressional committee in 1781 had recommended that
new states be formed out of the land, and that they be laid out into
townships six miles square, "the first appearance in Congress of a plan of
new states which should be subdivided into townships,"[15] although the
manner of their division was left unspecified.

Pelatiah Webster, a contemporary publicist, sought to influence
Congress's decision in favor of the New England arrangement of progressive tiers of township seating, suggesting that townships six, eight, or ten
miles square be laid out contiguous to the settled country.[16] Jefferson's
plan, however,

first definitely set forth the rectangular system of surveys as it
exists today. It was a wholly new thing to use parallels and

meridians bounding such townships uniformly over a great area regardless of the topography of the country. . . . The system of rectangular surveys was therefore a gradual evolution under conditions peculiar to American colonial life, modified in regard to boundary lines by the reforming doctrinaire mind of Jefferson.[17]

When Congress returned the following year to considering a policy for disposing of public lands, it had the benefit of Jefferson's draft ordinance of 1784. The great land ordinance adopted by Congress in 1785,[18] perhaps the most important single land law ever passed in our national history, closely followed in certain important particulars the survey plan proposed by Jefferson. It did not incorporate Jefferson's decimal system of land measurement or his system of land warrants based on irregular location. In every other respect, however, it was substantially similar.

At the head of the survey system, Congress placed a geographer, who was authorized to make necessary regulations for the conduct of the surveyors, one of whom was to be appointed by Congress from each state. The surveyors were directed to divide the territory into ranges of townships six miles square, beginning with the southwest corner of the boundary of Pennsylvania. The ranges were to be numbered progressively from that point westward, and no land was to be offered for sale until seven ranges of townships had been surveyed. The townships in turn were to be divided into "lots of one mile square, or 640 acres, in the same direction as the external lines, and numbered from 1 to 36." The township plats were to be transmitted to the Board of Treasury, which was to record them and then transmit copies of the original plats "to the commissioner of the loan office of the several States," where they would be made available to all prospective purchasers of the lands offered at a public sale.

Pressure was not lacking in the following decade for the repeal of the land survey system inaugurated by the act of 1785. Congress partially surrendered to this pressure when it opened the public lands for sale after only four ranges had been surveyed.[19] Opposition to the principle of prior survey continued until 1796. The land act of that year established the principle of prior rectangular surveys on so firm a basis that it could not later be overturned.[20]

The value to later generations of the system planned by Jefferson can never be estimated. Not only were Americans spared the evils of selling land according to indiscriminate location, but they never had to experience, during the coming century of expansion, the misfortunes accompanying overlapping private surveys and their attendant title disputes. For this we owe a debt of gratitude to the planful vision of Thomas Jefferson.[21]

Forerunner of the Northwest Ordinance

I have not intended to imply that Jefferson alone framed Congress's early land and territorial policy. The final policy adopted by Congress was an amalgam of Colonial precedent, contemporary practice, political compromise, and bold planning. No one man designed the structure that became the basis of later national policy. Yet, if any man deserves to be named as the planner of Congress's Western territorial policy, it is certainly Jefferson.

Jefferson had long realized that Virginia could not, single-handed, control the entire West. The territory that Virginia claimed under her charter was far too great to be administered by a single state.[22] He had complained bitterly in *Notes on Virginia* of the high-handed manner in which the eastern region of the tidewater obtained a legislative representation in the Virginia constitution out of proportion to its population (4: 275). Without governmental autonomy, the Western settler was destined to remain in a legislative minority and at the mercy of a preponderant East. He wanted to broaden the composition of the farming class and at the same time extend self-government to the frontier. It was in accordance with this view that he included in his draft of the Virginia constitution the following provision:

> The Western and Northern extent of this country shall in all other respects stand as fixed by the charter . . . until by the act of the Legislature one or more territories shall be laid off Westward of the Allegheny mountains for new colonies, on which colonies shall be established on the same fundamental laws contained in this instrument, and shall be free and independent of this colony and of all the world. (1: 25–26)

The purpose of the first clause was to frustrate the attempts of the land speculators to lay claim to any of this territory. The latter part discloses beyond question Jefferson's plan to organize the Western lands into self-governing and independent states.

In 1784, having just completed drawing up the final deed of cession of the Virginia lands, and as a member of Congress, Jefferson was requested to serve as chairman of a committee to frame a policy for the Western territories. The resulting document (4: 227–78), however brief, was of the greatest historical significance, for it served as a prototype of the territorial ordinance of 1784 and, later, the Northwest Ordinance.

The territorial ordinance of 1784 as enacted by Congress faithfully adhered to the pattern of territorial organization outlined by Jefferson. It stated that the "territory ceded or about to be ceded . . . shall be divided into distinct states" and defined the parallels of latitude that each state would comprehend. Congress would provide for a system of temporary government, and "when any such State shall have acquired twenty thousand free inhabitants," its people might call a convention of representatives to establish a permanent constitution and government for themselves."[23]

The better-known Northwest Ordinance of 1787 was substantially a revision of this ordinance. It acquires its importance from the fact that it remained on the statute books in succeeding years without alteration. Every state regularly admitted into the Union under the Constitution was formed under its territorial provision:

> There shall be formed in the said territory not less than three nor more than five states . . . and whenever any of the said States shall have sixty thousand free inhabitants therein, such State shall be admitted, by its delegates, into the Congress of the United States, on an equal footing with the original States in all respects whatever, and shall be at liberty to form a permanent constitution and State Government.[24]

Thus in the formulation of a system of government for the territories, Jefferson's planning had played a very important part.

Territorial Expansion: The Louisiana Purchase

At the time that Jefferson was developing plans for agricultural expansion in the West, no one could have foretold the exact manner in which the United States would acquire its vast territories by the Louisiana Purchase in 1803. The story of how Napoleon obtained control of Louisiana and how he finally relinquished his claim to the United States for $15 million reads almost like a fable. Jefferson's role in acquiring this great domain belongs also to the same chain of fortuitous events.

Yet the facts are clear that Jefferson acted according to a pattern of policy that he had urged for over a score of years. He believed that the foundation of freedom in the United States rested on the abundance of its lands. He had developed an attitude of agrarian imperialism: an anxious desire to extend American territorial boundaries to the west. As a member of Congress, he had offered to prohibit purchases "to be made by the individual States or persons, of lands on this continent not within the boundaries of these United States."[25] Only Congress would be allowed to buy lands beyond the boundaries of existing states, and only Congress would have the power of declaring the policies for the newly acquired areas.

Jefferson required no urging, therefore, when there was presented to him the unique opportunity of adding the vast territory of Louisiana to the United States. For years he had considered territorial expansion to the west as a real possibility. When the chance to acquire the new vast domains was placed within his reach, he seized it and extended our national boundaries as far as circumstances permitted.

The Abolition of Slavery

In the period immediately following the Revolution, the institution of slavery was under systematic attack. In the opinion of some historians, there existed at this time a better possibility of reaching an accord on the abolition of slavery than at any time before or afterward.[26]

Jefferson was in the vanguard of the opponents of slavery, although he was not alone. He favored its abolition not so much out of pity for the slave but because of its degrading and demoralizing effect on the slaveholders. Slave labor was inefficient and retarded the progress of agriculture by making the plantation owner indifferent to more modern methods of production. Furthermore, the internal security of the country was endangered by the slave system: "with what execrations should the statesman be loaded, who permitting one half the citizens thus to trample on the rights of the other, transforms those into despots, and these into enemies, destroys the morals of the one part, and the *amor patriae* on the other" (4: 83).

In his proposed drafts of the Declaration of Independence (2: 52,53), Jefferson roundly condemned the slave traffic. In *Notes on Virginia*, he explained his legislative program for the abolition of slavery in that state. All slaves born after the passing of the act were to be emancipated. All other slaves were to be gradually manumitted; after having reached the ages of eighteen and twenty-one for females and males respectively, they were to be colonized as "a free and independent people," being first furnished with "implements of household and of the handicraft arts, seeds, pairs of the useful domestic animals, etc." (4: 449–50).[27]

Most significant was Jefferson's plan in his draft territorial ordinance of 1784 to prevent the spread of slavery into the territorial lands. "That after the year 1800 of the Christian Era, there shall be neither slavery nor involuntary servitude in any of the states, otherwise than as punishment of crimes whereof the party shall have been convicted to have been personally guilty" (4: 277–78). The tragedy lies in the fact that Congress failed by a single vote to adopt a total prohibition of slavery in the territories. In the opinion of Ford, an editor of Jefferson's writings,

> Next to the Declaration of Independence (if indeed standing second to that), this document ranks in historical importance of all those drawn by Jefferson and but for its being superseded by the Ordinance of 1787, would rank among all American State Papers immediately after the National Constitution. . . . Jefferson proposed to interdict slavery in all the western territory as the Ordinance of 1787 did. Had it been adopted as Jefferson reported it, slavery would have died a natural death, and secession would have been impossible. (4: 277–78)

The proposal to keep slavery out of the territorial lands was partially adopted in the Northwest Ordinance. It formed the basis of federal policy for several decades thereafter. Jefferson always deplored the error of Congress; until his final breath, he hoped for the eradication of slavery.

The Rehabilitation of Southern Agriculture
In connection with Jefferson's plans for the disposition of the Western lands, it is worth examining his view on the rehabilitation of Southern agriculture. Jefferson was completely familiar with the problems of the Southern plantation owner. Except for a few years of practicing law in his early twenties, all his life had been spent as a planter. Managing his estate at Monticello was his most ardent interest. The future of American liberty, in his view, depended on prosperity of the farmer. Jefferson had thought deeply about how the condition of agriculture in Virginia could be improved.

Jefferson proposed a three-fold scheme for the solution of agriculture in his own state: 1. the gradual abolition of slavery, as has already been noted; 2. a gradual breaking away from the one-crop tobacco culture; 3. the introduction of household manufactures.

Jefferson was not limited to these proposals in planning for the nation's future prosperity. The idea that Jefferson was disposed to a passive acceptance of uncontrolled social change without attempting to direct it toward the improvement of the human lot is inaccurate. His views were far indeed from those of the nineteenth-century economists who glorified the status quo as an exemplification of the divine operation of certain "natural" economic laws.

Jefferson took a keen interest in contemporary developments of farm technology. He followed the latest accounts of agricultural experiments conducted both in Europe and America, and himself contributed articles based on his experience on his own estates. His invention, the Jefferson plow, was fairly well known.[28] Jefferson was known and respected in America's scientific circles, and for many years he held the eminent position of president of the American Philosophical Society. In addition, he helped organize a society for the dissemination of knowledge concerning agricultural problems (10: 233).

He was one of the first to test the growing of wheat in Virginia. On the basis of his experience, he recommended a diversification of products with a view toward giving greater strength and stability to the state's agricultural economy. In *Notes on Virginia*, he considered the danger of competition from the "fresh and fertile lands in abundance . . . in the western country on the Mississippi and the midlands of Georgia." Soil exhaustion and the competition with better lands

> would oblige them [Virginia planters] to abandon the raising of tobacco altogether. And a happy obligation for them it will be. It is a culture productive of infinite wretchedness. Those employed in it are in a continual state of exertion beyond the power of nature to support. Little food of any kind is raised by them; so that the men and animals on these farms are ill fed, and the earth is rapidly impoverished. (4: 88–89)

Jefferson saw our expanding agricultural economy as one in which every citizen would live on and derive most of his subsistence from his own land. At first, during the period when he was writing *Notes on Virginia,* he showed an unalterable hostility to having the United States engage extensively in manufactures. He then believed that the policy of free trade would best assure the security and prosperity of our republic. It would

> remove as much as possible the occasions of making war . . . to abandon the ocean altogether, . . . the element whereon we shall be principally exposed to jostle with other nations. . . . Our interest will be to open the doors of commerce and to knock off all its shackles, giving perfect freedom to all persons for the vent of whatever they may choose to bring into our ports, and asking the same in theirs. (4: 99)

Jefferson believed that "We have lands enough to employ an infinite number of people in their cultivation," and that "cultivators of the earth are our most valuable citizens" (4: 449–50). He doubted the wisdom of having this country carry on all its own manufacturing.

Yet, as Jefferson began to view the continued growth of industrial production, he began to see, to some extent, how it might be reconciled with his conception of a basically agrarian economy. The solution lay in the encouragement of household manufactures, in developing generally the kind of self-sufficient household he managed at Monticello. According to Gilbert Chinard, Jefferson's view was based "on his experience at Monticello, where he had proved that it was possible to manufacture tools, bake bricks, make furniture and to maintain a comparatively large family on the products of the soil."[29]

One of Jefferson's remarkable characteristics is the flexibility with which he adapted his thinking to changing social trends. Some writers have condemned him for his lack of consistency. But Jefferson was too much the realist and too much lacking in vanity to defend his earlier views when time had proved them wrong.

The earlier period of his life was spent almost entirely on the frontier and in the agricultural region of Virginia, remote from the scene of rapidly growing manufactures. As Jefferson became more familiar with the facts of America's growing industrialization, he came to acknowledge the necessity of taking a different view. Concerning the nation's reliance for its national security on its ability to produce its own armaments, Jefferson's later views were substantially similar to those of Hamilton in his Report on Manufactures. In 1816, for example, he acknowledged to Benjamin Austin his change of policy: "You tell me I am quoted by those who wish to continue our dependence on England for manufactures. There was a time when I might have been so quoted with more candor, but within the thirty years which have since elapsed, how circumstances changed!" (11: 50)

He insisted that one's views must be governed by conditions of time and place. The trend toward industrialization in the United States required corresponding adjustment of our national policies.

> To be independent for the comforts of life, we must fabricate for ourselves. We must now place the manufacturer by the side of the agriculturer; the former question is suppressed, or rather assumes a new form. Shall we make our own comforts, or go without them, at the will of a foreign nation? He, therefore, who is now against domestic manufacture, must be for reducing us either to dependence on that foreign nation, or to be clothed in skins, and to live like wild beasts in dens and caverns. I am not one of these; experience has taught me that manufactures are now as necessary to our independence as to our comfort. (11: 504)

Jefferson even raised the question of whether the growth of manufactures might some day permit going "beyond our own supply," and he characteristically concluded that no a priori answer could be made to that question.

> If it shall be proposed to go beyond our own supply, . . . will our surplus labor be then most beneficially employed in the culture of the earth, or in the fabrications of art? We have time yet for consideration, before that question will press upon us, and the maxim to be applied will depend on the circumstances which shall then exist; for in so complicated a science as political economy, no one axiom can be laid down as wise and expedient for all times and circumstances and for their contraries. (11: 504)[30]

It is significant that he did not utter an emphatic negative to this question. Once, in 1781 (in *Notes on Virginia*), he had castigated the idea that the United States should produce its own manufactured goods. Now, in 1816, he willingly entertained the suggestion that not only should this country produce for its own needs, but it might also become an exporter of industrial products. It was no accident, therefore, that when he was president, Jefferson's policy toward the encouragement of domestic manufactures was not essentially different from the earlier Hamiltonian policy. The tariff duties enacted under the Federalist administrations were not repealed. For the revenue produced by the tariff, Jefferson found new ones, as the following section will show. Industry continued to thrive during the Jeffersonian regime. By a policy of accommodation, industry was allowed to assume its place with agriculture as one of the twin pillars of the emerging American economy.[31]

Reduction of the National Debt

On his accession to the presidency, Jefferson continued to apply the logic of planning wherever possible to the conduct of national affairs. His record as a planner during his administration closely parallels his accomplishments during the previous years.

The objectives of Jefferson's first term were determined primarily by his previous opposition to Hamilton's policies. Jefferson regarded Hamilton as a confirmed monarchist, drunk with admiration for British institutions. In Hamilton's hands, American institutions were becoming increasingly perverted by excrescences typical of old-world tyrannies. A new class of paper speculators was threatening to corrupt republican virtue. Unless federal power was restored to its original design, in Jefferson's view, the promise of creating a democratic society in America would soon be destroyed.

Having recently overcome the Federalist opposition in the bitterly fought elections of 1800, Jefferson sought the widest possible support for his policies. To allay the violently partisan prejudices that divided the country, he appealed in his first inaugural address to the sentiment of national unity: "We are all Republicans; we are all Federalists." In a passage of notable merit, Jefferson describes what, in his view, is "the sum of good government." In addition to complete freedom of speech, there must be

> a wise and frugal government, which shall restrain men from injuring one another, which shall leave them otherwise free to regulate their own pursuits of industry and improvement, and shall not take from the mouth of labor the bread it has earned. This is the sum of good government, and this is necessary to close the circle of our felicities.[32]

He elaborated on the ultimate necessary for reducing the costs of government:

> Considering the general tendency to multiply offices and dependencies, and to increase the ultimate term of burden which the citizen can bear, it behooves us to avail ourselves of every occasion which presents itself for taking off the surcharge, that it never may be seen here that, after leaving to labor the smallest portion of its earnings on which it can subsist, government shall in itself consume the residue of what it was instituted to guard.[33]

Superficially, it might appear that Jefferson's entire policy consisted of narrowing the activities of government and reducing its power. It is certainly true that these constituted the main objectives of his first administration. As long as the federal power was in the hands of those whom Jefferson believed were opposed to republicanism, he was suspicious of anything that accentuated the authority of government. He believed the first object of policy was to fix in the public mind the cardinal principles of republicanism. By emphasizing in his conduct of office simplicity and frugality, both politically and personally, the president aimed to establish these principles beyond peradventure for all time to come.

But it will be seen from the discussion that follows that the reduction of the federal debt was only one aspect of Jefferson's policies, and only a means to a larger design of making the government an instrument for public improvement. When the public debt was well on its way to extinction, Jefferson might have elected to continue his announced policy of reducing the activities of government to the absolute minimum. But he did not choose this policy. Instead, as we shall see, he chose as his primary object not the further reduction of debt, but, on the contrary, a vast program of expenditures for public improvement.

When Jefferson came into power, he had scarcely an alternative to the course he followed. He distrusted the policies of the previous administration and especially the objects for which federal authority had been used. The offices were filled with appointees whose republicanism he doubted. The gravest danger of all in his mind was the extravagance of government, as indicated by the high level of the federal debt. On January 1, 1801 the national debt stood at $83,038,050, almost $30 million more than it had been in 1789 when Hamilton assumed his funding operation.[34] Both Jefferson and Gallatin were critical of the habit of recurring to loans instead of taxation. The debt had grown by profligacy and unnecessary expenditures. Instead of adding strength to the government, as Hamilton argued, Jefferson viewed debt as a canker on the body politic. He desired especially the early abolition of internal taxes such as those existing on carriages, liquors, sugar, houses, lands, and slaves. Hamilton had devised a complicated plan by which surplus revenues would be applied to the sinking fund, the interest of which was to be used toward extinguishing the principal of the debt. Gallatin, his secretary of the treasury, opposed the sinking fund procedure. He proposed instead a long-range fiscal plan "determinate in amount, simple in its execution and certain in its effect."[35] In the place of relying on interest accruing from debts owed to the government, Gallatin proposed to pledge to the payment of the debt a definite sum of revenue to be appropriated regularly each year, over and above the normal government expenditures.

The first requisite of Jefferson's debt-reduction policy was the consent of Congress to the general principle that the payment of debt was to take precedence over all other expenditures.[36] In both houses of Congress, the proposals for the reduction of the debt were accepted as first charges on the treasury and inviolably pledged. A fiscal plan was devised whereby it was estimated that, under conditions of peace, the national debt of $80 million could be paid off in sixteen years. The total annual revenues of government were estimated for this period at about $10.5 million. If the costs of government could be held at approximately $3 million, over $7 million would be regularly available for paying the interest and the capital of the public debt. A regular annual appropriation of $7.3 million was to be made, an amount fixed by Gallatin as adequate for the purpose.

It is hardly surprising that contingencies occurred—especially in a new government—that neither Jefferson nor Gallatin could have foreseen. Contrary to the wishes of the president, Congress eliminated the internal taxes at the behest of Representative John Randolph, before the condition of the exchequer could afford this relaxation in revenue. Troubles in the Mediterranean required expenditures that had not been anticipated. Finally, the indebtedness of the government was increased by the purchase of the Louisiana Territory by $13 million in addition to the original cash payment of $2 million.

Nevertheless, the plan of debt reduction was eminently successful. By the end of 1805, the principal was reduced by approximately $18 million, if we exclude the Louisiana purchase from consideration.[37]

The government had made remarkable progress toward extinguishing the debt. The prosperity of the country had resulted in revenue far greater than had been anticipated by the original fiscal plan. An actual surplus was looming for the first time the republic's history. It seemed now within the power of the government to decide whether it wished to continue its policy of drastic economy under the new conditions prevailing, or to embark on a new scheme.

CHAPTER VIII

Thomas Jefferson:

Internal Improvements

Social Improvement

The planning that took place during Jefferson's second term of office remains to this day so little known that the student of American history must marvel at this fact. So many facts of lesser note concerning Jefferson's life have obtained common currency, but, strangely, practically nothing is generally known concerning one of the largest projects entertained by Jefferson, one that for a time he must have held closest to his heart.

Jefferson's plans for social improvement were contingent upon the prosperity of the country and the resulting state of federal finances. The economic policies pursued by his first administration, in the words of Henry Adams, "had been marked by a complete success. Never before had the country enjoyed so much peace, contentment and prosperity." The burden of public debt had been materially reduced; as the administration commenced its second term of office, only $10.5 million of federal bonds remained to be immediately discharged. For the first time the country could afford to relax Gallatin's policy of stringent economy. The government could choose between a reduction of taxes or a diversion of the surplus revenues to other objects.

In order to understand why Jefferson adopted the latter course, it is necessary to understand the nature of the federal tax structure at this time. Of the approximately $11 million in annual revenue at the beginning of Jefferson's administration, about 90 percent was derived from customs duties. The government had, in effect, continued the tariff rates established by the previous administrations. Opposition to them was virtually nonexistent, even in the purely agrarian sections of the country. For the greater part, they bore chiefly on luxury imports. They afforded, further-more, some measure of encouragement to domestic industry. The internal taxes had been abolished in 1802, and so far as the mass of the people were concerned, taxes for the maintenance of the federal government hardly existed. Some additional revenue was derived from the sale of public lands, and from postage, but this was more in the nature of fees for services rendered. There could be few justifiable complaints against the continuation of the import taxes.

The problem of the surplus offered its own answer. The solution lay in a continuation of the existing taxes and a diversion of the surplus revenues to realizing objects of social improvement that would not otherwise be possible. In his second inaugural address, Jefferson indi-cated his intention of converting the federal surplus into a permanent fund for creating public improvements: "Redemption once effected, the reve-nues thereby liberated may, by a just repartition among the States, and a corresponding amendment to the Constitution, be applied, in times of peace, to rivers, canals, roads, arts, manufactures, education and other great objects within each State."[1]

It was proposed that the annual amounts set aside for debt payment be reduced from $8 million to $4.5 million, thereby leaving $3.5 million for public improvements and defense expenditures.[2] Again, in his annual message of December 2, 1806, Jefferson informed Congress that the goal of full redemption of the debt was rapidly being approached. Did Con-gress therefore propose to suppress the import duties on foreign goods? To his own question, he replied in the negative. The elimination of the tariff would only give an advantage to foreign manufactures over our own. He pointed, further, to the fact that the great mass of goods on which the import was paid consisted of luxuries, purchased only by those who were rich enough to afford them. "Their patriotism would certainly prefer its continuance and application to the great purposes of the public educa-tion, roads, rivers, canals, and such other objects of public improvement as it may be thought proper to add to the constitutional enumeration of Federal powers."[3]

Jefferson's political conceptions had traveled a long way from the ideal announced in his first annual message of "a wise and frugal government which shall restrain men from injuring one another, which shall leave them otherwise free to regulate their own pursuits of industry and improvement, and shall not take from the mouth of labor the bread it has earned."[4] Instead of regarding government as inherently oppressive and parasitical, he viewed it as an agency capable of achieving socially useful objects that could not be fully provided by private enterprise or state and local governments alone. He looked forward to the time when a continued wise utilization of surplus revenues would achieve on the federal level many of the reforms that Jefferson and his colleague Gallatin had separately fought to effect through action by the states.[5] Nowhere in his writings did Jefferson better express the policy he envisioned for the United States than in a letter of 1811 to his friend Pierre Samuel Du Pont de Nemours:

> We are all the more reconciled to the tax on importations, because it falls exclusively on the rich, and with the equal partitions of intestate's estates, constitutes the best agrarian law. In fact, the poor man in this country who uses nothing but what is made within his own farm or family, or within the United States, pays not a farthing of tax to the general government, but on his salt; and should we go into that manufacture as we ought to do, he will pay not one cent. Our revenues once liberated by the discharge of the public debt, and its surplus applied to canals, roads, schools, etc., the farmer will see his government supported, his children educated, and the face of his country made a paradise by the contributions of the rich alone, without his being called on to spare a cent from his earnings. The path we are now pursuing leads directly to this end, which we cannot fail to attain unless our administration should fall into unwise hands. (11: 203–04)

The public improvements planned by Jefferson during his second administration may be divided into three fields of activity: education, science and useful knowledge, and transportation. In the sections that follow, Jefferson's planning activities in these fields will be analyzed.

Jefferson believed a constitutional amendment necessary to effect his program of public improvements and he recommended it to Congress.[6] For reasons that are not altogether clear, Jefferson at no time described in detail which improvements he planned to make. It seems probable that he was waiting to ascertain how Congress would react to his program.[7] For example, although education was certainly one of the most important objectives of his program, he suggested alternatively the endowment of education by a grant of land to the states, the establishment of a national educational institution such as a university, and even the elaboration of a nationwide system of education as outlined by Du Pont de Nemours. Only in the field of transportation was there actually prepared a detailed program of specific long-term improvements accompanied by a discussion of the financial measures required. In this latter field, Jefferson relied extensively on the planning genius of Gallatin.

It has frequently been assumed that because Jefferson showed an unusually strong solicitude for the authority of the states, he was necessarily opposed to increasing federal authority even when legitimately exercised. It is no doubt true that Jefferson had a habitual preference for strict constitutional construction. The extension of federal powers made during the Hamiltonian regime gave him cause for alarm. In a letter to Peregrine Fitzhugh he gave his opinion: "I do not think it for the interests of the federal government itself, and still less of the Union at Large, that the State governments should be so little respected as they have been" (9: 377). In his well-known letter to President Washington in 1792, he bitterly assailed the loose interpretation of Hamilton, who defended the proposition that the federal government had the right to exercise all powers that concerned the general welfare and especially where money was employed (7: 1–39). Jefferson believed that the safest limitation was the requirement of an express grant of power in order to sanction any new activity. He supported the maxim, "if we have a doubt relative to any power, we ought not to exercise it" (12: 349–50). His faith in written constitutions was typical of that which had prevailed in the eighteenth century. He believed it possible to design a constitution that was both stable and flexible, acted to prevent arbitrary exercise of authority and, at the same time, permitted adjustments reflecting social changes. He was severely critical when his political enemies loosely construed the Constitution for their own purposes and he tried consistently to guide his own administration's conduct by the same canons of political rectitude.

It should not be supposed, however, that because Jefferson preferred political power to be defined by exact limits, he necessarily favored defining federal powers within extremely narrow limits. He believed in a written enumeration, to be sure, but the enumeration of powers was not intended to become a governmental straightjacket. Unfortunately, he did not prepare a written draft of his recommended constitutional amendment to make possible the program of public improvements. No one can say what specific powers he would have included. However, an answer to this question may be inferred from his action concerning the acquisition of the Louisiana Territory. At first he proposed that the territory be acquired by means of a constitutional amendment. When he saw that the opportunity to make the purchase had to be seized at once, before the Constitution could be amended, he did not hesitate to recommend this step. Nevertheless, his draft of an amendment for the government of the new territory is astonishing in the wide powers it would have forced on the federal government. In addition to empowering Congress to dispose of the land and to exchange lands with the Indians, he proposed

> to work salt springs, or mines of coal, metals and other minerals within the possession of the U.S. or in any others with the consent of the possessors; to regulate trade and intercourse between the Indian inhabitants and all other persons; to explore and ascertain the geography of the province, its productions and other interesting circumstances; to open roads and navigation therein where necessary for beneficial communications; and to establish agencies and factories therein for the cultivation of commerce, peace and good understanding with the Indians residing there. (10: 6–12)[8]

From this draft it is possible to infer that a wide field of new functions would have been secured for the federal government had Jefferson put his hand to drafting the proposed amendment for public improvements. The following sections analyze what improvements Jefferson's administration planned and accomplished even without benefit of an amendment to the Constitution.

Education

There prevails generally a popular, stereotyped view of Thomas Jefferson as exclusively concerned with state systems of education and a foe of all types of federal intervention in this field. Because Jefferson dreaded the effects of the centralizing policies of his political enemies, it has been frequently assumed that he favored a complete separation of function between those powers allotted to the federal government and those reserved for the states. The image of Jefferson gallantly striking down every proposal to expand federal functions has become ingrained in the popular mind. Nevertheless, the true story needs to be told, even though the facts are not complete (some of Jefferson's planning of education improvement did not get beyond recommendations). Congress manifested such meager enthusiasm for the administration's educational proposals that the president had little reason to formulate the details of his program. His program had not advanced much beyond the planning stage when foreign difficulties intervened with disastrous consequences for the treasury surplus toward which Jefferson and Gallatin had been striving. Whatever the indefiniteness of Jefferson's plans, the evidence, limited as it is, shows clearly that he attempted to improve education by federal endowment and subsidy.

It would be impossible to understand why Jefferson should have so interested himself in schemes for national promotion of education without understanding the educational conditions prevailing during his day. Jefferson was indeed a radical in his educational ideas. His first attempt, in 1779, to establish a state program of public school education supported by state taxes levied in proportion to property filled many of the propertied class with horror. During the whole of his lifetime, Jefferson consistently labored to improve educational opportunity on all levels. It is not surprising, therefore, that when he became president, he felt all the more impelled to use his powerful position to improve the low standard of education that prevailed almost everywhere.

Because the states later gradually assumed charge of public school education, it is often taken for granted that the problem of public education originally took the form of a conflict between state and federal authority, that is, between two forms of public education. But that is not the case. The problem was different at the time the Constitutional was drafted. It is probable that not a single member consciously visualized the powers reserved to the states as including the power to establish a public school system supported by state taxes. In not a single state did such a public school exist. One can scarcely generalize from the educational practices of the period that education was an affair of government at all. The omission of any reference to education in the Constitution is hardly surprising in view of the way this problem was handled in the state constitutions.

Of the first (unrevised) constitutions of the sixteen states admitted into the Union before 1800, only five made mention of education; of constitutions amended and revised before 1800, only eight mentioned it. The constitutions of Massachusetts and Vermont made mandatory a school in every town; Pennsylvania and Virginia, in every county; the New Hampshire legislature was pledged "to cherish" public schools; Delaware, to establish them "as soon as convenient"; North Carolina, to establish "a school or schools." Vermont alone made specific provisions requiring a school for every town and a university for the state. Outside of New England, where education was largely a local function, elementary education was left to private initiative, or to church or charity schools.[9] The states contributed nothing toward the maintenance of education; by 1800 only in Massachusets were local school districts given the power to tax. New York in 1795 was the first state to make a regular appropriation for the support of schools, but even this was allowed to lapse in 1800[10] since general consciousness of the need for education hardly existed. The high school, for example, did not make its appearance until 1827—in Massachusetts, one of the most advanced states educationally. Greater attention was paid to higher education as the prerogative of the children of the wealthy. Even so, colleges were invariably small, poorly endowed, and inadequately staffed. Jefferson was well aware of the backwardness of college education, in both its aims and methods. He had tried without success, as governor of Virginia, to infuse a new secular spirit into William and Mary College. Jefferson's bill for "the More General Diffusion of Knowledge," presented to the Virginia legislature in 1779, proposed the creation of a tax-supported school district in every community, making possible more widespread education opportunities. It was badly defeated.[11]

As one of the most enlightened persons of his time, Jefferson shared with other liberals the optimistic view that improvement of education would inevitably promote human progress. He believed that progress would become general when the minds of men ceased to be ignorant.[12] To Colonel Yancey he wrote in 1816, "If a nation expects to be ignorant and free, in a state of civilization, it expects what never was and never will be. The functionaries of every government have propensities to command it well—the liberty and property of their constituents. There is no safe deposit for these but with the people themselves; nor can they be free with them without information."[13] To Madison, he expressed the same thought more succinctly: To give "information to the people . . . is the most certain and the most legitimate insurance of government."[14] Democratic countries in particular have the responsibility of educating their citizens to the highest possible level. On the subject of extending equal opportunities, Jefferson wrote as follows: "The object is to bring into action that mass of talents which lies buried in poverty in every country, for want of the means of development, and thus give activity to a mass of mind, which, in proportion to our population shall be the double or treble of what it is in most countries."[15] Because private education served primarily the needs of the rich, and because church schools were usually parochial and illiberal in their points of view, Jefferson insisted that the educational practices be adapted to our democratic political institutions.[16] Jefferson struck at the heart of ecclesiastical education with his Statute of Virginia for Religious Freedom, one of his proudest achievements. The importance of the declaration of religious freedom and the disestablishment of churches during the period of the Revolution is hardly to be underestimated. When the amendment guaranteeing religious freedom was added to the Bill of Rights and the Constitution largely as a result of Jefferson's efforts, a great first step had been taken for wresting the control of education from the churches.[17]

The first official expression of interest in educational improvement by Jefferson's administration came in 1802 when the government committed itself to a policy of endowing new states with lands for public education. The policy of granting land to aid schools was hardly a new one. It had well-worn precedents in New England. The provision for the reservation of the sixteenth lot of every township for the maintenance of its schools made by the Land Ordinance of 1785 was merely the enactment of the New England practices into a federal statute.[18] Congress had also reserved the sixteenth section of every township for schools, as well as two complete townships for universities, when it arranged for the sale of lands in the Northwest Territory to the Ohio Company in 1787. Until the first new state formed out of territorial land was admitted into the Union, the land reservation policy for the support of education had behind it only these two precedents; no legal action existed binding the federal government to such a policy in the future. It was only when Ohio was admitted into the Union in 1802 that the action of Jefferson's government made land reservation for education a fixed and binding policy of the federal government. The newly admitted state, in this case Ohio, agreed to exemption for taxation of lands sold by the federal government until the last credit installment had been paid the government. The federal government, on the other hand, pledged to give the sixteenth section of every township or equivalent lands "for the use of schools."[19] According to Orfield, "With this act, land grants for the support of schools may be said to become firmly established as a national policy."[20] When the public lands in the southwest part of the Louisiana Purchase were offered for sale in 1806, the same policy was continued.[21] With the exception of the states of Texas, Maine, and West Virginia, every state admitted into the Union since 1802 has received a grant of land from the federal government for the endowment of its public schools.[22]

Education was thus early taken under the protection of the federal government as seen from the land reservation policy of Jefferson's administration. From the point of view of strict constitutional interpretation, the government had violated the Constitution by committing itself to a program involving the promotion of an object not mentioned in the enumerated powers. Whether Jefferson was greatly troubled by this inconsistency is not recounted. In any case, as president he continued to work for the same object of educational improvement that had animated him throughout his lifetime. Not long afterward, when there loomed a possibility of a federal surplus, the president and his secretary of the treasury began to consider a more comprehensive program of public improvement. (The circumstances explaining their volte-face with regard to revenues and expenditures were described in a preceding section.)

In his second inaugural address and in his sixth message to Congress, Jefferson proposed that with the authority of a constitutional amendment, Congress undertake a wide program involving "the great problems of education, roads, rivers, canals, and other such objects of public improvement as it may be thought to add to the constitutional enumeration of federal powers."[23] In a later message, he argued the necessity of public education because "public institutions can alone, [support] by those sciences which are . . . necessary to complete the circle, all parts of which, contribute to the improvement of the country."[24]

However vague in specifics, and shifting from time to time in what he proposed, there is never doubt as to Jefferson's enthusiasm and faith in the powers of educational improvement. At one time he suggested that Congress might endow "a national establishment of education" by a donation of public lands.[25] He entertained the idea of establishing a national system of education such as was prepared by Du Pont de Nemours, and indeed acknowledged Du Pont's work by saying that he had "read it with great pleasure." Du Pont's plan was one of the most highly centralized educational schemes of the many that were proposed during this period.[26] In a letter to Gallatin written soon after his second inauguration, Jefferson revealed the attractive prospects ahead: "But from whatever cause, the increase of revenue is a pleasing circumstance, as it hastens the moment of liberating our revenue and permitting us to begin canals, roads, colleges, etc."[27] Nowhere, however, did Jefferson formulate a clearly defined program as to what the educational improvements should be. He did, however, signify his approval in principle of the elaborate project proposed by his friend, Joel Barlow. It was modeled on the pattern of the National Institute of France, which included a huge organization combining research and teaching.[28] Jefferson wrote Barlow on December 10, 1807, saying that he hoped more than ever that the country might be spared going to war, so that his dream of improving science and education might be realized. "I had fondly hoped to set those enterprises into motion with the last legislature [Congress] I shall meet. But the chance of war is an unfortunate check" (9: 168–69).

Why did Jefferson leave so vague and undefined his plans for educational improvement? Why do his educational recommendations lack the deft touch and precision of design that characterize his earlier planning? Several reasons may be advanced in explanation. The first is that Congress had displayed indifference toward all proposals made thus far concerning federal advancement of education. Jefferson understood that time would be required to educate Congress to his point of view. In his letter to Joel Barlow, he wrote, "There is a snail-paced gait for the advance of new ideas on the general mind, under which he must acquiesce. A forty years' experience of popular assemblies has taught me that you must give them time for every step you take. If too hard pressed they balk, and the machine retrogrades" (9: 168–69). The record of Congress concerning its attitude to plans for educational improvement was one of apathy, if not hostility.

President Washington experienced the same indifference. He wrote the commissioners of the Federal District on January 28, 1795 offering his Potomac shares toward the initial endowment of a national university (11: 15, 22). Practically two years elapsed before the matter was even discussed in Congress, when James Madison on December 12, 1796 presented the subject afresh. Congress was not even lukewarm in considering the proposition, even in its diluted form, of a seminary for the District of Columbia.[29] It was almost ten more years before the issue was again mentioned in Congress—a memorial from Samuel Blodgett requesting that Congress grant a site for a national university "and such other patronage as they may think proper."[30] Following this isolated instance another decade slipped by until the subject was discussed on December 11, 1815.[31] Considering these facts, Jefferson would have been naive had he believed that his plans for educational improvement would be received as politically practicable. This probably explains why priority was given instead to the consideration of a comprehensive program for roads and canals. As we shall see, a magnificent conception of planning a national transportation system was presented to Congress in Gallatin's report of 1808. Jefferson himself suggested this explanation to Barlow: "People generally have more feeling for canals and roads than education." The president, however, mentioned that he still hoped "we can advance them with equal pace" (9: 168–69). Finally, as will be observed, financial exigencies of the treasury compelled the administration to give up all the improvement plans before they could be realized.

Whatever may be thought of the limitations in explicitness and detail of Jefferson's presidential plans for educational improvement, they manifest a clear intention to undertake a new class of duties for the federal government. Jefferson's views on government during his second administration were vastly removed from the simple design of frugal government that he announced in his final inaugural address. Had the fiscal surplus continued over a long period of time, as Jefferson hoped, one wonders into what new forms Jeffersonian democracy might ultimately have developed.

Science and Useful Knowledge

As Jefferson was in the vanguard of contemporary liberal educational thinkers, so also was he anxious to promote science and useful knowledge under government auspices. For practially twenty-five years, from 1795 to 1819, after Benjamin Franklin and David Rittenhouse, he served as president of the American Philosophical Society, whose members included almost all the leading scientific and humanist scholars of his period. Only Franklin compared with him in scope of intellectual interests. Throughout the whole of his lifetime, even when his mind was absorbed in public affairs, he continued to make contributions to science. It would be idle to detail here the studies that he made in such varied sciences as geography, paleontology, agriculture, entomology, and mechanics. Of himself, Jefferson wrote, "Nature intended me for the tranquil pursuits of science by rendering them my supreme delight."[32]

Prior to becoming president, Jefferson had made clear his belief that the government should encourage the development of science and make full use of scientific information. As secretary of state, he had brought about the adoption of a scientific monetary system, designing the decimal system. Acting as president of the American Philosophical Society, he had urged the government to expand the scope of the statistical information collected by the census. He specifically recommended that census compile information concerning the number of natives, citizens of foreign birth, and aliens, and also the number of persons engaged in each occupation. Still more did Jefferson reveal his attitude toward the governmental promotion of science and useful information by his administration of the first patent laws while he was secretary of state. He took the view that the constitutional provision securing temporary monopolies to authors and inventors was aimed "to promote the progress of science and useful arts." He believed that the particular method employed of granting temporary monopolies was altogether subordinate to the provision's larger purpose. Even though he granted only thirty-three letters patent in 1791 and twenty in 1792, still he regarded the act as serving its function.[33] Jefferson had vigorously opposed the amendment of the patent law in 1793, whereby his power of examination and discretion faded into a more ministerial duty of registration, with each applicant becoming the judge of his own invention. According to Jefferson, the original purpose of the constitutional provision was being degraded into a "ceremonial under which any gim-crack could masquerade as a genuine invention." He protested, "I might build a stable, bring into it a cutting-knife to chop straw, a hand mill to grind the grain, a curry-comb and brush to clean the horse and by a patent preclude anyone from evermore using these things without paying me."[34]

As president of the United States, his views were determined to a large degree by his appreciation of the need for developing the sciences in America. As one most familiar with the contemporary world of science both in Europe and in this country, he had a clear understanding of how far American science lagged behind European. Then, too, he believed that there existed an affinity between republicanism and science. A republican government had a special obligation to promote all forms of science and useful knowledge. He expressed this idea later when, following his retirement, he petitioned Congress to exempt from tariff duty imported books on scientific subjects, citing in support of his petition "the value of science to a republican people; the security it gives to labor by enlightening the minds of citizens; the protection it affords against foreign power; the virtues it inculcates; the just emulation of the distinction it confers on nations foremost in it; in short, its identification with power, morale, order and happiness."[35]

Jefferson's splendid hopes for the future of science were in strong contrast to its existing poverty in fact. Scientific research had hardly begun in the United States, and scholars could justifiably complain of the lack of facilities for carrying on investigations. Most scientific studies were conducted by learned laymen like Jefferson himself, who attempted to contribute to several branches of learning.[36] The idea of a university or research foundation specializing in scientific research was still unknown. There would not exist for several decades a single instance of a professorship devoted exclusively to science and research. One authority states that "the conception of a university as in fact a research institute was uncommon anywhere in the United States in 1854,"[37] practically a half-century after Jefferson's administration. Yale College was the first to establish a Department of Philosophy for postgraduate scientific study in 1847; in 1860 it announced that it would grant the Ph.D., a policy that Harvard adopted twelve years later. Prior to 1797 there was not one scientific journal in the United States, and there existed only two scientific societies, the American Philosophical Society and the American Academy of Arts and Sciences, founded in 1769 and 1780 respectively.

Those Americans who decided to devote their lives to some science, such as medicine or chemistry, had first to study abroad, since adequate training did not exist in America. With regard to materials for research, for books and instruments, the United States was dependent on Europe.

In both his accomplishments and his uncompleted plans, Jefferson reveals the breadth of his views concerning governmental action to aid science and increase useful knowledge. The first achievement of his administration was to carry out President Washington's recommendation for establishing a military academy. Although the United States Military Academy at West Point, established in 1802, was intended to train cadets and officers for the army, its instruction during its early years was largely in the field of engineering science. Until 1866, the academy was under the authority of the superintendent of engineers of the War Department. After 1812, when it established a separate Department of Engineering, engineering science remained an extremely important part of the academy's curriculum.[38] This is of special significance; until the Rensselaer Institute was established in 1824, there was not another engineering school in the country.

Another phase of Jefferson's interest in extending scientific knowledge is represented by his organization of the Lewis and Clark expedition in 1803–04, following the acquisition of the Louisiana Territory. As yet, little was known of that vast area's terrain and resources. Jefferson personally prepared the instructions for the expedition and made clear that he desired as full information as possible on such subjects as topography, resources, minerals, watersheds, forest and agricultural products, savage inhabitants, and customs of the aborigines.[39]

It was not until several years later, when the treasury showed signs of maintaining a surplus, that Jefferson began to conceive of more ambitious exploratory surveys. The opportunity of establishing surveys on a systematic and permanent basis, instead of dispatching an occasional expedition to obtain subjective and unsystematic information, lay before him.

A recommendation in favor of a coastal survey was included in the president's program of improvements announced in his annual message of 1806. Congress approved, and on February 10, 1807, an act was passed appropriating $50,000 to defray the initial costs. The execution of the statute was delegated to Secretary of the Treasury Gallatin, who invited scientists to submit plans. The task of organizing the survey was finally entrusted to Ferdinand R. Hassler, a Swiss scientist who had recently arrived in this country. The Coastal Survey, which inaugurated many of the methods still employed by the present geodetic survey, was "the first scientific bureau under the government."[40]

On the basis of the few facts available, it would be difficult to state categorically how far Jefferson planned to extend the scheme of surveys into the interior region. Judging from the fact that in 1807 he dispatched Zebulon Pike and a party of explorers to the headwaters of the Mississippi and its lower tributary waters, it seems probable that had finances permitted, the president would have made explorations and surveys a regular and systematic policy of the government. It may be recalled here that in his draft of a constitutional amendment for the governance of the territory of Louisiana, he had explicitly provided authority "to explore and ascertain the geography of the province, its productions and other interesting circumstances." On the basis of Jefferson's active interest in promoting measures to obtain more accurate knowledge of the economic geography of the interior, one is justified in hazarding a guess that had his policy been energetically continued by his presidential successors, the Geological Survey, established in 1879, would have been instituted far earlier. This might have had a profound effect on the government's policy for the West: On the basis of information thus accumulated, the government might have directed westward development far more intelligently than it did.

The evidence is hardly conclusive that Jefferson would have shaped federal policy for the promotion of the sciences according to the scheme of Joel Barlow mentioned in the previous section. Yet the president wrote Barlow approvingly of his project.

> The time is fast approaching when the United States, if no foreign disputes should induce an extraordinary expenditure of money, will be out of debt. From that time forward, the greater part of their public revenue may, and probably will, be applied to public improvements of various kinds, such as facilitating the intercourse through all parts of their dominion by roads, bridges, and canals; such as making more exact surveys and forming maps and charts of the interior country, and of the coasts, bays, harbors, perfecting the system of lights, buoys, and other nautical aids; such as encouraging new branches of industry, so far as may be advantageous to the public, either by offering premiums for discoveries, or by purchasing from their proprietors such inventions as shall appear to be of immediate and general utility, and rendering them free to the citizens at large; such as exploring the remaining parts of the wilderness of our continent, both within and without our own jurisdiction.[41]

In referring to the magnificent epoch to follow at the end of eleven years, Barlow, in alluding to Gallatin's fiscal program whereby the government would be free of debt in 1817, believed it wise to be planning for that era to come. A great catalog of public works projects would be available for public expenditure, and the best minds in the country should in the meantime be planning for that eventuality. The Barlow scheme probably had no more chance of success than Jefferson's other fine hope for the improvement of education by federal means. Nevertheless, it is important because it embodied Jefferson's scientific aspirations.

A National Transportation System

Jefferson's administration came closest to realizing its hopes of bequeathing to the future an inheritance of public improvements when it launched the construction of the Cumberland National Road, the largest public works project prior to the Erie Canal. It linked part of the Ohio Valley with the Eastern seaboard, which however limited for that era of transportation, nevertheless afforded a bridge across the formidable barrier of the Allegheny Mountains.[42]

In its other attempts at transportation planning, Jefferson's administration was less successful. The embargo intervened to abort Gallatin's great plan presented in his famous report of 1808.[43] In a long-term plan that was intended to outline federal public works policy for the next ten years, Gallatin proposed that the government commit itself to financing and constructing a national network of roads and canals. His plan envisaged nothing less than an integrated national system of transportation (in terms of the existing technology), which would promote the harmonious economic development of the whole of the nation's resources. Even though the change of economic circumstances occasioned by the embargo tendered Gallatin's plan impracticable, it remained the basis of all federal road and canal activity for the next twenty years. The presidential administrations succeeding Jefferson's referred constantly to it, and the plans of Monroe's secretary of war, John C. Calhoun, and of John Quincy Adams were largely based on it. Had the thinking of the administrations that followed kept pace with Jefferson's, it is not at all improbable that the federal government might have pursued a more active role in directing the early development of the railroads.

Although Jefferson stood committed by his final inaugural address to a policy of simple and frugal government, it should be remembered that his sympathies were mainly with the Western agriculturalist. The Western regions looked to his administration for help, and it was the farmer who was having trouble transporting his products to market and who needed the government's help most of all. The agrarian interest may have opposed a vigorous intervention of government in principle, but so far as transportation improvements were concerned, the farmer was anxious to obtain whatever help was available. Those sections that stood to gain by road and canal improvements willingly acceded even though contrary to their political principles.

The condition of the roads during this period reveals clearly how great was the need for their improvement. Jefferson and his secretary of the treasury were familiar with the problem, having themselves had to travel frequently over the tortuous Western roads. Both men had seen how the absence of commercial transportation had driven the desperate farmers of western Pennsylvania to the Whiskey Rebellion. The cost of shipping goods by wagon from Pittsburgh to Philadelphia ranged from $5.00 to $10.00 a hundredweight—far too high for farm produce.[44] During this period, the usual charge for hauling a barrel of flour for 150 miles was five dollars, for hauling a cord of wood twenty miles, three dollars.[45] In the absence of other modes of transport, hogsheads of tobacco were sometimes rolled thirty to forty miles to market.[46] The extent to which farmers were kept from expanding into the interior is shown by the fact that in South Carolina, as late as 1818, two-thirds of all cotton was grown within five miles of a river, and two-thirds of the remaining third was grown within ten miles.[47] The problem of transportation in the West was accentuated by the fact that improvements had to be built over great areas having sparse populations, and in a country both wild and rugged. J. B. McMaster has ventured the opinion that "the heaviest taxes that could have been laid down would not have sufficed to cut half the roads or build the bridges that were required.[48]

Toward the improvement of this condition, the previous Federalist administration had done nothing. The interests of the dominant groups in the Federalist party lay primarily in domestic and foreign trade. Furthermore, the war in Europe had lent an incentive to the investment of capital in shipbuilding, foreign trade, and banking—fields that offered more lucrative returns than investments in internal improvements.[49]

Nor was private enterprise alone capable of bearing the burden of making internal improvements. Private capital was scarce, and its market was poorly organized. Foreign capital for road building was not and would not be available for several decades.[50] Although a few state governments, notably that of Pennsylvania, had ventured to subsidize private construction, the states had not yet discovered that their securities were an adequate basis for obtaining large amounts of credit. Most turnpike companies were both local and small with respect to their capital and mileage, and on the whole, they were unprofitable. Corporations were still a novelty by and large; and turnpike corporations were chiefly local companies made up of a few shareholders who regarded their stocks more as a contribution to securing better roads than as an investment. According to Durrenburger, "at least one-third of the turnpike corporations chartered never built a mile of road, due chiefly to their inability to raise the necessary capital; at least one-third . . . were unable to sell the full amount of their capital stock or found their capital inadequate to construct their roads."[51] Larger road projects necessitated splitting longer roads into small segments, each of which was built and maintained by a separate company. The mortality rates among turnpike companies, even following the completion of a road, were exceedingly high. Poor management, high maintenance costs, and inadequate traffic contributed to their instability, and frequently "the road beds fell into disrepair and many of them were abandoned by the companies as worthless."[52]

The Western farmer, therefore, looked to Jefferson's administration for help. Whatever Jefferson and Gallatin may have believed concerning the limited powers of the federal government, they nevertheless found in the Constitution adequate authority to provide relief for the transportation needs of the West. Nor did they wait until there had accumulated in the treasury a substantial surplus to finance large-scale transportation improvements.

As in providing aid for education, Gallatin found a device for committing the federal government to a long-range transportation improvement program. In addition to offering to the newly admitted state of Ohio the sixteenth section of every township for the support of schools, Gallatin proposed that the state be given one-tenth of the net proceeds of all lands sold thereafter by Congress (after deducting the expense for making the sales) to "be applied towards laying out and making turnpikes and other roads, first from navigable waters emptying into the Atlantic to the Ohio and afterwards continued through the new States; such roads to be layed out under the authority of Congress and of the several States through which the same will pass."[53]

This provision was justified also as a means of compensating the Western states for their loss of revenue. As a condition to their entry to the Union, they had agreed not to tax lands in their states to which the federal government retained title. Under the credit system of land sales, the purchaser of public lands was allowed five years to complete payment, during which time his land was exempt from state taxes. Gallatin, therefore, devised this scheme for reimbursing the states, and also for obtaining future road improvements. Gallatin's proposal was accepted, although the grant of the net proceeds of the land sales was reduced from one-tenth to one-twentieth.[54] In a subsequent act, Congress remitted 3 of the 5 percent to the states for constructing roads within the state; the remaining 2 percent was retained by the federal government as a fund for the construction of the National Road.[55]

By 1805 that portion of the fund belonging to the federal government amounted to $12,662.[56] On March 29, 1806, under the leadership of

Gallatin, Congress appropriated $30,000 for a survey and authorized the president to appoint three commissioners to report a plan for the road.[57] The amount of money contained in the 2 percent fund was obviously not sufficient to construct a road of the dimensions planned. On April 13, 1807 Gallatin wrote President Jefferson that the "money already appropriated would be sufficient to construct about four or five miles of the road." He was determined to build the road "in the most complete manner just as many miles as the money will pay for." Once the road was begun, he felt sure that Congress would appropriate enough money to complete it. He regarded it "as a national object of primary importance." He estimated that the road would effect an annual savings of transportation costs of over $200,000: "ten thousand tons will be carried westward annually and perhaps one hundred thousand barrels of flour brought back."[58]

The Cumberland National Road represented the first completed part of Jefferson's national transportation program. Because of shortage of funds, the completion of the road was seriously delayed; the first ten miles of the road west of Cumberland, Maryland, were not completed until 1812. Jefferson and Gallatin planned to extend the road west as far as St. Louis on the Mississippi River.

The rapid growth of railways during the 1830s made unnecessary the extension of the road, and it was never built beyond Illinois. The National Road performed an important service during this period in reducing the existing freight rates by almost half. Furthermore, it established an important link across the hitherto impassable Alleghenies.

Gallatin's Report

As the condition of the treasury showed continued improvement, the president and his secretary of the treasury began to conceive of federal policy in more ambitious and comprehensive terms. In response to a resolution of the Senate passed on February 23, 1807, Gallatin presented a report on April 6, 1808 offering a comprehensive program for roads and canals in the coming year.[59]

Gallatin's report did not merely propose an expanded program of federal aid; it presented a comprehensive plan to establish a national system of transportation improvements, accompanied by a detailed financial program of ways and means. It was proposed that $20 million be appropriated from the anticipated federal surplus over a period of ten years for the construction of roads and canals. The specific improvements recommended were: great canals along the Atlantic seacoast, uniting New England with the South; communications between Atlantic and the Western waters; communications among the Atlantic, the St. Lawrence River, and the Great Lakes; interior canals and roads.

The first group of improvements comprehended the construction of canals along the Atlantic seacoast to connect the great inland buoys and coastwise rivers with canals cut through the forenecks of land between New England and the South. Under the second group there would be constructed canals in the Santee, Roanoke, James, Potomac, and Tennessee rivers. In the third group he urged the establishment of communications between the Great Lakes and the Atlantic by means of canals and roads connecting with the Hudson River and Lake Champlain, the Mohawk River and Lake Ontario, and including a canal around Niagara Falls. The last group enumerated a list of interior canals and roads ranging from New England to New Orleans.

Gallatin argued in his report that his transportation program would aid in promoting the economic development of the nation by making the maximum use of its natural and financial resources. The kind of projects outlined were on too large a scale for private organization alone; without subsidy from the government, they could not be built. Gallatin estimated that the transportation costs saved by new roads and canals would in the long run pay the costs of their construction. In addition, the value of the unsold public lands held by the government would be enhanced. The government could easily sell the improved lands at a higher price if the produce of the land could find better markets. Gallatin was not dogmatic as to the specific method by which these objects would be accomplished. The government might itself undertake the improvements, but Gallatin believed in private enterprise wherever possible. Under such circumstances, the government might make loans to private companies or, preferably, subscribe to shares of their stock. Detailed problems of this kind could be worked out in practice. As an immediate step, he urged that surveys be made to determine more definitely the feasibility of each project.

Gallatin's transportation program was also urged as a necessary measure for national security. Not only would roads and canals shorten distances and promote commercial intercourse, they would improve our defenses and provide an alternative to maintaining a large standing army and navy. Good roads would make possible mobility of our existing military forces and "afford the means of rapid concentration of that force and a formidable body of militia at any given point."[60]

Unfortunately, Gallatin had scarcely made his report when it became necessary to shelve his plans. The road and canal scheme was premised on the assumption that peace would continue and that only a small part of the national revenues would have to be devoted to national defense. Jefferson and Gallatin hoped that the friendly negotiations in which they were engaged with British Foreign Secretary Charles Fox would lead to a solution of our conflict with Britain. With the sudden death of Fox, conditions changed entirely. The new foreign secretary, George Canning, reverted to the earlier policy, attempting to crush America's growing commercial strength. On November 11, 1807 Canning issued his famous Orders in Council, which, with a stroke of the pen, suppressed the largest part of America's trade with Europe. In order to defend our commercial interest, Jefferson recommended an embargo law as a temporary precaution. This went into effect on December 22 and was not repealed until March 4, 1809. Meanwhile, trade was strangled, a circumstance that dried up the anticipated revenues from foreign imports. The precious sums hoarded by the treasury for inaugurating a wonderful new era of public improvements instead had to be spent on armaments. The great dream seriously entertained by Jefferson's administration of using the federal surplus toward objects of social and economic amelioration had come abruptly to an end.[61]

CHAPTER IX

Albert Gallatin

and John Quincy Adams:

Internal Improvements

Transportation and Communications in
American National Development: An Overview

The geography of the United States has always forced Americans to give preeminence to the needs of transportation and communications. Our history can be largely written in terms of the westward movement of the frontier and the restless mobility of our people. Great distances had to be traversed in a country of continental dimensions. Boundless resources awaited to be tapped and exploited if one could get there and encourage others to settle there. It is perhaps no accident that this country has pioneered and made such remarkable progress in improving means of transportation—railroads, automobilies, airplanes—and communications—telegram, telephone, radio, and television. Americans have become accustomed to thinking in terms of conquering space and moving across vast areas.

In the decade following our grant of political independence, there was also a remarkable awakening of interest in improved transportation and communications. Changes in technology presented new vistas of economic opportunity. The invention of the steam engine, improvements in the technique of road building, and new methods of canal construction resulted in what one historian calls a "burst of proposals for waterways and roads."[1] The steam engine was still in its infancy, yet a mind with Washington's prescience could guess at its economic portent:

I consider Rumsey's discovery for working boats against the stream, by mechanical powers principally, as not only a very fortunate invention for these States in general, but as one of those circumstances, which have combined to render the present time favorable above all others for fixing, if we are disposed to avail ourselves of them, a large portion of the trade of the western country in the bosom of this State irrevocably. (9: 69)

Similarly, when Gouverneur Morris of Pennsylvania visited the Caledonian Canal in Scotland in 1795, he wrote in his diary: "When I see this, my mind opens to a view of wealth for the interior of America, which hitherto I had rather conjectured than seen."[2] America was blessed with waterways, inlets, rivers, and bays in abundance. The new type of lock construction of canals offered opportunities for their use.

These were notable improvements over previous means of transportation and communications. Vigorous far-seeing minds were stirred by the possibilities of linking the trans-Allegheny region to the Atlantic seaboard. The Allegheny mountain range constituted the most formidable barrier to communications with the East. Because there was no way economically to ship the farm produce of the trans-Allegheny region to the Eastern seaports, the farmers of the Ohio River Valley were forced to ship their foodstuffs all the way to New Orleans via the Mississippi River. Unless some solution was found, the Western settlers would be driven to an alliance with the Spanish in order to obtain a continued use of the Mississippi River. Thus was involved also the problem of maintaining political unity with the West. The situation was sufficiently exacerbated for Washington to write to Governor Benjamin Harrison of Virginia in 1784, "The western states (I speak now from observation) stand as it were upon a pivot. The touch of a feather would turn them any way" (9: 63). Virginians in particular were worried about this situation, not only because of its political dangers, but also because of the loss of trade. They knew that the settlement of the Ohio River Valley had just begun; existing trade was but a trickle compared with what it might become. At the Constitutional Convention in 1787, the Virginia delegation revealed a pronounced interest in "pushing commerce ad libitum," in the words of its chairman, Edmund Randolph.[3] Virginia was well located as a possible commercial outlet for the produce of the West—if a satisfactory means could be found for bridging the Allegheny Mountains.

Washington assumed the most active role in promoting a commercial bond between the West and East. His interest in the matter dated from 1753 when as a subaltern in the British military service, he assisted in mapping out a preferred road route across the Alleghenies. Beginning in 1759 he tried to interest the Virginia legislature in a bill to incorporate a canal company as a voluntary enterprise. After the Revolutionary War, in 1784, he was finally successful in organizing the Potomac Company of which he was elected president. Although Washington was naturally partial to the Potomac River route that he fathered, he urged Congress and all the states to take whatever action was within their means to encourage and promote such projects.

> The extensive inland navigation with which this country abounds, and the easy communications which many of the rivers afford with the amazing territory to the westward of us, will certainly be productive of infinite advantage to the Atlantic States, if the legislatures of those through which they pass have liberality and public spirit enough to improve them. For my part, I wish sincerely that every door to that country may be set wide open, that the commercial intercourse with it may be rendered as free and as easy as possible. (9: 445)

To Richard Henry Lee, president of Congress and also a Virginian, he wrote urging that the government "open all the communications which nature has afforded, between the Atlantic States and the Western territory, and to encourge the use of them to the utmost" (9: 172). He was severely critical of the petty parochial jealousies that prevented the states from acting in concert toward improving the commercial potentialities of the Western region. In fact, he believed the greatest obstacle was not the difficulty of constructing the canal, but instead

> The *unfortunate jealousy* which ever has, and it is to [be] feared will ever prevail, lest one part of the State should obtain an advantage over the other parts, as if the benefits of the trade were not diffusive and beneficial to all. . . . Common policy, therefore, points clearly and strongly to the propriety of our

enjoying all the advantages, which nature and our local situation afford us. (9: 61)

As president of the United States, Washington refrained from involving the federal government in any of the Western canal or road projects, whatever might have been his personal inclination to lend them assistance. The federal treasury was too greatly in want of funds, and the amount of money that would be needed was far in excess of any figure the treasury could support for many years to come. Private capital, also in scarce supply, was finding its returns in shipbuilding, foreign trade, and banking too lucrative to risk its funds in questionable or long-range investments like canal or turnpike companies.[4] Nevertheless, in Washington's view, the progress being made was considerable. In a letter written to the Earl of Buchan on April 22, 1793 he took this optimistic view:

And we are at this moment deeply engaged and far advanced in extending the inland navigation of the River Potomac on which it [the new capital city] stands, and the branches thereof, through a tract of as rich country for four hundred miles, as any in the world. Nor is this a solitary instance of attempts of the kind, although it is the only one which is near completion, and in partial use. Several other very important ones are commenced, and little doubt is entertained, that in ten years, if left undisturbed, we shall open a communication by water with all the lakes northward and westward of us, with which we have territorial connection; and inland navigation in a very few years more from Rhode Island to Georgia inclusively; partly by cuts between the great bays and sounds, and partly between the islands and sand banks and the main from Albemarle Sound to the River St. Mary's. To these may be added the erection of bridges over considerable rivers and the commencement of turnpike roads, as further indications of improvements in hand. (10: 338)[5]

In a limited way, within its means, the Washington administration made an important contribution to the improvement of communications throughout the country and especially with the West, by its use of the postal powers. The post office, until taken over by the national government, operated over a restricted area with irregular and infrequent schedules and managed its affairs precariously with its small financial resources. In his annual address in 1791, Washington requested Congress to consider "the importance of the post office and post roads on a plan sufficiently comprehensive as they respect the expedition, safety and facility of communications."[6] The post office was accordingly reorganized on a permanent basis in 1794.[7] Postal service was extended for the first time to the whole of the Western country. As Rich states, "When the new government was established under the Constitution, the leaders showed more of a desire to extend the postal routes because of the service rendered by the mails in the general development of the country."[8]

During the administration of Thomas Jefferson, substantial progress was made in extending communications, principally roads, into the West. As we have observed, the Cumberland National Road was initiated by Jefferson's administration as a means of enabling the Western farmer economically to ship his produce to the Eastern seaports. Although freight transportation by means of wagon road was expensive, there is no doubt that it alleviated the marketing problem of the farmers to whom the road was accessible. But the National Road took too many years to build, and not for many years after it was first authorized were the farmers of the Ohio River Valley able to benefit by it.

Jefferson and Gallatin planned the National Road as only a part of a gigantic public works program of roads and canals to link every part of the country. Gallatin's report of 1808 envisaged a continuing program for a ten-year period during which time a definite sum of money would be budgeted for the construction of an integrated network of communications. Henry Adams describes Gallatin's program:

> The improvements thus contemplated were so laid out as to combine and satisfy local interests. The advantage which Mr. Gallatin proposed to gain was that of combining these interests in advance, so that they should cooperate in one great system instead of wasting the public resources in isolated efforts. He wished to fix the policy of government for at least ten years, and probably for an indefinite time, on the whole subject of internal improvements, as he had already succeeded in fixing it in regard to the payment of debt. But thus establishing a complete national system to be executed by degrees, the whole business of

annual chaffering and log-rolling for local appropriations in
Congress, and all its consequent corruptions and inconsistencies
were to be avoided.[9]

It is interesting to contemplate the effect on our future national transportation policy had Gallatin's program been at least satisfactorily initiated and to conjecture on its effect had it been fully realized. What might
its effect have been on the scope of federal powers? Might it have resulted
in further cooperative efforts between the federal government and the
respective states in undertaking jointly projects like the Erie Canal? Can
one also admit the possibility that the federal government might have
taken an active rather than passive role in directing and financing the
development of the railroads? Might not the success of the federal
venture in road and canal building have led to a more positive federal
policy on other fronts? Is it conceivable that the Civil War might have
been averted by a transportation and communications policy that bound
the South to the North by commercial ties of mutual benefit? In short, is
it not possible that the success of Gallatin's plan might, in turn, have
influenced other aspects of national public policy, and, therefore, replaced the later policy of social drift with some long-range programs of
positive action?

It is futile to conjecture on these questions; it seems idle even to raise
them. But it cannot be doubted that the frustration of Gallatin's program
by the events immediately preceding the War of 1812 had an important
effect of postponing and weakening the entire movement to build internal
improvements. As we shall see in the following section, Gallatin's plan
was revived a number of years later and some of its projected improvements were carried out. Nevertheless, the most opportune time for realizing such an ambitious national program had passed. New obstacles to its
passage had arrived in the meantime: apathy on the part of either or both
the executive and legislative branches; the growth of narrow constitutionalism that refused to find adequate authority in the Constitution except
with a specific grant of power; sectional or local jealousies that led each
state to rely on its own financial credit and resources for building roads
and canals, and to oppose federal assistance for rival trade areas.

Despite these obstacles, the government persisted in a growing
program of internal improvements, reaching a peak of expenditure during
the administration of John Quincy Adams. During Adams's four years of
office, more money was spent in building roads and canals than in the

previous thirty-six years of the national government's existence. But as Adams knew, the value of his internal improvements program depended on its permanence and continuity, and in this respect, he knew his administration had been a failure. Adams's successor, Andrew Jackson, was a sworn enemy to federal internal improvements, and Jackson's inauguration to the presidency symbolized the reversal of Adams's policy and the sweeping away of many years of effort spent in forming an organization for transportation planning. Shortly thereafter, on May 27, 1830, there followed President Jackson's famous Maysville veto,[10] which in less than plain words repudiated the policy of internal improvements that to greater or lesser degree had animated every president since Washington.

Until Jackson, whatever the obstacle, there always seemed to be a chance of successfully reviving and carrying out the original Gallatin plan. The administration of Jackson thus marked the beginning of a new era in national policy, and practically speaking, the start of a new era of laissez-faire.

Revival of Gallatin's Plan After the War of 1812

After the outbreak of the War of 1812, the United States had good reason to regret its failure to listen to Secretary of the Treasury Gallatin's advice. The nation found itself woefully unprepared to wage war with England. Having failed to heed the repeated entreaties of Gallatin that the charter of the Bank of United States be renewed, the government was condemned to wage a war without adequate finances and to pay heavy discounts for the privilege of borrowing.[11] Having delayed also in carrying out Gallatin's plan of transportation improvements, the country found itself unprepared to cope with the problem of moving men and material to the theater of war.

The coastwise roads were placed under excessively heavy traffic due to the British control of the sea.[12] These ordinary dirt roads had deteriorated rapidly under the constant use of four thousand baggage wagons regularly employed in the coastwise trade. Even civilian life became disordered by the delays and irregularities of travel and shipping. For example, even in summer when roads were at their best, two months were required to travel from Boston to Augusta, Georgia. On the military front the conditions were worse. The failure of the military campaign on the

Western front was tragic proof of Gallatin's argument of the military necessity of good roads. Roads had even to be built to reach the enemy. Major General Edmund Gaines estimated that "the impracticable state of the roads and the want of canals" were responsible for a "sustained greater loss of health, if not of life" than would have resulted from the "capture of the whole of Upper Canada, with the proposed improvement of the militia and of the means of transportation."[13]

The amount of money spent by the government only on transporting military supplies was fabulous; MacGill estimates it at $60 million. For example, a $500 cannon delivered on the Western frontier cost the government between $1,500 and $2,000. The delivered price of a barrel of flour was $100 and a bushel of oats $60. It is estimated that the total "wagonage" charges of $414,000 for transporting military freight between the Chesapeake and Delaware bays would have been sufficient to construct a canal between them. Similarly, the Allegheny River between Pittsburgh and Lake Erie could have been improved sufficiently for commercial and military needs by an expenditure of a little more than a fourth of the money spent on transporting military supplies over that route.[14]

When the war clouds had cleared after the Treaty of Ghent, the issue of federal participation in a program of internal improvements was revived. The war had demonstrated the crucial need for more adequate means of transportation, and now spokesmen for better roads and canals laid new importance on the federal military power. In fact, the War Department became during this period the national center of road and canal planning.

Throughout the period, the constitutional issue of whether the government possessed the power to engage in internal improvements was primary. Although nationalism was in full tide as the nation gloried in its wartime exploits, there existed no strong sentiment in favor of a constitutional amendment granting the government these specific powers. Leaders of the movement for federal internal improvements perceived that if the government was to engage in such a program, it would have to be by means of a liberal constitutional interpretation. Under the circumstances, finding an acceptable formula that could justify federal participation was uppermost in importance; developing specific road and canal projects was secondary.

Representative John C. Calhoun of South Carolina came forward with a proposal that the government simply earmark its bonus and prospective dividends from the reestablished national bank as an internal improvements fund.[15] There was involved here, he claimed, only an issue of the government's power to spend its own money. The amount of money involved, $650,000, was "doubtless too small to effect such great objects of itself; but it would be a good beginning."[16] The bill avoided mention of specific improvements and Calhoun even argued that the rights of states through which future improvements would pass were not involved and would not arise until the construction of actual improvements was begun. Speaker Henry Clay, a coauthor of the "American System," found other reasons for avoiding discussion of the bill's real purpose. "Everything is hazarded by encumbering the bill with too much detail. . . . Let us provide the ways and means. Let our successors judiciously apply them."[17] Calhoun explained to Congress the ultimate internal improvements program that he hoped they would achieve, in effect a revival of Gallatin's great plan.

> The first great object was to perfect the communication from Maine to Louisiana. This might be fairly considered as the principal artery of the whole system. The next was the connection of the Lakes with the Hudson River. In a political, commercial and military point of view, few objects could be more important. The next object of chief significance was to connect all the great commercial points on the Atlantic, Philadelphia, Baltimore, Washington, Richmond, Charleston, Savannah, with the Western States; and finally to perfect the intercourse between the West and New Orleans. These seemed to him the great objects. There were others, no doubt, of great importance, which would receive the aid of the government.[18]

This expedient was destined to have no success. Calhoun's bill was promptly vetoed by President Madison, close upon his last term of office.[19] Many years before, in 1787 at the Philadelphia convention, Madison had been one of the staunchest defenders of nationalism.[20] Now, however, he sensed a growing undercurrent of states' rights sentiment and feared that the continued and expanding exercise of the implied powers by the federal government would infringe upon the authority of the states. Madison's was the first presidential veto of an act of Congress exercised in defense of states' rights. Just as Madison had previously held that the reestablishment of the national bank and the High Tariff Act of 1816 could be constitutionally justified on the basis of historical precedent, Madison's own veto of federal internal improvements became one of the most effective legal precedents to be cited against undertaking a national road and canal program.

The years from 1817 to 1825, during the Monroe administration, should logically have settled the government's policy in favor of a gigantic internal improvements program. The era was marked by relative party harmony, economic prosperity, and a growing enthusiasm for more roads and canals. President Monroe announced himself in favor of internal improvements. In both his first inaugural and his first annual message he expressed faith in such improvements: "Never did a country of such vast extent offer equal inducements to improvements of this kind."[21] The most outstanding protagonist for internal improvements, moreover, was Monroe's secretary of war, John C. Calhoun. During this period, Calhoun was a nationalist of nationalists, and in his determined efforts to promote a national internal improvements program, he had the vigorous support of Henry Clay, who made this program a part of his "American System." The program of Calhoun, in its essentials, was similar to the earlier plan of Gallatin, although as secretary of war he relied to a greater extent on the government's military power in fostering it. Calhoun shrewdly appraised the possibility of Congress adopting a large-scale transportation program in the absence of a specific authorization of constitutional authority. In the absence of an amendment, he emphasized the military advantages of roads and canals and particularly of military roads.

In 1818 Congress provided Calhoun with an opportunity to present his views on the subject. The House of Representatives in that year had instructed the secretary of war to report in the following session "a plan for the application of such means as are within the powers of Congress for the purpose of opening and constructing such roads and canals as may deserve and require the aid of Government with a view to military operations in time of war . . . and the more complete defense of the United States."[22]

When Congress next convened, Calhoun presented his report.[23] His suggested projects consisted of the following: 1. a road extending north and south through the Atlantic states connecting Maine with Louisiana; 2. a system of inland canals connecting the great bays and sounds of the Atlantic coast with the coastal rivers; 3. a proportionate share of financial aid in the projects linking Albany to the Great Lakes, and Philadelphia, Baltimore, Washington, and Richmond to the Ohio River, Charleston and

Augusta to the Tennessee River; 4. some projects in northern New York linking that territory to the Northern frontier; 5. a system of military roads whose construction had already been begun, on the Western, Northern, and Southern frontiers.[24]

Calhoun emphasized the military usefulness of this program but he also comprehended that military power alone was too narrow a constitutional base on which to sustain such a broad program.

> The road or canal can scarcely be designed which is highly useful for military operations, which is not equally required for the industry or political prosperity of the community . . . they might be employed for other uses, which, in the event of war, would be necessary to give economy, certainty and success to our military operations, and which if they had been completed before the late war, would, by their saving in that single contest, in men, money and reputation, have more than indemnified the country for the expense of their construction.[25]

The report explained further that it was not proposing that the government alone assume responsibility for a road and canal program. Local projects would of course continue to be supported by the states and the commercial cities that sponsored them. The secretary of war stated that he was interested only in those larger projects in which "no one or two states have a sufficient interest," or those in which the "state or individual capacity . . . is inadequate," or those which "must be perfected by the General Government, or not to be perfected at all at least for many years."[26]

Calhoun's report offered no financial plan to show how these projects might be financed, or even estimates of their cost of construction. He realized that these amounts could only be guessed at; he therefore told Congress that their cost "could be ascertained with satisfaction only by able and skillful engineers, after a careful survey and examination." He believed strongly that the Department of War should be made the official agency for the planning and executing of the great improvements program, and he even suggested that soldiers be employed (with an appropriate raise of pay) in aiding the construction of these projects.

Calhoun's enterprising policy in promoting a national program of roads and canals was singular rather than characteristic of Monroe's administration. The president was personally in favor of internal improvements, but "proceeding always with a constitutional sanction." His views on national policy represent an ambivalence that was common during this period. Monroe favored the growth of industry, the extension of internal trade, the binding together of the Union by all possible ties of commercial intercourse. On the other hand, he was insistent that all government policy proceed within the specific limits of the Constitution, and that any extension of federal authority be authorized by an amendment. Monroe was influenced by a growing conservatism in interpreting the Constitution, an attitude exemplified by President Madison. The federal government could maintain a policy if there existed a precedent for it in previous legislation even if there existed no specific constitutional sanction for it. But it could not break ground and initiate a new policy without such a specific authorization by the Constitution. Thus, for example, Jefferson's administration could initiate the construction of the great National Road without a special grant of power in the Constitution, but a later government was constitutionally permitted only to provide the means for its proper maintenance and to create other similar improvements, but this only if it did not at all conflict with any rights asserted by the states concerned. In the absence of a constitutional amendment, it was considered necessary to furnish legal authority to meet the exigencies of each new situation.

The futility of this situation was revealed in 1821 when Congress passed an act providing for the preservation and repair of the National Road by the erection of tollhouses, gates, and turnpikes, the revenues of which would be used to keep the road in repair. President Monroe promptly vetoed the act as an infringement on the rights of the states. In a statement of forty pages, entitled "Views of the President on the Subject of Internal Improvements," Monroe explained in detail the reasons for his veto.[27] He did not doubt the need of repairing the National Road, but he believed the method adopted by Congress was unconstitutional. The power to erect tollhouses and enforce payment of tolls would bring the federal government into conflict with the powers of states. There was implied in this act the power to execute "a complete system of internal improvements," which could be predicted only on "the complete jurisdiction and sovereignty for all the purposes of internal improvements." Such a power could not be implied by an existing power of the federal government. The president agreed that the existing powers of Congress were sufficient to construct roads into the territories ("where their execution was of the coarsest kind"), but as soon as a territory became a state, the power of the federal government over the road ceased and it was obliged to surrender the road to the state.

Monroe was appreciative of the sentiment in favor of federal improvements, and when Congress failed to heed his recommendation in favor of a constitutional amendment,[28] he urged that Congress act within its existing powers. Putting the best face on necessity, he asked Congress to appropriate funds to prevent the National Road from falling into ruin.

> Should Congress, however, deem it improper to recommend such an amendment, they have, according to my judgment, the right to keep the road in repair by providing for the superintendence of it, and appropriating the money necessary for its repairs. Surely if they had the right to appropriate money to make the road, they have a right to appropriate money to preserve the road from ruin. From the exercise of this power no danger is to be apprehended. Under our happy system, the people are the sole and exclusive foundation of power.[29]

Planning by the Board of Internal Improvements

Despite Secretary of War Calhoun's strenuous efforts to launch a federal internal improvements program, little progress in that direction could be reported as President Monroe's administration neared its last year of office. An important change occurred in 1824, with the passage on April 30 of the Surveys Act, which established a system of prior surveys of roads and canals under the Corps of Engineers of the War Department.[30]

In his annual message of 1823, President Monroe (perhaps at the urging of Calhoun) recommended that the Corps of Engineers make surveys for a canal route to connect the Ohio River with Lake Erie to the north and Chesapeake Bay to the east.[31] For many years, virtually every advocate of internal improvements had interested himself in surveys of particular improvements. Secretary of the Treasury Gallatin had recommended that his federal program start with surveys to determine the practicability of various routes of roads and canals. The initiative in acting on President Monroe's proposal was taken by Representative Joseph Hemphill of Pennsylvania, who sought to convert the president's suggestion for a specific survey into a general system of surveys. For the latter, no additional constitutional power was needed. No improvements could be planned without the information that surveys would furnish. Knowledge was vital regardless of which branch of government would construct the improvements. Hemphill argued that:

> The execution of this measure will present Congress with a full view of the subject. It will lay the foundation of a well digested and regular system, and it will require but little money compared with the importance of the information. Nothing can be more useful than an accurate knowledge of the natural capacities of the country for improvements; to be made acquainted as well with the interior as exterior; to possess a knowledge of all the valuable streams, the distances of their tide waters, the impediments to navigation which may be in them, and their capacity of being connected with each other by good roads and canals.[32]

The discussion of Hemphill's bill led to a recommendation of national internal improvements in general. For three months Congress debated the issue. The opposition based its views on the unconstitutionality of federal internal improvements. Some states' rights advocates like Senator Thomas Hart Benton of Missouri argued that Congress, not the president, should have the power to decide which projects should be surveyed. Benton cleverly appealed to the fears of local interests planning roads and canal improvements. By presenting their proposals to Congress, he said, there was less of a chance that their claims would be overlooked. Henry Clay, among others, lent his powerful oratorical assistance toward passage of the measure. He championed the rights of the West to federal financial assistance and insisted that the government's power over interstate commerce was sufficient "to give practical effect" to the regulations made under it. If Congress was able to appropriate generously to build seawalls (in Clay's words, "a marine canal"), harbor improvements, dockyards, etc., in order to give effect to its jurisdiction over foreign commerce, then the exercise of similar powers was equally warranted to foster and promote domestic commerce.[33]

The passage of the Surveys Act on April 30, 1824 marked the beginning of a promising era in transportation planning. The president was authorized to "employ two or more skillful engineers and such officers of the corps of engineers" to make "the necessary surveys, plans and estimates . . . of the routes of such roads and canals as he may deem of national importance in a commercial or military point of view, or a necessity for the transportation of public mail." The act specified that when the surveys and plans were completed, they were to be laid before Congress by the president with his recommendations. Thirty thousand dollars was appropriated to defray the cost of the surveys.

Soon afterward, a separate Board of Internal Improvements was created by executive order. The personnel of the board consisted of General Bernard, Colonel Totten, and John L. Sullivan, all prominent engineers. The board was under the authority of Major General Alexander McComb, chief of engineers, who was, in turn, subject to the secretary of war. That the task of preparing the surveys of America's future transportation improvements was placed under the Corps of Engineers was fortunate in a number of respects. The corps dated its official existence from 1802, when the Military Academy at West Point was also established as a training school for military engineers. During this early period, before other engineering schools were founded, the Corps of Engineers "were to a great extent the repositors of this country of that knowledge, which was requisite for the purpose of making accurate surveys."[34] The consolidation of transportation planning under the army engineers gave Secretary of War Calhoun additional influence in preparing an expanded road and canal program.

Before a year had passed, the board had completed the preliminary investigation of the routes the president had assigned, and its report had been made to Congress with a favorable recommendation by the president.[35] Preliminary examinations had been made of the country between the Potomac and the Ohio Rivers, between Lake Erie and the Ohio River, between the Allegheny and the Schuylkill rivers, between the Delaware and Raritan rivers, between Buzzards and Barnstable bays, between Narragansett Roads and Boston Harbor. The report contained exploratory observations of each route. The board's report on the Chesapeake and Ohio canal project illustrates the procedure employed. The board had been instructed to make an examination of the "several routes for canals" and report its opinion of their "practicability." If the board was unable to decide "definitively on any particular route," it was requested to present its observations on the relative advantages of each. In the present instance, the board reported that it considered a canal connecting the Ohio and Potomac rivers as practicable "beyond all doubt," although further investigation would be necessary to determine which route was preferable. The general direction of the canal had been examined and valuable data had been obtained concerning the region's topography, soil, location of water reservoirs, etc. The board was able to say of its work:

> By following the successive series of operations, which we have just analyzed, nothing is left to conjecture; every part of the work is studied and ascertained, and no chance is left for mistakes of facts, or miscalculations, to endanger the success of its completion. This regular mode of proceeding is the surest way to avoid these illusive deceptions from whence such works have so frequently failed. The general project corresponds in its results with the details; the whole combines economy, solidity, and durability, and the estimates being founded upon positive and ascertained facts, their accuracy may be depended upon.[36]

The advantages of the method employed by the Board of Internal Improvements in planning national transportation improvements are patent. Whatever its limitations in either skill or experience, the board embodied some of the best civil engineering competence that the country possessed. This is attested by the fact that during the 1830s, when private capital was organizing the first railroads, the engineers of the board were loaned by the government to survey and lay out the roadbeds. The board acting as an ad hoc body was organized to achieve the specific object of surveying roads and canals. It was therefore free to concentrate its whole effort on this one major objective. The reports of the board indicate that within the limits of its knowledge, it viewed the transportation needs of the country both systematically and comprehensively from a national point of view. The historian of the Corps of Engineers says of the board's policy, "This was the only attempt ever made by the Corps of Engineers to view the country as a whole and to adopt a policy of internal improvements, or river and harbor improvements, in accordance with that view."[37] It should be added that the board was directed to survey only projects or routes of "national importance" from the viewpoint of commerce or military security. The aid of the surveys was to augment rather than to supplant state or private transportation improvements.

The final annual report of Secretary of War Calhoun projected a grand program for a national system of transportation, based on the great regional watershed basins. Calhoun's plan was Gallatin's original scheme, enlarged and brought up to date. For the Mississippi River Valley, the Great Lakes region, and the Atlantic coastal area to the Allegheny Mountains he proposed separate administrative regions, or in modern parlance, developmental authorities. As a Southerner, Calhoun had also emphasized the needs of the South in strengthening its commercial ties with the North both along the Atlantic coastal and the Mississippi River Valley regions. Calhoun's own statement best summarizes these plans and expectations:

> These three great works then (1) the canal to Ohio and Lake Erie, with the improvements of the Ohio, Mississippi, and the canal around the Muscle Shoals; (2) the series of canals connecting the bays north of the seat of Government . . . to New Orleans, uniting the whole of the Southern Atlantic States, are conceived to be the most important objects within the provisions of the act of the last session. The beneficial effects which would flow from such a system of improvements would extend directly and immediately to every State of the Union; and the expenditure that would be required for its completion would bear a fair proportion to the wealth and population of the several sections of the country—at least as they will stand a few years hence. When completed, it would greatly facilitate commerce and intercourse among the States, while it would afford to the Government the means of transmitting information through the mail promptly to every part, and giving effectual protection to every portion of our widely extended country.[38]

The Plans of John Quincy Adams

The movement for an extensive federal program of internal improvements was, it appears, always doomed to frustration at about the time its success seemed most assured. Fate always intervened when the maturation and adoption of a long-range program appeared imminent. Secretary of the Treasury Gallatin had seen his program suddenly dashed to ruin by the unexpected turn of international relations. After the War of 1812, when public sentiment seemed to be crystallizing in favor of federal participation in road and canal improvements, Calhoun's national bank bonus bill was vetoed by President Madison. It should be recalled that at the Philadelphia convention in 1787, and also afterward, Madison had indicated both his interest in and approval of federal aid for internal improvements. President Monroe's constitutional scruples also prevented him from permitting Congress to establish a system of tolls for the use of the National Road in the absence of a constitutional amendment. When Congress at length manifested no interest in sponsoring an amendment, Monroe was spurred to request congressional action even without additional constitutional power. Congress made provision for the maintenance and extension of the National Road and established the system of internal improvements surveys under the Corps of Engineers. For a decade, the chief obstacle to a vastly expanded federal program of internal improvements had been the restraints interposed by the executive branch.

Although opposition to internal improvements no doubt existed, public sentiment in favor of an expanded participation by the federal government appeared to be at high tide. At no time since 1808 did the moment seem more propitious for inaugurating a large-scale program. If the detailed planning of such a program had not yet matured, then at least the Board of Internal Improvements had made a beginning. A sound planning organization had been established, and there were reasons for believing that Adams's inauguration was the beginning of a new era. Frederick Jackson Turner writes, "The tide of sentiment in favor of internal improvements was so strong that, to insure its complete success, it would have been necessary only for the executive to have ceased to interpose the checks which Monroe had placed upon this movement."[39] In his inaugural address, President Adams cautiously used the language of his predecessors: He would "proceed in the great system of internal improvements within the limits of the constitutional power of the Union."[40] To Adams, this was part of his magnificent plan for the long-range development and conservation of his country's resources. He did not understand internal improvements to be simply a scheme of federal financial aid for building various roads and canals. At long last, it seemed that the new president would be successful in laying the foundation for an expanded internal improvements program.

Judging by the amount of federal investments and the extent of planning activity in internal improvements, this conclusion might seem warranted. In fact, more money was spent in road and canal building during Adams's four years in office than was spent in all of the previous thirty-six years of the national government's existence.[41] Over $2.3

million was appropriated during Adams's administration for roads, canals, and river and harbor improvements, compared with about $1 million for all the previous years. Dewey estimates that the probable cost of completing the improvements planned by 1830 would have amounted to $96 million. These figures would suggest that the federal government was definitely launched on a large-scale, long-range program of transportation improvements.

But however auspicious the beginning of his administration, before a year was over, Adams knew that he had failed. The success of his program depended on continued political acceptance. His total plan had many sides, and its achievement would require many years. He had only to realize that hardly had he passed into executive power when the balance of the political scales was weighed against him. A realist, he did not deceive himself with false hopes; he knew that his popularity was waning, and the strength of Jacksonians growing. By the middle of his term, the control of both houses of Congress passed to the opposition. The opposing coalition chose every convenient means to embarrass him. Because Adams enthusiastically advocated internal improvements, his enemies in Congress defeated his plans, even when, from the long-range point of view, their Western constituencies might have gained by these improvements. Looking backward in 1837, Adams blamed narrow sectional alignments and states' rights views for his failure:

> When I came to the presidency, the principle of internal improvement was swelling the tide of public prosperity. . . . I fell, and I fear, with my fall, I fear never to rise again, certainly never to rise again in my day, the system of internal improvement by means of national energies. The great object of my life therefore has failed. The American Union, as a mere person in the family of nations, is to live from hand to mouth, and to cast away instead of using for the improvement of its own condition, the bounties of Providence.[42]

Even before the middle of his term of office, Adams had lost the initiative in recommending legislation. His third and fourth annual messages to Congress were limited to giving an account of what had been done. He no longer urged on Congress his plans for the future. In his diary, he consoled himself with this rationalization: "Measures of detail should be matured in Congress, and it is time for the President to act upon them when they are brought to him in the form of bills for signature."[43]

It was unfortunate for Adams that the circumstances of his election to the presidency did not give him a clear mandate. He had come into office under the cloud of a disputed election, with fewer electoral votes than his chief opponent. Jackson's henchmen took delight in charging that Adams had won by a corrupt bargain with Clay. Adams acknowledged in his *Memoirs* that his election was "not by the unequivocal suffrages of a majority . . . , with perhaps two thirds of the whole people adverse to the actual result."[44]

Had Adams been differently constituted personally, or had he come from a different background, he might have been able to overcome these serious handicaps. He was poorly fitted to compete in the political arena of rough-and-tumble backwoods democracy. His intellectual brilliance and his broad training were ill-adapted for the transitional political era in which he lived. The coming era of frontier democracy offered relatively greater inducements for mass demagoguery than for hopes of preferment by competence and demonstrated ability. Adams, in short, could not speak the language of the masses of people, and he was unable to translate his plans for the future of America into terms appealing to the common man. He was lacking in personal warmth, and in the hostile atmosphere of the nation's capital, he felt himself more isolated than ever. Having seen so many recent examples of political treachery, he acted without the advice of his cabinet associates who were better qualified than he to judge how Congress and the public would react to his statements.

Adams's greatest mistake was made in his first annual message to Congress. Having failed to heed the advice of Clay and other of his supporters, he tactlessly laid before Congress a broad program of expanded federal functions. He enlarged on the theme of nationalism and the duties of government in a manner that was certain to antagonize those who were jealous of states' rights. "The spirit of improvement is abroad upon the earth," he said, and he went on to recommend a governmental program apparently without limit. The message included not only the expansion of internal improvements but also "laws promoting the improvement of agriculture, commerce and manufactures, and cultivation and encouragement of the mechanic and elegant arts, the advancement of literature, and the progress of the sciences, ornamental and profound." In proposing the establishment of astronomical observatories, he indiscreetly described them as "lighthouses of the skies," thus making himself the object of his enemies' ridicule and derision.[45]

Although considerable gains were made during Adams's administration in developing internal improvements, his program on the whole must be considered a failure. Adams, in any case, regarded his presidency as a failure. In his first message to Congress, he had stated his basic philosophy of the ends of civil government: "The great object of the institution of civil government is the improvement of the condition of those who are parties to the social compact, and no government, in whatever form constituted, can accomplish the lawful ends of its institution, but in proportion as it improves the condition of those over whom it is established." He included also the "moral, political and intellectual improvements" of man, which was a part of those ". . . duties assigned by the Author of our Existence to social no less than to individual men." In his opinion, government was "invested with power . . . for the fulfillment of these duties . . . and to the attainment of the end, the progressive improvement of the condition of the governed."

Adams would take no comfort in what little his administration had accomplished. In the main, he had failed to achieve his mission in life— establishing his grand plan on a sound footing. He knew that the chances of realizing his schemes were more remote at the end of his term of office than ever before. He viewed the future with grim pessimism. He was depressed more by his country's tragedy than by his personal failure. For he foresaw quite clearly the tragic outcome of the narrow, limited, and sectional views of the Jackson crowd. He had no faith that the main lines of the country's development could be worked out by means of political and sectional compromises. He had no faith in private, uncontrolled enterprise per se. Nor was he willing to commit the destinies of the country to any one economic group or section of the country. Although he was regarded by the West and the South as the spokesman of the Eastern commercial section, he was far from willing to give the business interests a free hand in exploiting the nation's resources. In his opinion, commerce ought to receive "the most distinguishing favor and the most liberal protection ought to be given." But he added, "Commerce is the very last interest in the nation upon which I would bestow power. Mercury made a very good messenger, but he would have made a detestable master."

To Adams, the victory of Jacksonian policies implied a reversal of all that he stood for. The philosophy of states' rights was in effect an abdication of the responsibilities and duties of government. Adams recognized the dangers of sectional conflict, and he believed they could be avoided only by a constructive national program. In a speech on the occasion of the fiftieth anniversary of Washington's inauguration, he said, "The Constitution itself had been extorted from the grinding necessity of a reluctant nation." He believed that the Constitution was an instrument for improving the social condition of the people. The Constitution's adoption had been won against "a stubborn, unyielding resistance" that had produced "a sullen, embittered, exasperated spirit . . . whose rallying cry was state rights—state sovereignty, state independence." In his opinion, the revival of states' rights views again threatened the structure of the Union and his great hopes for America's future.

It is unfortunate that John Quincy Adams, unlike his father, left no treatise on civil government. Although his writings are voluminous, they consist almost entirely of memoirs, letters, and speeches. These furnish evidence of his broad program of national planning and suggest the general framework of his ideas. Had Adams formulated his ideas in a clear and systematic manner as Hamilton, for example, had done, succeeding generations might better have appreciated the full stature of the man, his dreams, and the goals for which he was striving. Nevertheless, basing our analysis on the written fragments of his thought, it is clear that his objects of planning, taken together, constitute an important chapter of affirmative government in our history.

Important to an understanding of Adams is the fact that since childhood he had spent a considerable part of his life abroad in the diplomatic service. As a consequence, when he returned to the United States, he was singularly free of provincialisms or narrowly sectional points of view. For example, it was Adams who in 1807 as senator from Massachusetts initiated the resolution in the Senate that resulted in Gallatin's great report on internal improvements. When shipping and foreign trade temporarily collapsed as a result of Jefferson's embargo, Adams preferred to resign rather than represent the embittered opposition of the New England states. He was a nationalist from the beginning, and he viewed the United States as an integral union, not a composite of separate states.[46]

Nor can Adams's motives be fully understood without knowing how he was influenced by science and education. Beyond a doubt, he was then the foremost public figure in the United States who held also an illustrious place in the world of science. Brooks Adams writes that "science and education were passions and amounted to a religion"[47] with him. His

Report on Weights and Measures,[48] prepared while serving as Monroe's secretary of state, was a prodigious task and a century later could be described as still "a classic."[49] His long residence in Europe brought him into contact with scientific ideas in established centers of learning. By contrast, American standards were very poor indeed. In presenting his plans before Congress for establishing scientific institutions under governmental authority, it is unfortunate that Adams failed to show their practical utility to business, industry, and agriculture. Yet Adams's interest in science was profound and far-reaching. Brooks Adams writes: "He alone among public men of that period appreciated that a nation to flourish under conditions of modern economic competition, must organize its administrative as well as social system upon scientific principles."[50]

Adams's plans included a national university, an astronomical observatory, the promotion of education for women, and the establishment of such other agencies and media as would advance education and science. Adams reminded Congress in his first message that Washington's plan to establish a national university and a military academy was only partially fulfilled. He "earnestly recommended the establishment of seminaries of learning, to prepare for all the emergencies of peace and war."[51]

Having spent many years in training for the profession of political leadership, Adams had an extraordinarily high conception of public service. It was the duty of government to lead and to integrate and unite the various interests within the country by means of counstructive programs. He insisted on the power of government to make its own decisions without being dictated to by any sectional or economic interest. He hoped to make his administration a scientific one, with a trained staff of civil servants. While his policies were attacked with venomous hostility by his enemies, he steadfastly refused to dismiss capable government employees for political reasons. He asked only that public servants be politically neutral; it was not necessary, so far as he was concerned, that they be his political supporters. Concerning Major General McComb, he wrote that the chief engineer of the War Department had "maintained an exemplary neutrality."[52]

Adams foresaw for the United States a glorious future if its great resources were developed and husbanded. It was this promise of American life that he, as secretary of state, feared might be compromised or defeated by the intrusions of European wars or dynastic politics into the

New World, leading him to express the rights of the United States in the Monroe Doctrine.

Adams's plans for America's development included: 1. improvement of transportation and communications; 2. improvement of education and science; 3. conservation of forests and land resources; 4. creation of a governmental department for the management of these policies.

Adams believed so strongly in an expanded program of internal improvements that he was willing to make that issue the test of his popularity with the people. Although a New Englander, he believed in the future of the West as ardently as any frontiersman. "There is not upon this globe of earth a spectacle exhibited by man so interesting to my mind or so consolatory to my heart as this metamorphosis . . . into cultivated fields and populous villages which is yearly, daily, hourly, going on by the hands chiefly of New England men in our western states and territories."[53]

He believed our abundant inland waterways should be developed and utilized as highways of trade to and from the West. He believed that the larger road and canal projects should be developed "by means of national energies" rather than by "the limping gait of State legislatures and private adventure." Adams understood the merits of systematic planning, and he worked closely with Major General McComb in directing the work of the Board of Internal Improvements.[54] In 1825 the federal government for the first time purchased stock in a private company, the Chesapeake and Delaware Canal Company, thus establishing a precedent for a mixed corporation. The practice of subscribing stock was extended to the Dismal Swamp Canal Company of southern Virginia, and the Chesapeake and Ohio Canal Company.[55] In all, the government invested $1,293,555 in the stock of canal improvements corporations. Adams hoped that his policy would be extended so that all parts of the country would be able to benefit by means of these transportation improvements.

Adams's interest in science and education led him to suggest a federal program that was far beyond the grasp of the average legislator. Adams's desire to establish a national university and various scientific institutions stemmed from his realization that the United States, a new country, was lagging behind Europe in the advancement of science and learning. He simply could not understand why the public was willing to spend money for roads or bridges or for meetinghouses but was indifferent to science and culture. Nor did Adams feel that the federal government was constitutionally prohibited from advancing the cause of science and education because of an absence of enumerated powers. He suggests that he would have supported federal aid for education for women. To the head of a women's seminary he explained that,

> with regard to any assistance from Congress, I was sorry that she must expect nothing more. Congress, I was convinced, would now do nothing. They will do nothing for the education of boys, excepting to make soldiers. They will not endow a university. I hoped this disposition would change, but while it continues, any application to Congress for female education must be fruitless.[56]

In the absence of any encouragement from Congress, Adams refrained from outlining further his ideas on improving science and education.

Adams proved himself a pioneer in reforestation and conservation by undertaking the first important federal program for the maintenance of forest resources in relation to naval shipbuilding needs. The naval war with England made the country aware for the first time of the importance of preserving its live oak timber tracts. In 1819 when Adams was secretary of state, the United States had obtained by treaty with Spain a cession of Florida, which was known to contain valuable stands of live oak timber. This measure was followed by an act of Congress in 1819 that authorized the president to employ the military forces to prevent the cutting or stealing of the timber.[57] Few appreciated as keenly as Adams the importance of the live oak tracts. Out of his rich diplomatic experience, he understood better than any American of his day how indispensable live oak was to any nation that aspired to naval and sea power. He was familiar with the fact that England had established a live oak plantation on her own soil, and that the czar of Russia had imported live oak acorns with the intention of establishing a similar plantation in the Crimea. As long as naval power depended on wooden ships, America stood in an enviable position. The United States possessed a virtual monopoly of the serviceable live oak timber supply. The problem of the government was to preserve that position, by reservation and reforestation if necessary. Jenks Cameron, who studied Adams's forest policy, believes "that Mr. Adams was consciously and deliberately looking a long way ahead when he was engaged in the Florida negotiations"[58] as Monroe's secretary of state. During Adams's presidential administration, a naval yard was built at Pensacola, in the heart of the Florida live oak stands. Reconnaissances were conducted at the request of the president to learn if other live oak existed in South Carolina, Georgia, and Florida. Adams was informed that the live oak stocks were being depleted and that live oak was even "a staple export." As a result of this report, there was passed on March 3, 1827 one of the most significant forest conservation measures of our early history.[59] Under it, Congress appropriated $500,000 per annum for a period of six years for the purpose of gradually improving the navy. But although primarily a naval measure, the president was given power to take proper means to preserve live oak growing on timberlands and to reserve from sale such additional lands containing live oak as he found valuable for naval purposes. This act paved the way for a renewal of its terms; in 1833 another appropriation of the same amount was made available for another six-year period, enabling the government to expand its live oak reservation.

An important aspect of the act of 1827, however, was that it fired "the opening legislative gun for the first national attempt at reforestation made in America."[60] It set aside $10,000 to be used for the purchase of a tract for the artificial cultivation of live oak trees. At the suggestion of Colonel Joseph While, Adams in 1828 established the government's first reforestation project at Santa Rosa, immediately adjacent to the Pensacola Navy Yard.[61] One could attach little significance to the establishment of the live oak plantation were it not for the larger conceptions of forest policy that it reflected. The purchase of a 30,000-acre tract was to be the first step of a larger project that planned artificially to reforest some 60,000 live oak acres. Similar live oak plantations might follow if this proved successful. The evidence is incomplete, and it cannot be certain exactly what Adams had in mind when he engaged in this forest program with such interest. Adams personally was "a confirmed tree enthusiast" and maintained an amateur tree nursery at his country home at Quincy, Massachusetts. According to Cameron, the initial Florida experiments were to lead the way to a policy of "governmental forest management towards a conservational end: in word, forestry."[62] Cameron makes these deductions from what he believes to have been Adams's larger purpose:

It was perhaps . . . inevitable . . . that Mr. Adams should have reacted to the naval timber question with a magnificent, but— for the day—utterly impractical conception: that he should have envisioned himself as the inaugurator of a wise and orderly system that would enable America gradually to cut loose altogether from a dependence for naval timber upon natural growth, with its unavoidable Broad Arrow implications, its timber thieves, and its gouging contractors "willing to profit by the occasion"; and gradually to adopt a system of supply from tree plantations established for the purpose, and so conducted that their regular yearly increment would provide a safe margin in cubic content over the amounts ascertained to be necessary for new construction and new repairs. In a word, Mr. Adams was thinking along what are referred to as sustained yield lines. It was indeed, a magnificent conception, but it was many, many years ahead of its time. It was too orderly, too disciplined a conception for a people with the pine-tree flag only half a century behind them and with "inexhaustible" forests all about them.[63]

It is especially unfortunate that Adams left no comprehensive statement of his ideas on the subject of public administration because he, among American statesmen, was administratively minded to a singular degree. A study of his *Memoirs* and collected writings shows that he gave careful thought and attention to the administration and management of public policies.

There is no doubt that he was many decades ahead of his contemporaries in discerning the need of a disinterested, trained civil service. He would have established in the public service the same standard of integrity and public devotion he set for himself. He was bitterly opposed to the policy of recklessly giving away the public lands. He believed that the government should manage its land resources carefully and conservatively, as trustees of generations of Americans yet unborn. The land would gradually increase in value, and there would accrue to the government a heritage of wealth with which to endow all kinds of public benefactions: improved means of transportation, schools, colleges, and scientific institutions.

But Adams knew before long that he was defeated. He hoped that others might carry on the fight and that eventually it might be won. In a passage in his diary, he explained to his cabinet why he recommended projects to Congress even though he knew they had no chance of immediate acceptance: "I concurred entirely in the opinion that no projects absolutely impracticable ought to be recommended. But I would look to a practicability of a longer range than a simple session of Congress."[64]

And so John Quincy Adams urged Congress to consolidate various governmental functions of domestic management under a new executive department to be called the Home Department. Some of the existing executive departments, viz., State and War, were becoming too burdened with activities unrelated to their major purpose.[65] In the long run, the management of these domestic affairs must suffer from neglect. He proposed that the Home Department have charge of "the internal correspondence, the roads and canals, the Indians and Patents Office."[66] This would have been perhaps an effective beginning in devising an administrative structure consonant with the president's plans for an active and watchful management. To this plan, as to his others, Congress turned a deaf ear and chose instead the more easy solution of quick returns and a rapid, unfettered exploitation of the nation's resources.

Notes

Chapter I: Introduction

1. Gilbert Chinard, *Thomas Jefferson, The Apostle of Americanism* (Boston: Little, Brown, 1929), p. 75. That the words *pursuit of happiness* do not appear in the Constitution needs an explanation. They were not an accidental aberration of Thomas Jefferson's pen, however. The word *happiness* appeared in Virginia's bill of rights, although not in the same form. It appeared also in the famous Northwest Ordinace of 1787 as "Religion, morality and knowledge, being necessary to good government and happiness of mankind, schools and means of education shall forever be encouraged." S. E. Morison, H. S. Commager, and W. E. Leuchtenburg, *The Growth of the American Republic*, 2 vols. (New York: Oxford University Press, 1969), 1: 233. According to Catherine Drinker Bowen, when putting the Constitution in final form, the Committee on Style and Arrangement did consider "freedom and happiness" as part of the preamble, but its principal author, Gouverneur Morris, had a better inspiration with, "We, the People." *Miracle at Philadelphia* (Boston: Little, Brown, 1966), pp. 239–40. Also, when the convention finished its work and transmitted the Constitution to the Congress in 1787, its closing appeal contained the hope "that [the Constitution] may promote the lasting welfare of the country so dear to us all, and secure here freedom and happiness is our most ardent wish" (p. 228).

2. *America Was Promises* (New York: Duel Sloan, 1940), p. 1.

3. "From the beginning the Land of Democracy has been figured as the Land of Promise. Thus the American's loyalty to the national tradition . . . affirms . . . the imaginative projection of a better future. An America which is not the Land of Promise . . . would not be the America bequeathed to us by our forefathers. In cherishing the Promise of a better national future, the America is fulfilling . . . the substance of the national tradition." *The Promise of American Life* (New York: Macmillan, 1909), p. 6.

4. "Moved by the pressure of religious disabilities at home and by the fear of greater sufferings which were believed to be in store, the Puritans removed spontaneously and in large numbers to the New World. They did this under a common impulse, and as the result of agreements and widespread understandings. . . . The fact that a prospect was opened for escape from episcopal domination, for the establishment of their favorite ecclesiastical policy under the protection of a government of their own, was tacitly accepted as a sufficient guarantee of the rest. It was instinctively believed that comfort and prosperity would follow

in the wake of this much desired liberty." H. L. Osgood, *The American Colonies in the Seventeenth Century*, 3 vols. (New York: Macmillan, 1904), 1: 427.

5. The full quotation has a contemporary ring to it: "the dons, the bashaws, the grandees, the patricians, the sachems, the nabobs, call them by what name you please, sigh and groan and fret, and sometimes stamp, and foam, and curse, but all in vain. The decree is gone forth, and cannot be recalled, that a more equal liberty than has prevailed in other parts of the earth, must be established in America. That exuberance of pride which has produced an insolent domination in a few, insolent and monopolizing families, will be brought down nearer to the confines of reason and moderation than they have been used to. *Works*, ed. C. F. Adams, 10 vols. (Boston: Little, Brown, 1856), 9: 386–88.

6. *The Cycles of American History* (Boston: Houghton Mifflin, 1986), pp. 219–20. Subsequently, in a letter to me after I had acquainted him with my study from a summary paper, Dr. Schlesinger paid me the compliment of telling me that my work had preceded others, which made me "a true pioneer in the reconstruction of the early economy policy of the republic," to which he offered his "belated congratulations on your path-breaking work of nearly a half a century ago."

Chapter II: The Federal Convention Assembles

1. *The Critical Period of American History.*

2. The following is a partial list of the literature consulted for this chapter, most of which date from the time of writing: Beard, *Rise of the American Civilization;* Beard, *Economic Interpretation of the Constitution;* Beard, *Economic Origins of Jeffersonian Democracy;* Nevins, *American States During and After the Revolution;* Merriam, *The Written Constitution and the Unwritten Attitude;* Merriam, *History of American Political Theories;* Smith, *The Spirit of American Government;* McLaughlin, *The Confederation and the Constitution;* Read, *The Constitution Reconsidered;* Bowen, *Miracle at Philadelphia;* Hendrick, *Bulwark of the Republic;* Jensen, *The Articles of Confederation;* Farrand, *The Records of the Federal Convention of 1787* (hereafter cited as *Records*); Earle, *The Federalist;* Small, *The Beginnings of American Nationality;* Morison, Commager, and Leuchtenburg, *Growth of the American Republic.*

3. *The Washington Post*, September 11, 1987.

4. "When Washington Tried Isolation," p. 348.

5. *Confederation and Constitution*, pp. 154–68.

6. *Records*, 1: 413.

7. Ibid., 3: 32–33.

8. Ibid., 3: 46.

9. *Writings*, P. L. Ford, ed., 1: 254–56.

10. *Writings*, H. A. Washington, ed., 2: 429.

11. *The Federalist*, No. 9, p. 48.

12. Ibid., No. 14, p. 85.

13. *Works*. See Dunning, *History of Political Theories*; chap. 5. Allan Nevins recounts that as late as 1881–82, Herbert Spencer visited the United States, and declared similar views. He thought our Constitution was not working well, "declaring that this proved the truth of his conviction that no Constitution could be an artificial creation, like ours and succeed." *The American States*, p. 118.

14. "English Opinion of the American Constitution and Government," pp. 57, 66, 67, 73, 85.

15. *Liberalism and American Education*, pp. 12–13.

16. *The Federalist*, No. 14, p. 84.

17. *Liberalism and American Education*, p. 234.

18. The pamphlets of Noah Webster and Benjamin Rush are quoted in full in Goode, *National Scientific and Educational Institutions*, pp. 82–85.

19. *The Written Constitution and the Unwritten Attitude*, p. 3.

Chapter III: Mercantile Influences

1. See Walton H. Hamilton, "Constitutionalism," *Encyclopedia of the Social Sciences*. When this was written in 1941–42, it would probably have been regarded as a mild form of heresy. Its truth is now recognized by eminent historians, for example Arthur M. Schlesinger, Jr.: "The Founding Fathers, in short, had no doctrinal commitment to the unregulated marketplace. They were not proponents of laissez-faire. Their legacy was rather that blend of public and private initiative known in our day as the mixed economy." Schlesinger quotes E. A. J. Johnson, a most careful student of economic policy in the early republic: "it is difficult to find any thoroughgoing eighteenth-century proponents of *laissez-faire*, and even harder to find much explicit evidence of legislative acceptance of a theory of economic freedom." *Cycles of American History*, pp. 222–23, 220.

2. *Records*, 2: 10.

3. The literature on mercantilism is voluminous. Some of the important works consulted are: E. F. Heckscher, *Mercantilism*, 2 vols. (London: Allen & Unwin, 1935); J. W. Horrocks, *A Short History of Mercantilism* (London: Methuen, 1925); G. B. Hertz, *The Old Colonial System* (Manchester, England; 1905); C. L. Beer, *The Commercial Policy of England Toward the American Colonies* (New York: P. Smith, 1893); C. L. Beer, *British Colonial Policy* (New York: Macmillan, 1907); C. L. Beer, *The Old Colonial System*, 2 vols. (New York: Macmillan, 1912); O. M. Dickerson, *American Colonial Government,*

1696–1765 (Cleveland, 1912); A. H. Basye, *The Lord Commissioner of Trade and Plantations, 1748–1782* (New Haven, 1925); R. P. Bieber, *The Lords of Trade and Plantations, 1675–1696* (Allentown, Pa.: H. R. Haas, 1919); E. C. Kirkland, *A History of American Economic Life* (New York: F. S. Crofts, 1939); E. L. Bogart, *The Economic History of the American People* (New York: Longmans, 1930); J. T. Adams, *Provincial Society: 1690–1763* (New York: Macmillan, 1927); Osgood, *The American Colonies in the Seventeenth Century*; C. M. Andrews, "England's Commercial Policy," *The Colonial Period of American History*, vol. 4 (New Haven: Yale University Press, 1934–1939); V. S. Clark, *History of Manufactures in the United States*, 2 vols. (New York: McGraw-Hill, 1929), vol. 1; E. R. Johnson et al., *History of Domestic and Foreign Commerce in the United States*, 2 vols. (Washington: Carnegie Institution, 1915), vol. 2; A. A. Biesecke, *American Commercial Legislation Before 1789* (New York, 1910); Findlay MacKenzie, ed., *Planned Society* (New York, 1937); McLaughlin, *Confederation and Constitution Reconsidered*: Walton H. Hamilton and Douglas Adair, *The Power to Govern* (New York: Norton, 1937).

    4. *The Power to Govern*, pp. 70–71. The comments of two other scholars on mercantilist practice are worth noting. J. U. Nef affirms the presence of mercantilist considerations in the framing of the Constitution, but he regards the political considerations leading to the formation of the Union, rather than the economic, as the more compelling. Max Lerner, on the other hand, points to the "curious contradictions" involved in the framing of the Constitution: "The mercantilist economic policy" of the convention members "with all the close and comprehensive controls . . . over economic life" and with its "resulting concentration of authority" came into conflict with their "atomistic" political thought that emphasized "governmental dangers. . . . Their conservative economic interests dictated a strong central mercantilist government, the prevailing political ideas of the time, fortifying their fear of democracy, made them place that government of expanded powers in an intellectual framework of limited powers." Read, *The Constitution Reconsidered* .

    5. *The Power to Govern*, pp. 180–81.

    6. *The Federalist*, No. 14, p. 82.

    7. *Records*, 2: 142–44. The consideration of this power was committed to the Committee of Eleven. It was stricken by that committee, and finally defeated by the Southern agrarian interest in a vote of seven to four. Ibid., 2: 375, 400, 448–53. The issue was decided wholly on the basis of sectional advantage. The Southern agrarian states were unwilling to grant the Eastern commercial interests the important advantage of having a navigation act to promote the shipping interests. The result does not imply therefore any decision concerning the abstract question of the wisdom of navigation acts, or the right of the state to interfere in the commerce and shipping of the nation. The real issue was the sectional conflict

between the Eastern trading and shipping interests and the Southern planters concerned over the retention of slavery. This was resolved by Article I, Section IX, by which importation of slaves was not prohibited until 1808.

8. Ibid., 2: 324–26. I have combined here the proposals of both Madison and Pinckney where they are duplicative. Farrand believes that others—Gerry, Rutledge, and Mason—collaborated with Pinckney in the preparation of his list. This is remarkable in view of their states' rights predilections, and confirms Bancroft's observation that after the small states were assured of equal votes in the Senate, they exceeded all others in giving powers to the national government. Cited in Brown, *The Commercial Powers of Congress*, pp. 113–14. Brown writes that in his opinion, if the small states had been allowed to control Congress, its delegated powers would have been even greater (p. 108).

9. *Records*, 3: 520–21; see also 3: 477.

10. Ibid., 1: 615.

11. Ibid. This reference to "the free intercourse now to be opened" without doubt refers to the enlarged possibilities of trade brought about by the introduction of the steamboat. Although the steamboat was not yet developed to the level of being practicable commercially, the convention was acquainted with it and already suspected its future trade potentialities. See Brown, *Commercial Powers of Congress*, pp. 62–63.

12. Mason of Virginia promptly objected to the proposition, saying that "he was afraid of monopolies of every sort." *Records*, 1: 615.

13. *The Federalist*, No. 14, p. 83. It is ironic that it was James Madison who as president in 1817 vetoed the internal improvements bill for extension of the national road, thereby setting a precedent for beginning the decline in federal internal improvements.

14. In a letter written in 1831, long after Madison had adopted a strict constructionist position, he was able to write "that in the case of canals, particularly, the power would have been properly vested in Congress. It was more than once proposed in the Convention of 1787, and rejected from an apprehension, chiefly that it might prove an obstacle to the adoption of the Constitution. Such an addition to the Federal powers was thought to be strongly recommended by several considerations." Madison then proceeds to list four reasons Congress should have had this power. 1. "Congress would possess, exclusively, the sources of revenue most productive and least unpopular, that body ought to provide and apply the means for the greatest and most costly works." 2. "There would be cases where canals would be highly important in a national view, and not so in a local view." 3. Cases where a state would interpose its objections to a canal "highly important in a State through which they would pass." 4. Cases where a chain of canals would pass through a number of states, thus forming an outlet for their foreign commerce and "at the same time a ligament for the Union, yet be hopeless

of attainment if left to the limited faculties and joint exertions of the States possessing the authority." *Records*, 3: 494–95.

15. For example, that multiple purposes may be served by a single grant of power was fully understood by Madison, as is revealed in his argument that Congress should have the power to tax exports. "As we ought to be governed by national and permanent views, it is sufficient argument for giving ye power over exports that a tax, tho' it may not be expedient at present, may be so hereafter. A proper regulation of the same purposes may and probably will be necessary hereafter, and for the same purposes as the regulation of imports; viz. for revenue—domestic manufactures—and procuring equitable regulations from other nations. An embargo may be of absolute necessity, and can alone be effectuated by the Genl. Authority." Ibid., 2: 361. See also 2: 305–08, 357–63.

16. *The Power to Govern*, p. 120.

17. Brown, *Commercial Powers of Congress*, pp. 18ff, 120, 133–35.

18. See Chief Justice Marshall in Gibbons v. Ogden, 9 Wheaton 1, 6 L. ed. 23 (1824); E. S. Corwin, *The Commerce Power Versus States Rights* (Princeton: Princeton University Press, 1936).

19. *Politics and the Constitution*, 2 vols. (Chicago: University of Chicago Press, 1953), 1: 47, 83, 229.

20. Ibid., 2: 144, 166, 188, 344–45.

21. Quoted in ibid., 2: 182–83.

22. The idea of an amendment clause originated in Randolph's introductory resolutions. Ibid., 1: 22. The detailed form of the amendment was that of the Committee on Detail (2: 84, 133, 148, 159, 174, 188, 467, 557–59). Harry D. Gideonse has said, "the chief distinction between constitutional and other forms of government is the *explicit* provision for legal methods of change and the amending clause is therefore the very heart of the Constitution." "An Economist Looks at the Constitution," *University of Chicago Magazine*, 28 (March 1936): 3.

Chapter IV: The Executive Office

1. See W. E. Binkley, *The Powers of the President* (Garden City: Doubleday, 1937); N. J. Small, *Some Presidential Interpretations of the Presidency* (Baltimore: Johns Hopkins University Press, 1932); E. S. Corwin, *The Presidency* (New York: New York University Press, 1940); Herbert Agar, *The People's Choice* (Boston: Houghton Mifflin, 1933); Arthur M. Schlesinger, Jr., *The Imperial Presidency* (Boston: Houghton Mifflin, 1973), also *Cycles of American History,* chap. 11.

2. Morison, Commager, and Leuchtenburg, *Growth of the American Republic*, 1: 255.

3. It is interesting to observe how closely our conception of the presidency follows the character and leadership of whoever currently occupies the office. See Binkley, *The Powers of the President*. During the New Deal, when Roosevelt's leadership overwhelmed the other branches, Harold J. Laski reacted by accepting the interpretation that "fear of executive despotism" was the dominant consideration of the Constitutional Convention in the construction of the presidency. *The American Presidency: An Interpretation* (New York: Harper, 1940), p. 12. More recently, Arthur M. Schlesinger, Jr. described the presidency under Richard Nixon as "The Imperial Presidency." Then after Nixon's downfall, followed by the weak leadership of presidents Ford and Carter, the office was considered fragile or unworkable. Schlesinger concludes: "Whatever else may be said about Ronald Reagan, he quickly showed that the reports of the death of the Presidency were greatly exaggerated. . . . By 1986, the lamentations of 1980 seemed overwrought and irrelevant. A comparison of Reagan with his immediate predecessors was instructive." *Cycles of American History*, p. 293.

4. See Nevins, *The American States*, p. 166; F. G. Bates and O. P. Field, *State Government*, rev. ed. (New York: Harper, 1939), pp. 236–37; Leslie Lipson, *The American Governor from Figurehead to Leader* (Chicago: Univeristy of Chicago Press, 1939), pp. 12–15; Merriam, *A History of American Political Theories*, pp. 80–82. For detailed provisions, see W. C. Webster, "A Comparative Study of the State Constitutions of the American Revolution," *Annals of the American Academy of Political and Social Sciences*, 9 (1897): 395–401; W. C. Morey, The First State Constitutions," *Annals of American Academy of Political Science*, 4 (1893): 225–29; C. C. Thach, *The Creation of the Presidency, 1775–1789* (Baltimore: Johns Hopkins University Press, 1922), chap. 11.

5. *The Separation of Governmental Powers* (New York: Sabiston Murray, 1896), p. 74

6. *Writings*, Federal Edition, 3: 225, also 211. (Unless otherwise noted, all subsequent references to Jefferson are from this edition.) See also *The Federalist*, Nos. 47, 48, 50, 51; Adams, "Defense of the American Constitution" in *Works*.

7. Thach, *Creation of the Presidency*, pp. 51–52.

8. *Writings*, 1: 425.

9. *Writings*, 3: 12.

10. Cited in Thach, *Creation of the Presidency*, p. 64.

11. "Our own experience with boards, if brief, was nonetheless bitter. It is positively pathetic to follow Congress through its aimless wanderings in search of a system for the satisfactory management of its executive departments. At no period between 1774 and 1781 can we find it pursuing any consistent line of action with reference to them." J. C. Guggenheimer, "The Development of the

Executive Departments," in Jameson, *Essays in the Constituional History of the United States*, p. 148

12. Ibid., pp. 126, 137, 142, 146.

13. Thach, *Creation of the Presidency*, pp. 52–53.

14. Ibid., pp. 72–74. Robert Morris resigned as superintendent of finance in 1784, and his duties were assumed by a three-man Board of Treasury.

15. Ibid., pp. 171, 169. It is so often repeated that the Founding Fathers failed to understand the stage of development reached by the cabinet in the British constitutional system, and therefore accepted Montesquieu's misinterpretation of it, that were that problem not beyond the province of this study, it would warrant examination. Binkley writes as though the Founding Fathers were deliberately trying to create a system resembling the British, but did not understand it. *Powers of the President*, pp. 7–9. It is easy to understand why Montesquieu, in his *Spirit of the Laws* (1748), fell victim to the error, but it is less probable that the framers of the Constitution were unaware of the significance of the relationship of Pitt's ministry to Parliament. The truth is that the Fathers were not trying to copy the British Constitution, or draft one based on Montesquieu's maxims. The functional overlapping present in the federal Constitution is obvious, and it was just as obvious to the men who framed it. They were trying to construct an effective instrument, and the fact that what they did violated certain doctrinal precepts did not seem to disturb them.

16. Thach, *Creation of the Presidency*, p. 176; see also pp. 34–43, 85–88. I am greatly indebted to this excellent monograph, the author of which really understands the conception that resulted in the creation of the presidency.

17. In the process of drafting a new constitution in Massachusetts following the rejection of the proposed one in 1778, a number of interesting recommendations were made, the following of which is taken from the so-called Essex Result, drawn by Theophilus Parsons. It is an especially interesting conception of legislative leadership by the executive, and calls to mind Hamilton's later practice. "All the business of the legislative body will be brought to one point, and subject to an impartial consideration on a regular and consistent plan. As the Governor will have it in charge to state the situation of the government to the legislative body at the opening of every session, as far as his information will qualify him therefore, he will know officially all that has been done, what design the laws were enacted, how far they have answered the proposed end, and what still remains to complete the intention of the legislative body." Quoted in ibid., pp. 359ff.

18. Quoted in ibid., pp. 35–37. It may be noted that the New York constitution provided also for a senatorial council of appointment and a council of revision. During the Philadelphia convention, James Wilson, the foremost advocate of the New York executive scheme, argued for the creation of such a council

of revision. Thach, however, states that neither of these two agencies was effective in materially reducing the governor's authority.

19. *Records*, 1: 21, 244, 23, 292; 3: 599–600, 622–25.

20. See Thach, *Creation of the Presidency*, pp. 86–88, 177.

21. Ibid., pp. 81–84. Cf. *Records*, 1: 66–67.

22. *Records*, 1: 65.

23. Ibid., 1: 65, 68. The degree to which Sherman would decentralize political power is further clarified by certain memoranda found among his papers. Among his propositions is the requirement that "the laws of the United States ought . . . to be carried into execution by the judiciary and executive officers of the respective states, wherein execution thereof is required" (3: 616). But note how even Sherman had shifted his position from June 1, the date of the above speech, to July 17, when he seconded a motion in favor of executive ineligibility for reelection toward preserving executive independence, and offered no dissent to the motions embodying Wilson's ideas (2: 33, 499).

24. Ibid., 1: 65–67.

25. In the reference to linking the executive and judiciary in the power to veto legislative acts, Wilson was relying on the New York example. See Thach, *Creation of the Presidency*, pp. 35–40, 41, 82, 126. Having failed to obtain a more powerful check on the legislature by the executive branch alone, and being dissatisfied with the executive's qualified veto, he continued to argue in favor of the absolute joint veto by a council of revision, although earlier he was opposed to such a council, "which oftener serves to cover, than to prevent malpractices." *Records*, 1: 103–04, 138–39; 2: 73–80; 1: 97.

26. Ibid., 1: 191; 2: 79, 83.

27. Ibid., 2: 132, 185. Wilson: "The separation of the departments does not require that they should have separate objects but that they should act separately though on the same objects" (2: 78).

28. Ibid., 2: 183, 392–94, 497, 498, 499, 538, 539, 540, 541.

29. Corwin, *The Presidency*, p. 12.

30. *Records*, 2: 35; see also 56, 110, 113, 612; *The Federalist*, No. 48, pp. 321–26, especially p. 323.

31. Ibid., 2: 52; also 103, 105, 404, 500. See also Dickinson on 2: 86–87.

32. Ibid., 2: 104.

33. Ibid., 1: 68, 69; 2: 29, 31, 56, 102, 106, 402; also G. Morris on 2: 53–54, Madison on 2: 56.

34. Ibid., 2: 58, 59.

35. Ibid., 1: 21, 88, 230, 244; cf. 2: 58.

36. Ibid., 2: 57.

37. Ibid.

38. Ibid., 2: 55.

39. Ibid., 2: 33.

40. Ibid.

41. Ibid.

42. Ibid., 2: 57.

43. *A Study of "Monarchical" Tendencies in the United States from 1775 to 1801* (Urbana: University of Illinois Press, 1922), pp. 76–99.

44. *Records*, 1: 86–87.

45. Ibid., 1: 83.

46. Ibid., 2: 34–35.

47. Ibid., 2: 102–03.

48. Ibid.

49. Ibid., 2: 104. See also Sherman, 2: 33–34.

50. Ibid., 2: 64–69.

51. Ibid., 2: 65.

52. Ibid., 2: 67.

53. Ibid., 1: 176; 2: 57.

54. Ibid., 2: 57. This provision was incorporated into the Constitution, Article II, and it was added thereto, that no persons "holding an office of trust or profit under the United States" may be appointed electors.

55. Ibid., 2: 101.

56. Ibid., 2: 108–09, 111. Wilson had in the meantime even proposed selection of the executive by drawing electors from the national legislature by lot.

57. Ibid., 2: 115, 121; Committee on Detail: 2: 132, 171, 185; Committee of Eleven: 2: 401, 404, 497, 511, 525.

58. H. B. Learned, *The President's Cabinet* (New Haven: Yale University Press, 1912), p. 379.

59. For an analysis of the various councils proposed, see ibid., chap. iii; Thach, *Creation of the Presidency*, pp. 118–25.

60. Thach, *Creation of the Presidency*, p. 138.

Chapter V: Credit and Finance

1. Henry Adams measures Hamilton's achievement by "the mass and variety of legislation and organization which characterized the first administration of Washington. . . . The results—legislative and administrative—were stupendous and can never be repeated. A government is organized once and for all, and until that of the United States fairly goes to pieces, no man can do more than alter or improve the work accomplished by Hamilton and his party." *The Life of Albert Gallatin* (Philadelphia: Lippincott, 1879), p. 268.

2. For example, when Hamilton was a receiver of taxes in New York, he suggested to Robert Morris that the amount of the tax be fixed by a definite

valuation of the land so as to assure a definite revenue instead of the careless methods then employed by the state legislature. Another example is Hamilton's plan for a military establishment under the confederation at the conclusion of the peace treaty of 1783: "even if the resources of the United States were at this time equal to the undertaking of construction and equipping a navy, it would be ineligible to enter upon it, till a plan, deliberately combined in all its parts, had been digested and approved for that purpose."

3. *Works,* Lodge ed., 2: 319ff; 1: 301, 305ff. See also "The Continentalist" papers, 1: 1. (Unless otherwise noted, all subsequent references to Hamilton are from this edition.)

4. For example, Hamilton's fears of the larger states were not quoted even at the height of his centralizing policies. In May 1792, he wrote to his friend, Colonel Carrington: "If the States were all the size of Connecticut, Maryland or New Jersey, I should decidedly regard the local governments as both safe and useful. As the thing now is, however, I acknowledge the most serious apprehensions, that the Government of the United States will not be able to maintain itself against their influence. I see that influence already penetrating into the National councils and preventing their direction. Hence, a disposition on my part towards a liberal construction of the powers of the national government, and to erect a fence, to guard from depredations which is, in my opinion, consistent with constitutional propriety" (9: 533–34).

5. On March 5, 1783, Hamilton wrote to Washington: The "plan in agitation in Philadelphia, that combinations have been talked of between the public creditors and the army, and that members of Congress had encouraged the idea. . . . I have myself urged in Congress the propriety of uniting the influence of the public creditors, and the army as part of them to prevail upon the States to enter into their views" (9: 326). See also 9: 310.

6. *Annals of Congress,* 1st Cong., 1st sess., 1: 893, 904. The resolution developed as a result of a memorial of public creditors of Pennsylvania presented by Fitzsimmons of that state. I would venture a bold guess that Hamilton himself was the author of the memorial. The arguments that the memorial uses to suggest his whole later debt-funding program, and many of its phrases, bear almost unmistakable earmarks of being written by Hamilton.

7. Henry Cabot Lodge, an ardent supporter of Hamilton's views, says of the report: "There is probably no single State paper in the history of the United States, with the exception of the Emancipation Proclamation, which was of such immense importance. . . . In [Hamilton's] first report, he embodied the financial policy which organized and brought out our resources, rendered us strong and prosperous at home, established our credit, and made us respected in every money market in Europe. . . . It was the cornerstone of the Government of the United States, and the foundation of the National Movement" (2: 289).

8. The dates of his main reports are as follows: Report on the Public

Credit, January 9, 1790; Report on a National Bank, December 5, 1790; Report on the Establishment of a Mint, May 1, 1791; Report on Manufactures, December 5, 1791.

9. In his Report on the Public Credit of January 16, 1795, Hamilton elaborates: "But credit is not only One of the main pillars of public safety; it is among the principal engines of useful enterprise and internal improvement. As a substitute for capital, it is a little less useful than gold or silver, in agriculture, in commerce, in the manufacturing and mechanic arts" (3: 296).

10. *Fiscal Policy and Business Cycles* (New York: Norton, 1941), p. 162.

11. See also T. R. Dewey, *Financial History of the United States* (New York: Longmans Green, 1934), pp. 89–94.

12. Hansen, *Fiscal Policy and Business Cycles*, p. 166.

13. In his Report on Manufactures, Hamilton wrote: "Neither will it follow that an accumulation of debt is desirable, because a certain degree of it operates as capital. There may be a plethora in the political as in the natural body; there may be a state of things in which any such artificial capital is unnecessary. The debt, too, may be swelled to such a size as that the greatest part of it may cease to be useful as capital, serving only to pamper the dissipation of idle and dissolute individuals; and that the sums required to pay interest upon it may become oppressive" (4: 125).

14. *The Economic Origins of Jeffersonian Democracy* (New York: Macmillan, 1915), p. 116.

15. Jefferson later tried to absolve his feeling of guilt at having been the willing tool and accomplice of Hamilton in winning legislative support for the assumption of the state debts. Jefferson claimed that he had been ignorant of the significance of the assumption, being unfamiliar with matters of high finance. This may well be doubted. What Jefferson could not have known, however, was that the funding scheme was but the beginning of a comprehensive financial program with which he could never sympathize. See *Writings*, 1: 162, 163; 5: 184, 185, 6: 17s.

16. The United States had already had occasion to borrow $1.25 million from the Bank of North America in Philadelphia. C. L. Prather, *Money and Banking* (Chicago: Business Publications, 1937), pp. 185–200.

17. For example, John Adams, who was to become the beneficiary of Hamilton's banking system, described his views: "My opinion is that . . . a circulating medium of gold and silver only ought to be introduced and established; that a national bank of deposit only, with a branch in each State, should be allowed, that every bank in the Union ought to be annihilated, and every bank of discount prohibited to all eternity. Not one farthing of profit should ever be allowed on any money deposited in the bank." *Works*, 9: 638–39. Jefferson, who was also to inherit Hamilton's creation, had the following to say: "And I sincerely

believe with you, that banking establishments are more dangerous than standing enemies; and that the principle of spending money to be paid by posterity under the name of funding, is but swindling futility on a large scale" (11: 533). See also 11: 495, 301, 304–05; 5: 353, 276, 459. One may recognize with Jefferson the possibility of a centralized money power corrupting a democratic government or exercising undue pressure on it. But the solution was surely not the destruction of banks as such, or even Jefferson's attempt to "make all banks Republican, by sharing [government] deposits among them in proportion to the dispositions they show" (10: 15–16).

18. Although this chapter does not consider the later history of the national bank, its actual operations, or its revival in the second National Bank of the United States, it is worth noting that Hamilton's worthy successor, Albert Gallatin, who did not agree with Hamilton's social views, likewise favored the retention of the national bank. See Chien Tsent Mai, *"The Fiscal Policies of Albert Gallatin,"* (Ph.D. diss., Columbia University, 1930), chap. v.; *The Writings of Albert Gallatin*, Henry Adams, ed., 3 vols. (Philadelphia: Lippincott, 1879), vol. 3; R. C. H. Catterall, *The Second Bank of the United States* (Chicago: University of Chicago Press, 1903). The disorganization of the national finances during and after the War of 1812 could probably have been prevented had the charter of the First National Bank been renewed in time, as Gallatin recommended. This might also have made possible the undertaking the proposed internal improvements in time to have launched them successfully before the states' rights movement made such progress.

19. Compare this view with a statement of Jefferson. In decrying the exorbitant rate of interest charged on the national war loans, he said, "in such a nation there is one and only one resource for loans, sufficient to carry them through the expense of a war. . . . The fund I mean is the mass of circulating coin. Everyone knows that although not literally, it is nearly true, that every paper dollar emitted banishes a silver one from circulation" (11: 301).

20. Only three banks were in existence in the United States when Hamilton wrote his banking report. None of these, not even the largest, the Bank of North America with $2 million capital, did he regard as qualified to become a national bank. Its charter, besides being too brief, left it subject to state control and with too small a capital. Its organization was defective in that its directing board was self-perpetuating, and it was too much like a bank run merely for private profit.

21. The governing board was to consist of twenty-five directors (of whom not more than three-fourths were to be eligible for reelection for the succeeding year) to be elected by a voting procedure that reduced the proportionate number of votes of the larger stockholder in order to enhance, relatively, the voice of the smaller stockholder. In order to protect the bank against foreign control, only United States citizens could be elected as directors.

22. The plan provided that three-fourths of the bank stock to be subscribed would be paid in 6 percent recently funded government securities, one-fourth in gold and silver. Thus the bank stock offered a favorable market for Hamilton's newly funded bonds.

23. Hamilton's national bank proposal became law on February 25, 1791. In all important particulars, and even in almost all details, it conformed completely with the proposition outlined in his report. See I *U. S. Statutes at Large*, 191, chap. x.

24. *A History of Currency in the United States* (New York: Hamilton, 1924), p. 41.

25. "But as our object is to get rid of these currencies, the advantage derived from this coincidence will soon be past, whereas the inconvenience of this unit will remain forever." In a later report, Jefferson hoped to persuade Congress to adopt the decimal system for weights and measures, too. "Plan for Establishing Uniformity in the Coinage, Weights and Measures of the United States." *American State Papers, Miscellaneous*, 1: 13–19.

26. *History of Currency in the United States*, p. 38.

27. C. F. Dunbar, "Some Precedents Followed by Hamilton," *Quarterly Journal of Economics* 3 (1888–89): 35.

28. Ibid., p. 38.

29. Ibid., p. 39.

Chapter VI: Industrial Development

1. William Hill, "The First Stages of the Tariff Policy of the United States," *Publications of the American Economic Association*, 8, 6 (1893).

2. *Works*, Jared Sparks, ed. 12 vols. (Boston: Little Brown, 1855), 9: 464. (Unless specified otherwise, all references to Washington are from this volume.)

3. See also Hill, "First Stages of the Tariff Policy."

4. *Works*, J. C. Hamilton, ed. (New York, 1851), 2: 11,12.

5. *Growth of the American Republic*, 1: 219. Also Beard, *Economic Origins of Jeffersonian Democracy*, pp. 129–30.

6. *Economic Origins of Jeffersonian Democracy*, pp. 159–60.

7. W. G. Sumner, *Life of Alexander Hamilton* (New York: University Society, 1891), p. 175; Hamilton and Adair, *The Power to Govern*, pp. 240–41.

8. See H. A. Cole, *Industrial and Commercial Correspondence of Alexander Hamilton* (Chicago: A. W. Shaw, 1929).

9. F. S. Oliver, an English biographer of Hamilton, emphasizes this aspect of Hamilton's conception of national policy. Oliver says that Hamilton was "fortunate in having left behind him enough work—done, half-done, and at-

tempted—to make us certain of the vision which possessed his mind. . . . He held no brief for manufactures, merchanting, or agriculture. His aim was a balance, and his idea of the duty of the state was to regulate a just and proportionate development all along the line. He was no advocate of protection for the benefit of any trade or interest unless the advantage of the community as a whole appeared to him to be involved in such a course. If it be true that the tendency of modern American legislation has been to consider the prosperity of certain classes as an end in itself, and to ignore the equal and concurrent development of other branches of industry, his name cannot be invoked." *Alexander Hamilton: An Essay on American Union* (New York: Putnam, 1906), pp. 466–67; also pp. 144–45.

10. Cole, *Industrial and Commercial Correspondence of Alexander Hamilton,* p. 231.

11. It is barely possible that Hamilton may have prepared some memoranda on the subject that have not been included in his collected writings. At the time that his writings were being edited for publication, the interest of editors centered primarily on political policy and not on its execution. See L. K. Caldwell, *Ideas on Public Administration of Hamilton and Jefferson* (Chicago: University of Chicago Press, 1944).

12. Historians have commonly viewed Hamilton as the advocate of the protective tariff. Bounties for the encouragement of production were afterward forgotten in the same manner as the patent right replaced the suggestion of premiums for useful inventions and discoveries. In Hamilton's period, however, bounties were commonly employed as one of the devices of a mercantilistic economy. Hamilton said of the bounty, "This has been found one of the most efficacious means of encouraging manufactures and is, in some views the best" (4: 146).

13. Two students of Hamilton's economic policies have likewise emphasized that his conclusions were inferences based on specific facts described in his report. E. C. Lunt says: "Hamilton's conclusions, drawn from data representing historical and industrial facts, are strictly contingent on the reality of those facts; and the validity of his reasoning, in general, is rightly conditioned by the continued truth of those premises from which such reasoning proceeds." Worth noting is that Hamilton gave the device of tariff duties "a comparatively unimportant place in his scheme, and lays most stress on the granting of bounties." "Hamilton as a Political Economist," *Journal of Political Economy,* 3(1894–95): 300–02. J. T. Morse, author of a popular biography of Hamilton, states likewise that it is "impossible to predicate from anything contained in this report [Report on Manufactures] what would be the writer's opinion as to the proper policy in the present circumstances of the country." *Alexander Hamilton* (Boston: Little, Brown, 1876), p. 101.

14. I have relied heavily on J. S. Davis's *Essays in the Earlier History of American Corporations*, 2 vols. (Cambridge: Harvard University Press, 1917), 1: 349–520.

15. Davis states, "There was a connection, in origin at least, between the Report on Manufactures and the New Jersey scheme. It was not highly unreasonable to interpret as referring particularly to such institutions as the S.U.M. such a suggestion in the Report as that the bounties and the premiums should be granted only to those undertakings which made a regular business of the manufacture. The promoters had not despaired of aid from the federal government, and there was nothing but public opinion to stand in the way." Ibid., 1: 450.

16. Ibid., 1: 435.

17. In Davis's opinion, the insinuations against Hamilton and the society were unwarranted. Because of the general unfamiliarity with corporate enterprise, the S.U.M.'s privileges granted in its charter were "exclusive" only in the sense that they were not enjoyed by everyone. As events later proved, the opposition greatly underestimated the obstacles that such an establishment had to encounter. Its charter's special features were deliberately contrived to buttress the corporation so that it could sustain itself against the many trials and crises that it would have to meet. Ibid., 1: 450.

18. Ibid., 1: 525.

19. Hamilton's plan offered exceedingly attractive terms to people who had large amounts of money to invest in Western lands and who would in turn sell these lands in small parcels to the farmer on long-term payments. The plan was, quite frankly, a revenue scheme, as Hamilton believed the condition of the treasury justified measures that made fiscal considerations paramount and the needs of the farmer secondary. For a more tolerant view of Hamilton's policy, see Roy L. Robbins, *Our Landed Heritage* (Princeton: Princeton University Press, 1942). Robbins does not interpret Hamilton's land policy as a short-range expedient of treasury replenishment. He believes it was dictated by a long-range program of land colonization in which the investor class would be given a stake in helping to obtain an early settlement of the land. This view apparently gives some regard to Hamilton's plan to induce European emigration on a large scale.

Chapter VII: Public Land Policies

1. It is observed that the policy of free land had adequate precedents during the Colonial period. As stated by A. C. Ford, historian of colonial land practices, "No principle in the land history of our entire country is older and of more general application than that of giving away public land." *Colonial Land Precedents of the National Land System* (Madison: University of Wisconsin Press, 1910), pp. 95, 102–03, 113, 140.

2. The urgencies of the exchequer, both Virginia's and Congress's later, forced Jefferson to sanction the policy of land sales. See T. P. Abernethy, *Western Lands and the American Revolution* (New York: Appleton, 1937), pp. 224–28. See also Jefferson, *Writings,* 4: 391–92, 451, 454, 457, 472.

3. *Writings,* Washington, ed., 13: 399–400.

4. See T. P. Abernethy, *From Frontier to Plantation in Tennessee* (Chapel Hill: University of North Carolina Press, 1932); Jensen, *The Articles of Confederation;* Shaw Livermore, *Early American Land Companies* (New York: Commonwealth Fund, 1939); A. M. Sakolski, *The Great American Land Bubble* (New York: Harper, 1932).

5. "No group of people in America was more deeply affected by the Declaration of Independence than were the land speculators. All their plans were changed by that event. . . . Speculation in land was the absorbing American enterprise during the later colonial Revolutionary and the early Republican Period." Abernethy, *Western Lands and the American Revolution,* pp. 162, 45.

6. "Ohio and Indiana and Kentucky were perhaps as capable physically of organization into great estates as Virginia and Carolina, but by the time the swarms of settlers debouched upon those great Western plains, the habit of the small farm in the main was already fixed and the United States was to be a land of peasant proprietors." Jameson, *Essays in the Constitutional History of the United States,* p. 67.

7. See Sakolski, *Great American Land Bubble,* pp. 55–80.

8. F. E. Thorpe, *The Federal and State Constitutions, Colonial Charters and Other Organic Laws,* 7 vols. (Washington, D. C.: GPO, 1909) 7: 3818–19. "It is worthy to note that this was the first sweeping assertion by Virginia of her right to jurisdiction over all the land remaining within her boundaries fixed by the Charter of 1609. Until Jefferson propounded a contrary theory in 1774, it was admitted that the King might change the boundaries when he chose." Abernethy, *Western Lands and the American Revolution,* p. 148.

9. According to Abernethy, "The struggle, then, was not between the large states and the small ones but between those having Western Claims and those possessing none. It was rather a contest between certain states claiming Western Lands for themselves on one hand, and those claiming it in the interest of certain land companies on the other, the middle group of States being controlled largely by members of the Great Land Companies." Ibid., p. 172. He notes also that "proponents of the Maryland cause" uttered "not a word to the prejudice of the land companies' claims." Jensen adds: "The landed states may be pardoned their refusal to sacrifice their interest to the 'good of the whole' when it is recognized that they saw nothing in such phrases but the program of the land speculators of the landless States, or at best, the jealousy of the other States." *The Articles of Confederation,* p. 153.

10. Jensen, *The Articles of Confederation,* pp. 151, 154.

11. Act of October 10, 1780, *General Public Acts of Congress Respecting the Sale of Disposition of the Public Lands* (Washington, D.C.: Gales and Seaton, 1838), I, 7–8. (Hereafter referred to as *Public Land Laws*.) Also act of 1784, I, 8–9.

12. P. J. Treat, *The National Land System, 1785–1820* (New York: E. B. Treat, 1910), p. 75.

13. One may well doubt whether Jefferson's ideas on a government-controlled settlement of the Western lands would have been possible in the later nineteenth century, but there is no doubting that he intended the government to continue to have a positive role.

14. Tracing in detail the development of our early land policies, Ford shows conclusively "the continuity that exists between colonial land system and that system, framed by the national legislators from 1775. . . . [S]eemingly new legislation was founded on the best colonial precedents." *Colonial Land Precedents,* p. 59.

15. Ibid., p. 55.

16. Ibid.

17. Ibid., p. 82.

18. *Public Land Laws*, I, act of 1785.

19. Treat, *The National Land System*, pp. 43–44.

20. *Public Land Laws*, I, act of May 18, 1796.

21. Treat, *The National Land System*, pp. 90–91.

22. Abernethy, *Western Lands and the American Revolution*, p. 223.

23. *Public Land Laws*, I, 8–9, act of April 23, 1784.

24. Ibid., 8, act of July 13, 1787.

25. On this subject, see Jensen, *Articles of Confederation*.

26. Nevins, *The American States During and After the Revolution*, pp. 446ff. "Probably in no other period would our south have agreed to the constitutional compromise that required Federal prohibition of our trade in 1808." L. C. Gray, *History of Agriculture in the Southern United States to 1860*, 12 vols. (Washington: Carnegie Institution, 1933), 2: 615–17.

27. For a detailed analysis of Jefferson's antislavery activities, see A. C. Holland, "The Anti-Slavery Activities of Thomas Jefferson" (M.A. thesis, University of Chicago, 1927).

28. F. W. Hirst, *Life and Letters of Thomas Jefferson* (New York: Macmillan, 1909).

29. *Thomas Jefferson,* pp. 394–95.

30. See also 8: 13; 11: 72, 260–61.

31. "Agriculture, manufacturers, commerce and navigation, the four pillars of our prosperity. . . . Protection from casual embarrassments, however may sometimes be seasonably interposed." Jefferson's first annual message to Con-

gress, December 8, 1801, J. D. Richardson, ed., *Messages and Papers of the Presidents, 1789–1877*, 10 vols. (Washington, D.C.: GPO, 1896–99), 1: 318–19.

32. Hirst, *Life and Letters of Thomas Jefferson*, p. 379.

33. Ibid., p. 288.

34. Mai, *Fiscal Policies of Albert Gallatin.*

35. Ibid.

36. Henry Adams, *History of the United States of America During the Administrations of Thomas Jefferson and James Madison*, 6 vols. (New York: Scribners, 1889–91), 1: 232, 238, 240.

37. Mai, *Fiscal Policies of Albert Gallatin;* Adams, *Life of Albert Gallatin*, p. 310; Adams, *Administrations of Jefferson and Madison*, 3: 19, 238–40.

Chapter VIII: Internal Improvements

1. Richardson, *Messages and Papers of the Presidents*, 1: 367.

2. The regular annual appropriation for payment of the principal and interest on the public debt was increased from $7.3 million to $8 million on the purchase of Louisiana. Ibid., 1: 367ff.

3. Richardson, *Messages and Papers of the Presidents*, 1: 397. See also the annual message of October 27, 1807, 1: 417; annual message of November 8, 1808, 1: 444.

4. Ibid., 1: 367.

5. See Adams, *Life of Gallatin*, pp. 85, 90, 350; R. J. Honeywell, *Educational Work of Thomas Jefferson* (Cambridge: Harvard University Press, 1931).

6. In this respect, Jefferson's secretary of the treasury, Gallatin, was of a different opinion. He believed the federal authority ample to make such changes. For example, Gallatin believed that an amendment to acquire the Louisiana Territory was unnecessary, in contrast to Jefferson's opinion that it could not be acquired without amending the Constitution. Adams, *Life of Gallatin*, p. 320.

7. Jefferson tried to observe a strong separation of powers and he preferred, so far as possible, to leave the initiative of determining legislative programs to the legislative body. See Ralph V. Harlow, *History of Legislative Methods to 1825* (New Haven: Yale University Press, 1917), pp. 140, 165, et passim.

8. Jefferson emphasized his conception of national leadership to his friend James Sullivan, a Republican who had recently been elected governor of Massachusetts: "The harmony it has introduced between the legislative and executive branches, between the people and both of them and between all and the General Government, are so many steps towards securing that union of action and effort in all its parts, without which no nation can be happy or safe. . . . Your opinion of

the propriety and advantage of a more intimate correspondence between the executives of the several States, and that of the Union, as a central point, is precisely that which I have ever entertained; and on coming into office, I felt the advantages which would result from that harmony" (10: 420–21). In 1785, even before the adoption of the Constitution, Jefferson acknowledged his strong nationalist sentiment, writing to Monroe that he opposed a plan of supporting separate state land offices and having the state individually sell the land. "It separates still more the interests of the States, which ought to be made joint in every possible instance, in order to cultivate the idea of our being one nation, and to multiply the instances in which the people shall look up to their Congress as their head." *Writings*, Washington, ed., 1: 247.

9. Paul Monroe, *Founding of the American Public School System*, 2 vols. (New York: Macmillan, 1940), 1: 210–11.

10. Ibid., 1: 215.

11. See Honeywell, *Educational Work of Thomas Jefferson*, p. 10, appendix.

12. Hansen, *Liberalism and American Education*, p. 253.

13. Quoted in S. K. Padover, ed., *Thomas Jefferson's Democracy* (New York: Appleton, 1939), p. 137.

14. *Writings*, Washington, ed., 2: 332.

15. Ibid., 7: 94.

16. Although Jefferson accepted charity schools as better than none at all, he believed that they were no substitute for public schools. For example, he wrote to Washington in 1786 suggesting that the probable passage of his bill for the diffusion of knowledge would make unnecessary Washington's proposed charity schools (19: 23–25); see also Honeywell, *Educational Work of Thomas Jefferson*, p. 14.

17. Jefferson attributed the defeat of his educational program in some measure to the opposition of the churches and church-controlled schools.

18. *Public Land Laws*, 245, 6, act of May 20, 1785; M. N. Orfield, *Federal Land Grants to the States, With Special Reference to Minnesota* (Minneapolis: University of Minnesota Press, 1915), pp. 36–37.

19 *Public Land Laws*, 1: 85, act of April 30, 1802.

20. *Federal Land Grants to the States*, p. 41.

21. *Public Land Laws*, 1: 142, act of April 21, 1806.

22. Orfield, *Federal Land Grants to the States*, p. 42.

23. Richardson, *Messages and Papers of the Presidents*, 1: 397–98.

24. Ibid.

25. Ibid., 1: 398.

26. Du Pont de Nemours, *National Education in the United States of America*, Bessie G. Du Pont, trans. (Newark: University of Delaware Press,

1923). Hansen is of the opinion that Du Pont reported Jefferson's views on national education during this period. *Liberalism and American Education*, pp. 178–80, 198.

27. Gallatin, *Writings*, 1: 232.

28. Joel Barlow, "Prospectus of a National Institution To Be Established in the United States," in Goode, *National Scientific and Educational Institutions*, pp. 85–97.

29. *Annals of Congress*, 4th Cong., 2d sess., 6: 1600, 1601, 1698–1711.

30. *Annals of Congress*, 9th Cong., 1st sess., 301.

31. *Annals of Congress*, 14th Cong., 1st sess., 29: 21; 30: 33.

32. Quoted in Goode, *National Scientific and Educational Institutions*, p. 25.

33. Walton H. Hamilton, "Patents and Free Enterprise," Temporary National Economic Committee, Monograph No. 31 (Washington; D.C.: GPO, 1941), p. 25.

34. Quoted in ibid., pp. 25–26.

35. *Annals of Congress*, 17th Cong., 1st sess., 1: 532.

36. For an understanding of the development of the natural sciences at that period, see, C. R. Hall, *Samuel Latham Mitchell, 1764–1831, A Scientist in the Early Republic* (New York: Columbia University Press, 1934); J. G. Crowther, *Famous American Men of Science* (New York: Norton, 1927); E. S. Dana et al., *A Century of Science in America, With Special Reference to the American Journal of Science, 1818–1918* (New Haven: Yale University Press, 1918); Thomas C. Johnson, Jr., *Scientific Interests in the Old South* (New York: Appleton, 1936).

37. Johnson, *Scientific Interests in the Old South*, p. 36.

38. W. S. Holt, *The Office of the Chief of the Corps of Engineers of the Army* (Baltimore: Johns Hopkins University Press, 1923); *The Centennial of the United States Military Academy at West Point, N.Y., 1802–1902* (Washington, D.C.: GPO, 1904), pp. 223–424.

39. See Max Meisel, *A Bibliography of American Natural History, 1769–1865*, 3 vols. (Brooklyn: Premier, 1924–29).

40. "Ferdinand R. Hassler," *Dictionary of American Biography*, 8: 385–386. See also G. A. Weber, *The Coast and Geodetic Survey* (Baltimore: Johns Hopkins University Press, 1923).

41. Barlow, "Prospectus of a National Institution," pp. 86–87; see also C. B. Todd, *Life and Letters of Joel Barlow* (New York: Putnam, 1886).

42. A. B. Hulbert, *The Cumberland Road* (Cleveland: A. H. Clark, 1904); T. B. Searight, *The Old Pike: A History of the National Road* (Uniontown, Pa., 1894).

43. *American State Papers, Miscellaneous*, 1: 721–921.

44. W. F. Gephart, *Transportation and Industrial Development in the Middle West* (New York: Columbia University Press, 1909), p. 44.

45. J. A. Durrenburger, *The Turnpike Era: 1800–1830* (Valdosta, Ga., 1931), p. 33.

46. Avery O. Craven, *Soil Exhaustion in Maryland and Virginia* (Urbana: University of Illinois Press, 1926), p. 70.

47. U. B. Phillips, *A History of Transportation in the Eastern Cotton Belt to 1860* (New York: Columbia University Press, 1908).

48. *A History of the People of the United States*, 8 vols. (New York: Appleton, 1893–1913), 2: 461.

49. F. A. Cleveland and F. W. Powell, *Railroad Promotion and Capitalization in the United States* (New York: Longmans Green, 1909), p. 15.

50. Ibid., pp. 39ff.

51. *The Turnpike Era,* pp. 98, 107–08.

52. Ibid., p. 112.

53. *Writings,* 1: 78. Adams records that Gallatin later endorsed his letter in his own hand as "Origin of National Road."

54. II *U.S. Statutes at Large,* 173, act of April 30, 1802.

55. II *U.S. Statutes at Large,* act of March 3, 1803.

56. *American State Papers, Miscellaneous,* 1: 432.

57. II *U.S. Statutes at Large,* 357, act of March 29, 1806.

58. *Writings,* 1: 335; also *American State Papers, Miscellaneous,* 1: 718.

59. *American State Papers, Miscellaneous,* 1: 721–921. The report is ably summarized in C. E. MacGill et al., *History of Transportation in the United States Before 1860* (Washington, D.C.: Carnegie Inst., 1917), pp. 133–35.

60. *American State Papers, Miscellaneous,* 1: 741.

61. Adams, *Life of Gallatin,* pp. 355, 367, 372, 391.

Chapter IX: Internal Improvements

1. Nevins, *The American States During and After the Revolution,* p. 469.

2. Quoted in A. B. Hulbert, *The Great American Canals* (Cleveland: A. H. Clark, 1903), 1: 20–21; see also 2: 43–45.

3. *Records,* 1: 19. According to James McHenry's notes of the convention, the following was detailed: "Under this head may be considered the establishment of great national works—this improvement of inland navigation—agriculture—manufactures—a freer intercourse among the citizens" (1: 26). According to C. H. Ambler, "the paternity" of the Constitution "has been generally attributed to Virginia, but few have appreciated her interest in its commercial provisions." *History of Transportation in the Ohio Valley* (Glendale,

Ca.: A. H. Clark, 1932), p. 68. See also Brown, *The Commercial Powers of Congress*.

4. Cleveland and Powell, *Railroad Promotion and Capitalization*, pp. 16–22.

5. See also 11: 7.

6. Richardson, *Messages and Papers of the Presidents*, 1: 107.

7. I *U.S. Statutes at Large*, 357, May 8, 1794.

8. W. E. Rich, *The History of the United States Post Office to the Year 1829* (Cambridge: Harvard University Press, 1924), p. 91; see also pp. 71, 109, 169.

9. *Life of Gallatin*, p. 352.

10. See Richardson, *Messages and Papers of the Presidents*, 3: 1046–56.

11. Thomas R. Dewey, *Financial History of the United States* (New York: Longmans Green, 1939), pp. 126–50.

12. McMaster, *A History of the People of the United States*, 4: 218. See also MacGill, *History of Transportation*, p. 59.

13. Quoted in MacGill, *History of Transportation*, p. 59. See also "Message Respecting the Causes of the Failure of the American Army on the Northern Frontier," February 2, 1814, *American State Papers, Military Affairs*, 1: 452, 453, 459, 462, 471.

14. MacGill, *History of Transportation*, p. 81.

15. *Annals of Congress*, 14th Cong., 2d sess., 296–97. In introducing this first bill on internal improvements since the War of 1812, Calhoun stated, "We have now an abundance of revenue, and are now in a state of peace, giving leisure to Congress to examine subjects connected with domestic affairs" (297).

16. Ibid., 857.

17. Ibid., 866–68.

18. Ibid., 857.

19. Richardson, *Messages and Papers of the Presidents*, 2: 568–70. In his annual address on December 3, 1816, Madison had admonished Congress that a constitutional amendment was necessary to permit the federal government to engage in internal improvements. The vote on Calhoun's bill was close: 20–15 in the Senate, 86–84 in the House of Representatives. *Annals of Congress*, 14th Cong., 1st sess., 282, 1219. An attempt to override the president's veto was defeated. 14th Cong., 2d sess., 1062.

20. See *Records*, 2: 324–26; 3: 520–21.

21. Richardson, *Messages and Papers of the Presidents*, 2: 577, 587. Note, however, that Monroe studiously avoided mention of internal improvements in his messages of 1818, 1819, 1820, 1821, and also in his inaugural address of 1821 (2: 608ff, 642ff, 655ff, 667ff).

22. *Annals of Congress*, v. 32, 15th Cong., 1st sess. This resolution was passed by a vote of 76–57.

23. *Annals of Congress,* v. 33, 15th, Cong., 2d sess., 544, 2443–52; also *American State Papers, Miscellaneous,* 2: 533–37.

24. This was the beginning of the vastly extended program of military road construction in the decades that followed. At the time of this report, the only military roads in existence were from Plattsburg to Sackets Harbor, New York, from Muscle Shoals to Madisonville, Louisiana, and from Detroit, Michigan, to Fort Meigs, Ohio.

25. *American State Papers, Miscellaneous,* 2: 533–37.

26. Richardson, *Messages and Papers of the Presidents,* 2: 587.

27. Ibid., 2: 711, 713–52; also *Annals of Congress,* 16th Cong., 1st sess., 1659; v. 36, 17th Cong., 1st sess., v. 2, 1732, 1803, 1809–13, 1872.

28. A single attempt was made in the Senate to initiate an amendment: "That Congress shall have power to adopt and execute a system of internal improvements, confined to great national purposes." The resolution was indefinitely tabled after being read for a second time. *Annals of Congress,* v. 40, 17th Cong., 2d sess., 200, 227, 290. See also H. V. Ames, *The Proposed Amendments to the Constitution of the United States During the First Century of Its History* (Washington, D.C.: GPO, 1897), pp. 260–61. The proponents of internal improvements refused to admit the need of a constitutional amendment and refused to be ensnared by a proposition that had little chance of passage. Henry Clay, for example, urged his supporters to oppose the resolution. *Annals of Congress,* v. 31, 15th Cong., 1st sess., 1119–20, 1359ff.

29. Richardson, *Messages and Papers of the Presidents,* 2: 540; also *Annals of Congress,* 14th Cong., 1st sess., 282, 1219.

30. IV *U.S. Statutes at Large,* 22, act of April 30, 1824.

31. *Annals of Congress,* 18th Cong., 1st sess., v. 1, 998; also Richardson, *Messages and Papers of the Presidents,* vol. 2.

32. *Annals of Congress,* 18th Cong., 1st sess. v. 1, 998. For the progress of this bill in the House of Representatives, see 808, 829, 990, 994, 998–99, 1042, 1230, 1254, 1468; for the Senate, 242, 253, 336, 419, 534–70.

33. Speech of January 16, 1824, in Henry Clay, *Life and Speeches,* 2 vols. (Philadelphia: Leary Getz, 1860), 2: 179. In my opinion, Clay's "American System" cannot be considered planning, although it was a skillful appeal to unite particular sections of the country in support of protectionism and internal improvements. Clay was notoriously lazy, and his speeches are filled with inaccuracies and exaggerations. In the qualities of detailed analysis and patient investigation—qualities necessary in effective planning—Clay was generally deficient. See Carl Schurz, *Life of Henry Clay,* 2 vols. (Boston: Houghton Mifflin, 1887), 1: 216, 307, 324.

34. Statement of General A. A. Humphreys, in a letter to the secretary of war, September 4, 1876, quoted in Holt, *Office of the Chief of the Corps of Engineers,* p. 5.

35. 18th Cong., 2d sess., doc. 83.

36. Ibid. The report's attempt at thorough investigation may be judged by the divisions into which its engineering data were divided: sections, mountain, ground, results of the line of level, measurement of water, expense of water, evaporations, reservoirs, feeders, dams, tunnels, considerations of descent from summit, preferable route, etc. It may be noted that although General Bernard's high estimate of the cost of constructing the Chesapeake and Ohio canal shocked the optimistic promoters, when the canal was finally built, his estimates proved very nearly correct. See G. W. Ward, *The Early Development of the Chesapeake and Ohio Canal Project* (Baltimore: Johns Hopkins University Press, 1899), pp. 73–80.

37. Holt, *Office of the Chief of the Corps of Engineers*, p. 6.

38. *American State Papers, Military Affairs*, 2: 698ff. During his secretaryship of the War Department, Calhoun had carried out a number of administrative reforms, making that department a more efficient instrument of realizing his transportation improvement plans. See Herman von Holst, *John C. Calhoun* (Boston: Houghton Mifflin, 1899), pp. 41ff.

39. *The Rise of the New West* (New York: Harper, 1906), pp. 275–76.

40. Richardson, *Messages and Papers of the Presidents*, 2: 864.

41. Turner, *Rise of the New West*, p. 288; T. R. Dewey, *Financial History of the United States*, p. 215. In Adams's last annual message to Congress, he reported: "For the preparation of five additional reports of reconnaissances and surveys since the last session of Congress, for the civil construction upon 37 different public works commenced, eight others for which specific appropriations have been made by acts of Congress, and 20 other incipient surveys under the authority given by the act of 30th April 1824, about one million more of dollars has been drawn from the Treasury." Richardson, *Messages and Papers of the Presidents*, 2: 983.

42. Quoted by Brooks Adams in Henry Adams, *The Degradation of the Democratic Dogma* (New York: Macmillan, 1919), p. 25.

43. *Memoirs*, C. F. Adams., ed., 12 vols. (Philadelphia: Lippincott, 1877), 7: 355.

44. Ibid., 7: 98.

45. Richardson, *Messages and Papers of the Presidents*, 2: 882, 879.

46. For virtually the next twenty years, following his resignation from the Senate, John Quincy Adams was almost exclusively engaged in foreign affairs. His introduction of the resolution that led to Gallatin's report shows that he was interested in a vigorous internal improvements program for a score of years before he became president. This is of special interest in view of the fact that Adams's grandsons, Henry, Brooks, and Charles Francis Jr., all historians and all keenly interested in their grandfather's career, somehow overlooked this fact and also its significance. Henry Adams, Gallatin's brilliant biographer and historian

of Jefferson's administration, credits Senator Worthington with introducing the resolution that resulted in Gallatin's report. *Life of Gallatin,* p. 350; Brooks Adams, in Henry Adams, *Degradation of the Democratic Dogma,* p. 25; cf. J. Q. Adams, *Memoirs,* 8: 444. *Annals of Congress,* 9th Cong., 2d sess., 77–78, 97. Charles Francis Adams, Jr., who wrote the penetrating and provocative analysis of the ills of our early railroads, accepted uncritically the conventional inference from the fact that the federal government had not concerned itself with directing the development of the railroads. He wrote: "The railroad system of the United States with all its excellence and all its defects is thoroughly characteristic of the American people. It grew up untrammelled by any theory as to how it ought to grow; and developed with mushroom rapidity, without reference to government or political systems. In this country alone were the principles of free trade unreservedly and fearless applied to it." *Railroads: Their Origin and Problems* (New York: Putnam, 1888), pp. 116–17. Adams's statement is true only insofar as it is applied strictly to railroads; it ignores the essential fact that railroads must be regarded as but part of the nation's system of transportation, not as ends in themselves. In this larger context, he overlooked the fact that his grandfather was vitally interested in having the government plan and direct the building of an integrated national transportation system. No one could have foreseen the future of railroads—carriages pulled by horses, driven by sails, etc.—in Adams's time. Even so, President Adams lent the first railroads the skilled services of the engineers. Charles Frances Adams overlooked the most important fact, that if John Quincy Adams's ideas had won in directing road and canal improvements on a national scale, this scheme could also have been adapted for planning and directing the development of railroads.

47. Adams, *Degradation of the Democratic Dogma,* p. 53.

48. *American State Papers, Miscellaneous,* 2: 656–701; also 16th Cong., 2d sess., S. Doc. 119.

49. G. A. Weber, *The Bureau of Standards* (Baltimore: Johns Hopkins University Press, 1925), p. 7.

50. Adams, *Degradation of the Democratic Dogma,* p. 61.

51. Richardson, *Messages and Papers of the Presidents,* 2: 878.

52. *Memoirs,* 7: 480.

53. Ibid., 4: 526–27.

54. Ibid., 8: 13, 15, 18.

55. IV *U.S. Statutes at Large,* 124, 162, 168, 292, 353. See Adams's diary jottings concerning the Chesapeake and Ohio Canal, *Memoirs,* 7: 191, 266; 8: 6, 23–24, 33, 39, 41, 44–45, 49–50.

56. *Memoirs,* 7: 146.

57. III *U.S. Statutes at Large,* 651, act of February 23, 1822.

58. *The Development of Governmental Forest Control in the United States* (Baltimore: Johns Hopkins University Press, 1928), p. 37.

59. IV *U.S. Statutes at Large,* 242, act of March 3, 1827.

60. Cameron, *Development of Governmental Forest Control,* p. 39.

61. Ibid., pp. 44–45.

62. Ibid., p. 65.

63. Ibid., p. 40.

64. *Memoirs,* 7: 63.

65. Richardson, *Messages and Papers of the Presidents,* 2: 880. President Madison had recommended a similar change, but with no more success.

66. *Memoirs,* 7: 83–84.

Selected Bibliography

Abernethy, T. P. *From Frontier to Plantation in Tennessee*. Chapel Hill: University of North Carolina Press, 1932.

_____. *Western Lands and the American Revolution*. New York: Appleton, 1937.

Adams, Charles Francis, Jr. *Railroads: Their Origin and Development*. New York: Putnam, 1888.

Adams, H. B. *Maryland's Influence Upon Land Cessions in the United States*. Baltimore: Johns Hopkins University Press, 1885.

Adams, Henry. *The Degradation of the Democratic Dogma*. New York: Macmillan, 1919.

_____. *History of the United States of America During the Administrations of Thomas Jefferson and James Madison*. 6 vols. New York: Scribners, 1889–91.

_____. *The Life of Albert Gallatin*. Philadelphia: Lippincott, 1879.

Adams, James Truslow. *The Adams Family*. Boston: Little, Brown, 1930.

_____. *Provincial Society: 1690–1763*. New York: Macmillan, 1927.

Adams, John. *Works*. C. F. Adams, ed. 10 vols. Boston: Little, Brown, 1856.

Adams, John Quincy. *Memoirs*. C. F. Adams, ed. 12 vols. Philadelphia: Lippincott, 1877.

Agar, Herbert. *The People's Choice*. Boston: Houghton Mifflin, 1933.

Ambler, C. H. *George Washington and the West*. Chapel Hill: University of North Carolina Press, 1936.

_____. *History of Transportation in the Ohio Valley*. Glendale, Ca.: A. H. Clark, 1932.

Ames, H. V. *The Prosposed Amendments to the Constitution of the United States During the First Century of Its History*. Washington; D.C.: GPO, 1897.

Andrews, C. M. "England's Commercial Policy," *The Colonial Period of American History*. Vol. 4. New Haven: Yale University Press, 1934–39.

Annals of the American Academy of Political and Social Science. "The First State Constitutions." Vol. 9. 1897.

Ball, J. C. *Opening a Highway to the Pacific, 1836–1846*. New York: Columbia University Press, 1921.

Barlow, Joel. "Prospectus of a National Institution To Be Established in the United States." G. B. Goode, ed., *National Scientific and Educational Institutions*. New York: G. P. Putnams Sons, 1890.

Barrett, J. S. *Evolution of the Ordinance of 1787*. 1871.

Bassett, J. S. *The Federalist System, 1789–1801.* New York: Harper, 1906.

———. *The Life of Andrew Jackson.* 2 vols. New York: Macmillan, [1911] 1931.

Basye, A. H. *The Lord Commissioner of Trade and Plantations, 1748–1782.* New Haven, 1925.

Bates, F. G. and O. P. Field. *State Government.* New York: Harper, 1928.

Beard, Charles A. *The Economic Interpretation of the Constitution.* New York: Macmillan, 1913.

———. *The Economic Origins of Jeffersonian Democracy.* New York: Macmillan, 1915.

———. *The Supreme Court and the Constitution.* rev. ed. New York: Macmillan, 1938.

Beard, Charles A. and Mary R. Beard. *The Rise of the American Civilization.* 2 vols. New York: Macmillan, 1930.

Beer, C. L. *British Colonial Policy.* New York: Macmillan, 1907.

———. *The Commercial Policy of England Toward the American Colonies.* New York: P. Smith, [1893] 1948.

———. *The Old Colonial System.* 2 vols. New York: Macmillan, 1912.

Benton, E. J. *The Wabash Trade Route in the Development of the Old Northwest.* Baltimore: Johns Hopkins University Press, 1903.

Bieber, R. P. *The Lords of Trade and Plantations, 1675–1696.* Allentown: H. R. Hass, 1919.

Biesecke, A. A. *American Commercial Legislation Before 1789.* New York, 1910.

Binkley, W. E. *The Powers of the President.* Garden City: Doubleday, 1937.

Bishop, A. L. *The State Works of Pennsylvania.* New Haven: Connecticut Academy of Arts & Sciences, 1907.

Bishop, J. L. *History of American Manufactures.* 2 vols., 3rd ed. Philadelphia: E. Young, 1868.

Blackmar, F. W. *The History of Federal Aid to Higher Education in the United States.* Washington, D.C.: GPO, 1890.

Bogart, E. L. *Internal Improvements and State Debt in Ohio.* New York: Longmans Green, 1924.

———. *The Economic History of the American People.* New York: Longmans Green, 1930.

Bondy, William. *The Separation of Governmental Powers.* New York: Sabiston Murray, 1896.

Boudin, L. B. *Government by Judiciary.* 2 vols. New York: W. Goodwin, 1932.

Bowen, Catherine Drinker. *Miracle at Philadelphia.* Boston: Little, Brown, 1966.

Brown, D. W. *The Commercial Powers of Congress.* New York: Putnam, 1910.

Burke, Edmund. *Works.* 12 vols. 9th ed. Boston: Little, Brown, 1889.

Caldwell, L. K. *Ideas on Public Administration of Hamilton and Jefferson.* Chicago: University of Chicago Press, 1944.

Cameron, Jenks. *The Development of Governmental Forest Control in the United States.* Baltimore. Johns Hopkins University Press, 1928.

Carter, C. F. *When Railroads Were New.* New York: Henry Holt, 1909.

Catterall, R. C. H. *The Second Bank of the United States.* Chicago: University of Chicago Press, 1903.

Channing, Edward. *The Jeffersonian System.* New York: Harper, 1906.

Chinard, Gilbert, *Thomas Jefferson, the Apostle of Americanism.* Boston: Little, Brown, 1929.

Clark, C. Bennett. *John Quincy Adams.* Boston: Little, Brown, 1932.

Clark, V. S. *History of Manufactures in the United States.* 2 vols. New York: McGraw-Hill, 1929.

Clay, Henry. *Life and Speeches.* 2 vols. Philadelphia: Leary Getz, 1860.

Cleveland, F. E. and F. W. Powell. *Railroad Promotion and Capitalization in the United States.* New York: Longmans Green, 1909.

Cole, H. A. *Industrial and Commercial Correspondence of Alexander Hamilton.* Chicago: A. W. Shaw, 1929.

Conover, Milton. *The Federal Power Commission.* Baltimore: Johns Hopkins University Press, 1923.

_____. *The General Land Office.* Baltimore: Johns Hopkins University Press, 1923.

_____. *Office of Experiment Stations.* Baltimore: Johns Hopkins University Press, 1924.

Corwin, E. S. *The Commerce Power Versus States Rights.* Princeton: Princeton University Press, 1936.

_____. *Court Over the Constitution.* Princeton: Princeton University Press, 1938.

_____. *The Presidency.* New York: New York University Press, 1940.

Coxe, Tench. *A Statement of the Arts and Manufactures of the United States of America.* Philadelphia: William Hall, 1794.

Craven, Avery O. *Soil Exhaustion in Maryland and Virginia.* Urbana: University of Illinois Press, 1926.

Crenson, Mathew. *The Federal Machine: Beginnings of Bureaucracy in Jacksonian America.* Baltimore: Johns Hopkins University Press, 1975.

Croly, Herbert. *The Promise of American Life.* New York: Macmillan, 1909.

Crosskey, W. W. *Politics and the Constitution.* 2 vols. Chicago: University of Chicago Press, 1953.

Crowther, J. G. *Famous American Men of Science.* New York: Norton, 1937.

Cubberley, E. B. *Public Education in the United States.* Boston: Houghton Mifflin, [1919] 1934.

Curti, Merle. *The Social Ideas of American Educators*. New York: Scribners, 1935.

Dana, E. S. et al. *A Century of Science in America, With Special Reference to the American Journal of Science, 1818-1918*. New Haven: Yale University Press, 1918.

Davis, J. S. *Essays in the Earlier History of American Corporations*. 2 vols. Cambridge: Harvard University Press, 1917.

Dewey, Thomas R. *Financial History of the United States*. New York: Longmans Green, [1934] 1939.

Dickerson, O. M. *American Colonial Government, 1696-1765*. Cleveland, 1912.

Donaldson, Thomas. *The Public Domain*. Washington, D.C.: GPO, 1884.

Dunbar, L. B. *A Study of "Monarchical" Tendencies in the United States from 1775 to 1801*. Urbana: University of Illinois Press, 1922.

Dunnaway, W. F. *History of the James River and Kanawha Company*. New York: Columbia University Press, 1922.

Dunning, W. A. *History of Political Theories: From Rousseau to Spencer*. New York: Macmillan, 1920.

Du Pont de Nemours. *National Education in the United States of America*. Bessie G. Du Pont, trans. Newark: University of Delaware Press, 1923.

Durrenburger, J. A. *The Turnpike Era: 1800-1830*. Valdosta, G., 1931.

Earle, E. M., ed. *The Federalist Papers*, by James Madison and Alexander Hamilton. Washington: National Home Library, 1937.

Edwards, Everett E. *Washington, Jefferson, Lincoln and Agriculture*. Washington, D.C.: Bureau of Agricultural Economics, Department of Agriculture, 1937.

Elazar, Daniel J. *American Federalism: A View From the States*. New York: Crowell, 1966.

———. *The American Partnership: Intergovernmental Cooperation in the 19th Century*. Chicago: University of Chicago Press, 1962.

Fainsod, Merle and L. Gordon. *Government and the American Economy*. New York: Norton, 1941.

Farrand, Max. *The Framing of the Constitution of the United States*. New Haven: Yale University Press, 1913.

———. ed. *The Records of the Federal Convention of 1787*. 3 vols. New Haven: Yale University Press, 1911.

Fish, Carl R. *The Civil Service and Patronage*. Cambridge: Harvard University Press, 1905.

Fiske, John. *The Critical Period of American History, 1783-1789*. Boston: Houghton Mifflin, 1889.

Folmsbee, S. J. *Sectionalism and Internal Improvements in Tennessee, 1796-1845*. Knoxville: East Tennessee Historical Society, 1939.

Ford, A. C. *Colonial Land Precedents of the National Land System.* Madison: University of Wisconsin Press, 1910.

Fraser, Leon, "English Opinion of the American Constitution and Government." Ph.D. diss., Columbia University, 1915.

Fremont, J. C. *Report of the Exploring Expedition to the Rocky Mountains in the Year 1842 and to Oregon and Northern California in the Years 1843–1844.* Washington, D.C.: Annals of American Geographers, 1845.

Gallatin, Albert. *Writings.* Henry Adams, ed. 3 vols. Philadelphia: Lippincott, 1879.

Gates, Paul W. *The Illinois Central Railroad and Its Colonization Work.* Cambridge: Harvard University Press, 1934.

Gephart, W. F. *Transportation and Industrial Development in the Middle West.* New York: Columbia University Press, 1909.

Giesecke, A. A. *American Commercial Legislation Before 1789.* New York: Appleton, 1910.

Goode, G. Brown. *The Beginnings of American Science.* Washington: National Museum Report, 1897.

_____. "Genesis of the United States National Museum." *Annual Report of the U. S. National Museum.* Washington, D.C., 1892.

_____, ed. *National Scientific and Educational Institutions.* New York: Putnam, 1890.

_____. *The Smithsonian Institution, 1846–1896: The History of Its First Half Century.* Washington, D.C.: Smithsonian Institution, 1897.

Gray, L. C. *History of Agriculture in the Southern United States to 1860.* 12 vols. Washington: Carnegie Institution, 1933.

Haase, Adelaide R. *Reports of Explorations Printed in the Documents of the United States Government.* Washington, D. C.: GPO, 1899.

Haines, C. G. *The American Doctrine of Judicial Supremacy.* 2nd rev. ed. Berkeley: University of California Press, 1932.

Hall, C. R. *Samuel Latham Mitchell, 1764–1831, A Scientist in the Early Republic.* New York: Columbia University Press, 1934.

Hamilton, Alexander. *Works.* J. C. Hamilton, ed. 10 vols. New York, 1851.

_____. *Works.* H. C. Lodge, ed. 12 vols. New York: Putnam, 1903.

Hamilton, Walton H. "Patents and Free Enterprise." Temporary National Economic Committee, Monograph No. 31, Washington, D.C.: GPO, 1941.

Hamilton, Walton H. and Douglas Adair. *The Power to Govern.* New York: Norton, 1937.

Haney, L. H. *A Congressional History of Railways in the United States to 1850.* Madison: University of Wisconsin Press, 1908.

Hansen, Alvin H. *Liberalism and American Education in the Eighteenth Century.* New York: Macmillan, 1926.

————. *Fiscal Policy and Business Cycles.* New York: Norton, 1941.

Harlow, A. F. *Old Towpaths: The Story of the American Canal Era.* New York: Appleton, 1926.

Harlow, Ralph V. *History of Legislative Methods to 1825.* New Haven: Yale University Press, 1917.

Haskins, C. H. *The Yazoo Land Companies.* New York: American Historical Association, 1891.

Haworth, P. L. *George Washington, Farmer.* Indianapolis, 1915.

Heckscher, E. F. *Mercantilism.* 2 vols. London: Allen & Unwin, 1935.

Hendrick, Burton J. *Bulwark of the Republic, A Biography of the Constitution.* Boston: Little, Brown, 1937.

Hepburn, A. B. *A History of Currency in the United States.* New York: Hamilton, 1924.

Hertz, G. B. *The Old Colonial System.* Manchester, England, 1905.

Hibbard, H. B. *A History of the Public Land Policies.* New York: Macmillan, 1924.

Hirst, F. W. *Life and Letters of Thomas Jefferson.* New York: Macmillan, 1909.

Holland, A. C. "The Anti-Slavery Activities of Thomas Jefferson." M.A. thesis, University of Chicago, 1927.

Holt, W. Stull. *The Bureau of the Census.* Washington, D. C.: Brookings Institution, 1929.

————. *The Office of the Chief of the Corps of Engineers of the Army.* Baltimore: Johns Hopkins University Press, 1923.

Honeywell, R. J. *Educational Work of Thomas Jefferson.* Cambridge: Harvard University Press, 1931.

Horrocks, J. W. *A Short History of Mercantilism.* London: Methuen, 1925.

Hughes, Charles Evans. *The Supreme Court of the United States.* New York: Columbia University Press, 1928.

Hulbert, Archer B. *The Cumberland Road.* Cleveland: A. H. Clark, 1904.

————. *The Great American Canals.* 2 vols. Cleveland: A. H. Clark, 1903.

————. *The Paths of Inland Commerce.* New Haven: Yale University Press, 1921.

————. *Washington's Road.* Cleveland: A. H. Clark, 1903.

Hungerford, Edward. *The Story of the Baltimore & Ohio Railroad, 1827–1927.* 2 vols. New York: Putnam, 1928.

James, Marquis. *Life of Andrew Jackson.* 2 vols. Indianapolis: Bobbs Merrill, 1938.

Jameson, J. Franklin. *The American Revolution Considered as a Social Movement.* Princeton: Princeton University Press, 1926.

————. *Essays in the Constitutional History of the United States in the Formative Period, 1775–1789.* Boston: Houghton Mifflin, 1889.

Jefferson, Thomas. *Writings.* P. L. Ford, ed. Federal edition. 12 vols. New York: Putnam, 1904–05.

_____. *Writings.* H. A. Washington, ed. 13 vols. New York: Riker Thorne, 1855.

Jensen, Merrill, *The Articles of the Confederation: An Interpretation.* Madison: University of Wisconsin Press, 1940.

Johnson, E. R. et al. *History of Domestic and Foreign Commerce in the United States.* 2 vols. Washington, D.C.: Carnegie Institution, 1915.

Johnson, Thomas C., Jr. *Scientific Interests in the Old South.* New York: Appleton, 1936.

Jones, C. L. *The Economic History of the Anthracite Tidewater Canals.* Philadelphia: University of Pennsylvania Press, 1908.

Kirkland, E. C. *A History of American Economic Life.* New York: F. S. Crofts, 1939.

Knight, George W. *History and Management of Land Grants for Education in the Northwest Territory.* New York: Putnam, 1885.

Laski, Harold J. *The American Presidency: An Interpretation.* New York: Harper, 1940.

Learned, H. B. *The President's Cabinet.* New Haven: Yale University Press, 1912.

Leopold, R. W. *Robert Dale Owen.* Cambridge: Harvard University Press, 1940.

Lipson, Leslie. *The American Governor from Figurehead to Leader.* Chicago, University of Chicago Press, 1939.

Livermore, Shaw. *Early American Land Companies.* New York: Commonwealth Fund, 1939.

Lyon, L. S., M. W. Watkins and V. Abramson. *Government and Economic Life.* Washington, D.C.: Brookings Institution, 1939.

MacGill, C. E. et al. *History of Transportation in the United States Before 1860.* Washington, D. C.: Carnegie Inst., 1917.

MacKenzie, Findlay, ed. *Planned Society.* New York, 1937.

MacLeish, Archibald. *America was Promises.* New York: Duel Sloan, 1940.

Madison, James. *Writings.* G. Hunt, ed. 9 vols. New York: Putnam, 1900–10.

Mai, C. T. "The Fiscal Policies of Albert Gallatin." Ph.D. diss., Columbia University, 1930.

Malone, Dumas. *Jefferson and His Time.* 6 vols. Boston: Little, Brown, 1948–81.

Martin, W. E. *Internal Improvements in Alabama.* Baltimore: Johns Hopkins University Press, 1903.

Mason, E. S. *The Veto Power.* Boston: Ginn, 1890.

McLaughlin, Andrew C. *The Confederation and the Constitution, 1783–1789.* New York: Harper, 1905.

McMaster, J. B. *A History of the People of the United States.* 8 vols. New York: Appleton, 1883–1913.

McReynolds, R. A. "A History of the United States Post Office, 1607–1931." Ph.D. diss., University of Chicago, 1935.

Meisel, Max. *A Bibliography of American Natural History, 1769–1865.* 3 vols. Brooklyn: Premier, 1924-29.

Merriam, Charles E. *A History of American Political Theories.* New York: Macmillan, 1903.

————. *The Written Constitution and the Unwritten Attitude.* New York: R. R. Smith, 1931.

Merrill, G. P. *The First One Hundred Years of American Geology.* New York: Hafner, 1924.

Monroe, James. *Writings.* S. M. Hamilton, ed. 7 vols. New York: Putnam, 1898-1903.

Monroe, Paul. *Founding of the American Public School System.* 2 vols. New York: Macmillan, 1940.

Morison, S. E., H. S. Commager and W. E. Leuchtenburg. *The Growth of the American Republic.* 2 vols. New York: Oxford University Press, 1969.

Morse, J. T. *Alexander Hamilton.* Boston: Little, Brown, 1876.

————. *John Quincy Adams.* Boston: Houghton Mifflin, [1882] 1898.

Nevins, Allan. *The American States During and After the Revolution, 1775-1789.* New York: Macmillan, 1924.

Oliver, F. S. *Alexander Hamilton: An Eassay on American Union.* New York: Putnam, 1906.

Orfield, M. N. *Federal Land Grants to the States, With Speical Reference to Minnesota.* Minneapolis: University of Minnesota Press, 1915.

Osgood, H. L. *The American Colonies in the Seventeenth Century.* 3 vols. New York: Macmillan, 1904-07.

Owen, D. D. "Report of a Geological Exploration of Parts of Iowa, Wisconsin and Illinois in the Year 1839." 28th Cong. 1st sess., Senate document 407 Washington, D.C., 1844.

————. "Report of a Geological Reconnaissance of the Chippewa Land District of Wisconsin and the Northern Part of Iowa." Washington, D.C., 1848.

Padover, S. K., ed. *Thomas Jefferson's Democracy.* New York: Appleton, 1939.

Phillips, U. B. *A History of Transportation in the Eastern Cotton Belt to 1860.* New York: Columbia University Press, 1908.

Poor, H. V. *Sketch of the Rise and Progress of the Internal Improvements and of the Internal Railroads of the United States.* New York: H. V. and H. W. Poor, 1881.

Powell, J. W. *Bureau of Animal Industry.* Baltimore: Johns Hopkins University Press, 1927.

_____. *Bureau of Plant Industry.* Baltimore: Johns Hopkins University Press, 1922.

_____. *On the Organization of Scientific Work of the General Government.* Washington, D.C.: GPO, 1885.

Prather, C. L. *Money and Banking.* Chicago: Business Publications, 1937.

Putnam, J. W. *The Illinois and Michigan Canal: A Study of Economic History.* Chicago, 1918.

Rathburn, Richard. *The Columbian Institution for the Promotion of the Arts and Sciences.* Washington, D. C.: GPO, 1917.

_____. *National Institution for the Promotion of Science, Constitution and By-Laws.* Washington, D. C.: Gales and Seaton, 1940.

Read, Conyers, ed. *The Constitution Reconsidered.* New York: Columbia University Press, 1938.

Rhees, William J., ed. *The Smithsonian Institution: Documents Relative to Its Origin and History, 1835–1899.* 2 vols. Washington, D.C.: Smithsonian Institution, 1901.

Rich, W. E. *The History of the United States Post Office to the Year 1829.* Cambridge: Harvard University Press, 1924.

Richardson, J. D., ed. *Messages and Papers of the Presidents, 1789–99.* 10 vols. Washington, D. C.: GPO, 1896–99.

Ringwalt, J. L. *Development of Transportation Systems in the United States.* Philadelphia: Railway World, 1888.

Robbins, Roy M. *Our Landed Heritage: The Public Domain.* Princeton: Princeton University Press, 1942.

Sakolski, A. M. *The Great American Land Bubble.* New York: Harper, 1932.

Sanborn, J. B. *Congressional Grants of Land in Aid of Railways.* Madison: University of Wisconsin Press, 1899.

Sanford, Albert H. *The Story of Agriculutre in the United States.* New York: Scribners, 1916.

Schlesinger, Arthur M., Jr. *The Age of Jackson.* Boston: Little, Brown, 1945.

_____. *The Cycles of American History.* Boston: Houghton Mifflin, 1986.

_____. *The Imperial Presidency.* Boston: Houghton Mifflin, 1973.

Schmeckebeir, L. F. *Catalogue and Index of the Publications of the Hayden, King, Powell and Wheeler Surveys.* U.S. Geological Survey bulletin No. 322. Washington, D. C., 1904.

Schurz, Carl. *Life of Henry Clay.* 2 vols. Boston: Houghton Mifflin, 1887.

Scott, J. B. *Sovereign States and Suits Before Arbitral Tribunals and Courts of Justice.* New York: New York University Press, 1925.

Searight, T. B. *The Old Pike: A History of the National Road.* Uniontown, Pa., 1894.

Small, A. W. *The Beginnings of American Nationality.* Baltimore: Johns Hopkins University Press, 1890.

Small, N. J. *Some Presidential Interpretations of the Presidency.* Baltimore: Johns Hopkins University Press, 1932.

Smith, G. O. *The Classification of the Public Lands.* U.S. Geological Survey bulletin No. 537. Washington, D. C., 1913.

Smith, J. Allen. *The Spirit of American Government.* New York: Macmillan, 1911.

Sumner, William Graham. *Life of Alexander Hamilton.* New York: University Society, 1891.

Tanner, H. S. *A Description of Canals and Railroads in the United States.* New York: Tanner & Disturnell, 1940.

Thach, C. C. *The Creation of the Presidency, 1775–1789.* Baltimore: Johns Hopkins University Press, 1922.

Thorpe, F. E. *The Federal and State Constitutions, Colonial Charters and Other Organic Laws.* 7 vols. Washington, D.C.: GPO, 1909.

Todd, C. B. *Life and Letters of Joel Barlow.* New York: Putnam, 1886.

Treat, P. J. *The National Land System, 1785–1820.* New York: E. B. Treat, 1910.

Turner, Frederick Jackson. *The Rise of the New West.* New York: Harper, 1906.

Van Metre, T. W. *Transportation in the United States.* Chicago: Foundation Press, 1939.

Von Holst, Herman. *John C. Calhoun.* Boston: Houghton Mifflin, 1899.

Ward, G. W. *The Early Development of the Chesapeake and Ohio Canal Project.* Baltimore: Johns Hopkins University Press, 1899.

———. *Report to the Stockholders of the Chesapeake and Ohio Canal Co.* Frederick, Md., 1851.

Warren, Charles. *Bankruptcy in United States History.* Cambridge: Harvard University Press, 1935.

———. *Congress, the Constitution and the Supreme Court.* Boston: Little, Brown, 1925.

———. *The Supreme Court and the Sovereign States.* Princeton: Princeton University Press, 1924.

Washington, George. *Works.* Jared Sparks, ed. 12 vols. Boston: Little, Brown, 1855.

———. *Writings.* P. L. Ford, ed. 14 vols. New York: Putnam, 1889–93.

Weaver, C. C. *Internal Improvements in North Carolina Previous to 1860.* Baltimore: Johns Hopkins University Press, 1903.

Weber, G. A. *Bureau of Chemistry and Soils.* Baltimore: Johns Hopkins University Press, 1928.

———. *The Bureau of Standards.* Baltimore: Johns Hopkins University Press, 1925.

_____. *The Coast and Geodetic Survey.* Baltimore: Johns Hopkins University Press, 1923.

_____. *The Hydrographic Office.* Baltimore: Johns Hopkins University Press, 1926.

_____. *The Naval Observatory.* Baltimore: Johns Hopkins University Press, 1926.

_____. *The Patent Office.* Baltimore: Johns Hopkins University Press, 1924.

_____. *The Plant Quarantine and Control Administration.* Washington, D.C.: Brookings Institution, 1930.

_____. *The Weather Bureau.* New York: Appleton, 1922.

Webster, Pelatiah. *A Political Dissertation on the Political Union and Constitution of the Thirteen United States of North America.* Hartford: Hudson & Goodwin, 1783.

West Point, The Centennial of the United States Military Academy at West Point, New York, 1802–1902. Washington, D.C.: GPO, 1904.

White, Leonard D. *The Federalists, 1789–1801.* New York: Macmillan, 1963.

_____. *The Jacksonians, 1828–1861.* New York: Macmillan, 1948.

_____. *The Jeffersonians, 1801–1829.* New York: Macmillan, 1948.

Whitford, N. E. *History of the Canal System of the State of New York.* 2 vols. Albany: Brandon, 1906.

Wirth, Freemont P. *The Discovery and Exploration of the Minnesota Iron Lands.* Cedar Rapids: Torch Press, 1937.

Woodruff, George W. "Classification of the Public Lands." *Annals of the American Academy of Political and Social Science.* 33(1909).

Wright, C. D. and W. C. Hunt. *The History and Growth of the United States Census.* Washington, D.C.: GPO, 1900.

Index

Adair, Douglas, 39, 40, 45–46, 47, 48
Adams, Charles Francis, 178 n5
Adams, Henry, 152–53, 186 nl
Adams, John, 20
Adams, John Quincy, 20; attacks on, 170; concern with science and education, 169–70, 171–72; failure of administration of, 166–68; on internal improvements, 165, 166, 167–68; internal improvements during administration of, 153–54; perception of states' rights, 168–69; on public land policy, 174; relationship with Henry Clay, 167
Affirmative role: of government, 25, 28, 34, 45, 169; of president, 50
Agricultural factions: appeal by Hamilton to, 91–95; opposition to Hamilton's industrial policy, 91, 105, 106
Agriculture: incidence compared to industry of, 74; Jefferson's policy for Southern, 119–23; support of Jefferson for Western, 142
American Academy of Arts and Sciences, 139
American Philosophical Society, 137, 138, 139
Articles of Confederation: powers of Continental Congress, 28–29; practise of laissez-faire under, 50

Banking. See National bank
Barlow, Joel: plan for promotion of science, 136, 141
Beard, Charles A., 30, 76, 89

Bimetallism: Hamilton's proposals for, 78–79, 80, 82–83
Binkley, W.E., 183 n3
Blackstone, William, 53
Board of Internal Improvements, 162–63, 165, 171
Bondy, William, 51
Bowen, Catherine Drinker, 177 nl
Broom, Jacob, 60, 61
Brown, D.W., 46, 182 n17
Burke, Edmund, 32

Calhoun, John C.: interest in internal improvement of, 155–56; military aspect of improvements of 157–59; plan for national transportation system of, 163–64
Cameron, Jenks, 173–74
Canal improvement, 171
Capital, private: lack in federal government of, 24
Chinard, Gilbert, 177 nl
Clay, Henry: interest in internal improvements, 156, 157, 161; and J.Q. Adams, 167
Clinton, George: activities as governor of New York, 54–55
Coinage. See Currency
Commager, Henry Steele, 88–89, 177 nl
Commerce clause, 45–47
Committee of Eleven, 63, 180–81 n7; See also Constitutional Convention
Committee on Detail, 40–41, 42, 47, 57, 63; See also Constitutional Convention

Confederation: executive and legislative powers under, 51, 52; *See also* Continental Congress

Congress: power to allocate improvement funds of, 181–82 nn14, 15; reaction to proposals for public education, 136

Conservation: John Quincy Adams' position on, 171, 172–73

Constitution: attacks and comments on, 30, 32–33; concept of laissez-faire in, 37–38, 50; design for Article II of, 49, 50–51, 57; effect of, 32–33; influences leading to creation of, 29–30; proposed powers of government under, 40–44; provision for alteration of, 47–48, 182 n22

Constitutional Convention, 28; attention to power of the executive, 52; notion of monarchy in debates of, 61; participants' expectation of commercial expansion, 181 n11; role of Committee on Detail in, 40–1, 47

Continental Congress: powers of 28–29, 50–53; practise of laissez-faire under, 50; role of executive in debates of, 50–51

"Continentalist" paper, 89, 90

Corporations: for canal improvement, 171

Corps of Engineers, 161, 162, 165

Corwin, E.S., 182 n18

Credit: extension by means of national banking of, 80, 88; Hamilton proposals to expand, 79–80; Hamilton's proposals for policy for, 71–76; Hamilton's view of importance of, 67–68; *See also* Debt, public; Hamilton, Alexander; Report on the Public Credit

Croly, Herbert, 19

Crosskey, W.W., 23, 47

Cumberland Road. *See* National Road

Currency: effect of national bank on problems of, 79–80; Hamilton's plan for national, 81–83

Debt, public: funding of foreign, 84; Hamilton proposal for assumption of states', 73–74, 77, 188 n15; Hamilton proposals for funding, 70–71, 72, 75, 76, 77, 83–85, 88, 188 n15; Jefferson opposition to funding of, 125; policy of Jefferson for reduction of, 125–26, 128; *See also* Fiscal policy

Defense: Gallatin on, 146–47; Hamilton on, 95

Dickinson, John, 61

Dodd, W.E., 30

Dunbar, L.B., 61, 83, 84

Du Pont de Nemours, Pierre S.: national educational system of, 135

Durrenburger, J.A., 143–44

Economic policy. *See* Industrial policy

Education: Jefferson's view of importance of, 133–34; in U.S. before 1800, 132–33

Education, public: Jefferson's plans for, pre–1789, 132; Jefferson support for idea of, 135–36, 137; John Quincy Adams' plan for, 170, 171–72; land grants to establish facilities for, 134–35; Madison's interest in, 136; position of Congress on policy for, 136; Washington's interest in, 136; *See also* Improvements, internal; Public land policy; Schools

Elazar, Daniel, 23

Electoral college: proposal for creation of, 59, 62–63

Ellsworth, Oliver, 59, 62–63

Enlightenment philosophy: effect on design of Constitution of, 25, 33

Executive branch: debates on relationship to legislative branch, 57–59; Virginia and New Jersey plans for 55, 58

Executive powers: under Confederation, 51; example of George Clinton of New York, 54–55; proposals for, 55–60; and term of office, 61–62, 63; *See also* Monarchy; Powers; Presidency

Exploration: government sponsorship in Jefferson administration of, 140–41

Export tax: Madison opinion of Congressional power for, 182 n15

Federal Authority. *See* Commerce clause; Powers

First Bank of the United States. *See* National bank

Fiscal policy: in Jefferson administration, 127–28; *See also* Debt, public; Gallatin, Albert

Forest policy. *See* Conservation

Founders: on the Constitutional Convention, 30–33; creation of strong executive, 64; design of office of president, 50; goal for strong government of, 37, 40; on reelection of the executive, 50; use of mercantilist concept by, 37, 38–40

Framers. *See* Founders

Franklin, Benjamin, 44, 61

Fraser, Leon, 33

Freedom: Jefferson perception of, 108–9

Gallatin, Albert: fiscal plan of, 125, 127–28; plan for transportation system, 142, 144, 145–47, 152–53

Gerry, Elbridge, 59, 60, 61, 63

Gideonse, Harry D., 182 n22

Gold. *See* Bimetallism

Goodrich, Carter, 23

Hamilton, Alexander, 28, 32, 38; appeal to agricultural factions by, 91–95; "Continentalist" paper of, 89, 90; on defense, 95; on funding public debt, 70–71, 72, 75, 76, 77, 83–85, 88, 188 n15; goal for centralized government, 67; goals for development of national government, 67–68; on loans for land purchase, 80; mercantilist position of, 89; opposition to, 105; plans for strong national policy, 67, 69–70; on power of Continental Congress, 53; proposal for national bank, 77–81; proposal for power of executive of, 55; proposals for currency, 81–83; protectionist position of, 88, 94, 96, 98; Report on Manufactures of, 88, 98–100, 102–103, 104, 105; Report on the Establishment of a Mint of, 81; Report on the Establishment of a National Bank of, 77, 78; Report on the Public Credit of, 70, 71–76, 187 nn7, 8, 9; on social class and property, 69, 70; states' debt assumption proposals of, 73–74; use of public policy to achieve economic balance, 74–75

Hamilton, Walton H., 39, 40, 45–46, 47, 48

Hansen, Alvin H., 33, 34, 73

Happiness, pursuit of, 19, 108, 177 n1

Hemphill, Joseph: bill for internal improvements, 160–61

Hume, David, 90

Impeachment, 62, 63

Improvements, internal: James Monroe on, 157, 158–59; during J.Q. Adams' administration, 153–54, 165–66; plans of John Quincy Adams for, 171–72; proposed by Calhoun, 157–59; public interest in government participation in, 165; *See also* Board of Internal Improvements; Improvements, social; Surveys Act of 1824; Transportation system, national

Improvements, social: Jefferson's plans for, 127, 128, 129–30; *See also* Education, public; Schools

Indirect election. *See* Electoral college; Ellsworth, Oliver; Gerry, Elbridge

Industrial policy: of Hamilton, 70, 75, 86–89, 97–98; Hamilton's proposal for administration of, 100–101; objections to, 91, 96–97, 104–5, 106; *See also* Credit; Debt, public; Hamilton, Alexander; Protectionism; Report on Manufactures

Infant industry. *See* Hamilton, Alexander; Protectionism; Trade

Jackson, Andrew: internal improvements during administration of, 154; as proponent of laissez-faire, 22

Jefferson, Thomas, 20; on agriculture, 119–21; currency proposals of, 82; debt-reduction policy of, 125–26; on education, post–1789, 133–34; educational proposals by, 131–37, 135–36; executive office proposals of, 53; on free trade, 121; on industrial policy, 121–23; land policy, post–1789, of, 113–14, 117–18; land policy, pre–1789, of, 109–13, 114–15, 116–17; as national planner, 123, 127, 129; opposition to debt funding of, 125; opposition to

Hamilton of, 74, 130; public land policy of, 107, 108, 109–23; science and technology interest of, 137–39; on slavery, pre–1789, 118–19; on states' power and federal intervention, 130–31; support for Western agriculture of, 142

Judiciary: Madison on independence of, 59–60; powers and purpose of federal, 50

King, Rufus, 44, 61, 62

Laissez-faire: definition of, 22; as a doctrine of national policy, 22, 23, 28, 37, 179 nl; Hamilton's lack of belief in, 90; lack in Constitution of concept of, 37–38; policy in Jackson administration, 22, 154; as practised under Articles of Confederation, 50

Land Ordinance of 1785: adopted by Congress of the Confederation, 115; policy of land for educational facilities under, 134

Land policy: of Jefferson, pre–1789, 109–11

Land speculation: pre–and post–1789, 111–13, 193 n5

Laski, Harold J., 183 n3

Legislature: strength under Articles of Confederation of, 51–53; *See also* Continental Congress; Powers

Lerner, Max, 180 n4

Leuchtenburg, W.E., 88–89, 177 nl

Lewis and Clark expedition, 140

Live oak timber project. *See* Conservation

Lodge, Henry Cabot, 187 n7

Louisiana Purchase, 117–18, 125, 131, 140

Lunt, E.C., 191 n13

McClurg, James, 60, 61
McLaughlin, Andrew A., 30
McMaster, J.B., 143
Madison, James, 28, 32,; on balance of power in government, 52; on benefits of acceptance of Constitution, 44–45; on Congressional power to allocate improvement funds, 181–82 nn14, 15; on nationalism, 34; on nature of federal authority, 40; position on power of executive of, 55–56, 58, 59–60, 61; proposal for additional powers under Constitution, 41–44, 181 n14; veto of internal improvement bill, 156, 157, 181 n13
Malone, Dumas, 23
Marshall, Thurgood, 29–30
Martin, Luther, 61
Mason, George, 31, 181 n12
Mercantilism: acceptance by Hamilton of, 89; as tool of federal government, 24; as used by framers of Constitution, 37, 38–40, 180 n4
Merriam, Charles E., 20–21, 27, 35, 49–50
Monarchy: notion raised in Constitutional Convention of, 56, 61
Monroe, James, 20; on internal improvements, 157, 158–59; on role of federal government, 159-60
Montesquieu, Charles de, 53, 54
Morison, Samuel Eliot, 88–89, 177 nl
Morris, Gouverneur: on power of executive, 58–59, 60, 62, 63
Morris, Robert, 77; on activities of Continental Congress, 53; proposals for currency, 82
Morse, J.T., 191 n13

National bank: Hamilton's proposals for, 77–81; law creating, 190 n23;

size of, 103
Nationalism: of Calhoun, 157; changing position of Madison on, 156–57; effect on design and acceptance of Constitution of, 33–34; of John Quincy Adams, 165–69; *See also* States' rights
National Road, 142, 144–45, 152, 159, 160, 165
Navigation, 31
Nef, John U., 180 n4
Nevins, Allen, 179 n13
New Jersey: and commerce clause, 46–47; plan for powers of executive of, 55, 58
New York State: example of strong executive of, 54–55
Northwest Ordinance of 1787, 117, 119; policy of land for educational facilities under, 134

Oliver, F.S., 190–91 n9
Osgood, H.L., 177–78 n4

Patent laws, 138
Pike, Zebulon: government-sponsored exploration by, 140
Pinckney, Charles C.: proposal for additional powers under Constitution of, 41–42; proposal for executive powers of, 55
Planning, national, 27; John Quincy Adams' program of, 169
Postal service: effect on transmission of information, 151–52
Powers: attention by Continental Congress to government, 52; of Continental Congress, 29, 50; formulation of presidential, 50–63; Madison on sources of, 52; Madison's opinion of Congressional, 181–82 nn14, 15; nature and enumeration of proposed

Powers, (Continued) governmental, 40–45; of presidency, 50; *See also* Commerce clause; Executive powers; Separation of powers theory

Presidency: formulation of constitutional powers of, 50–63; Founders' design of office of, 50; *See also* Executive branch; Executive powers; Powers

Property: notions of Hamilton on importance of, 69, 70

Protectionism, 88, 90–91, 101–2; ideas of Hamilton for support of, 68, 88, 94

Public land policy: grants for establishment of schools under, 134–35, 144; grants for road construction under, 144; Hamilton report on, 105, 192 n19; of Jefferson, 107, 108, 109–23; pre-and post–1789 survey system, 115–16

Public lands: Hamilton's perception of, 84; role of federal government in sale of, 25; value and importance of, 24–25

Public policy: Hamilton opinion on use of, 74–75, 95; *See also* Credit; Debt, public

Public work. *See* Improvements, internal; Transportation system, national

Randolph, Edmund, 28, 182 n22; on power of executive, 60

Reeligibility. *See* Executive powers; Founders; Presidency

Reforestation. *See* Conservation

Rensselaer Institute, 139

Report on Manufactures, 90, 91, 98–101, 102–3, 104, 105, 121

Report on the Establishment of a Mint, 81

Report on the Establishment of a National Bank, 77, 78

Report on the Public Credit, 70, 75–76, 77, 187 nn7, 8, 9

Robbins, Roy L., 192 n19

Rutledge, John, 60–61

Schlesinger, Arthur M., Jr.: on laissez-faire, 23, 179 n1; on presidential power, 183 n3

Schools: grants of land for establishment of, 134, 144

Science: ideas of Joel Barlow for promotion of, 136, 141; interest of J.Q. Adams in, 169–70, 171–72; Jefferson's interest in development of, 137–39, 140

Separation of powers theory, 51–52, 53–54

Shays' Rebellion, 29, 34

Sherman, Roger: on executive power, 56

Silver. *See* Bimetallism

Slavery: Jefferson's position on, 118–19

Smith, Adam, 23, 24, 37

Smith, J. Allen, 30

Social class: notions of Hamilton on, 69, 70

Society of Useful Manufactures (S.U.M.), 103–05; *See also* Hamilton, Alexander; Industrial policy

States' rights, 22, 168–69 Jackson, Andrew; Laissez-faire

Surveys: government-sponsored coastal, 140; *See also* Exploration

Surveys Act of 1824, 160, 161–62; *See also* Board of Internal Improvements

Technology: Jefferson's interest in, 120

Territorial Ordinance of 1784, 115, 117

Thach, C.C., 54

The Wealth of Nations, 23, 24, 37

Trade; before 1789, 86,87; after 1789, 88; effect of suspension with Europe of, 147; Hamilton's ideas for regulation of, 89–90

Transportation: cost of, 143, 154–55; pre–1789 requirement for improved, 149–50; private investment in, 143–44; technological developments in, 148–49

Transportation system, national: plans for, 137, 141, 163–64

Turner, Frederick Jackson, 165

United States Military Academy: educational goals of, 139

University, national: John Quincy Adams' plan for, 170, 171; Washington's position regarding establishment of, 136; *See also* Education, public

Veto power, 55; *See also* Executive power; Presidency

Virginia plan: for powers of executive, 28, 55–56, 58

War of 1812, 154

Washington, George, 31; on activities of Continental Congress, 52–53; on commercial expansion, 150–151; concern with transporation development, 150–151; on industrial policy and trade, 87; on maintaining political unity, 149; position on establishment of national university, 136; on steam navigation, 149

Western lands: land grants for schools and roads, 144; post–1789 Jefferson policy for, 113–14; pre–1789 Jefferson policy for, 109–10, 114–15, 116–17; *See also* Northwest Ordinance of 1787; Public land policy

West Point. *See* United States Military Academy

Whiskey Rebellion. 143

White, Leonard D., 23

Wilson, James, 30–31, 37–38; proposal for executive office under constitution, 55, 56–57, 59, 61–62

Witherspoon, John, 46–47